The Local State
and Uneven Development

The Local State
and Uneven Development

Behind the Local Government Crisis

Simon Duncan and Mark Goodwin

Polity Press

First published 1988 by Polity Press
in association with Basil Blackwell.

Editorial Office:
Polity Press, Dales Brewery, Gwydir Street,
Cambridge CB1 2LJ, UK

Basil Blackwell Ltd
108 Cowley Road, Oxford OX4 1JF, UK

British Library Cataloguing in Publication Data
Duncan, S.
   The local state and uneven development:
   behind the local government crisis.
   1. Central-local government relations
   Great Britain
   I. Title   II. Goodwin, Mark
   352.041   JS3137

   ISBN 0–7456–0241–X
   ISBN 0–7456–0486–6 Pbk

Typeset in 10.5 on 12 pt Times
by Photo·Graphics, Honiton, Devon
Printed in Great Britain by Page Bros, Norwich

Contents

Acknowledgements

We are grateful to all those who helped us develop our ideas and write this book. First and foremost, our thanks must go to Peter Saunders, our co-researcher on the pilot project 'Urban Policy and Local–Central Relations' from which much of the material is taken. This project and its follow-up were carried out under the aegis of the Urban and Regional Research Division at Sussex University, and we would like to thank other colleagues and friends in the Division for the stimulus and support they have provided. In particular Peter Ambrose, Peter Saunders, Mike Savage and Andrew Sayer have been generous with their time and have commented on chapter drafts. Thanks also to our typist, who wishes to remain anonymous for his patient and good-humoured processing of multiple drafts, to Gary Llewellyn for the artwork and to all those at Polity Press who helped prepare this volume for publication. Steve Fothergill and Jill Vincent kindly provided the data for figure 3.3, and Ray Forest and Alan Murie allowed us to use their material for figure 4.4. Finally, the Economic and Social Research Council gave financial support to the research projects, without which this book would not have been written.

S.S.D., M.A.G. London and Sussex

List of Figures and Tables

Figures

Tables

List of Acronyms

ACC	Association of County Councils
ADC	Association of District Councils
AMA	Association of Metropolitan Authorities
BMA	British Medical Association
CBI	Confederation of British Industry
CLA	Country Landowners Association
CND	Campaign for Nuclear Disarmament
CSE	Conference of Socialist Economists
DC	District Council
DHA	District Health Authority
DHSS	Department of Health and Social Security
DOE	Department of Environment
DOI	Department of Industry
EEC	European Economic Community
GATT	General Agreement on Tariffs and Trade
GLC	Greater London Council
GREA	Grant Related Expenditure Assessment
GRP	Grant Related Poundage
HIDB	Highlands and Islands Development Board
HMSO	Her Majesty's Stationery Office
ILEA	Inner London Education Authority
IMF	International Monetary Fund
LCC	London County Council
LDDC	London Docklands Development Corporation
LTE	London Transport Executive
MDC	Metropolitan District Council
MSC	Manpower Services Commission
MTF	Merseyside Task Force
NATO	North Atlantic Treaty Organisation
NFU	National Farmers Union
OPEC	Organisation of Petroleum-Exporting Countries

PESC	Public Expenditure Survey Committee
PTA	Passenger Transport Authority
PTE	Passenger Transport Executive
RC	Regional Council
RSG	Rate Support Grant
RWA	Regional Water Authority
SDA	Scottish Development Agency
SNP	Scottish National Party
SO	Scottish Office
TINA	'There is no Alternative'
TSG	Transport Supplementary Grant

Preface

How to Use this Book

Aims and Issues

Since 1979 local government and the local state have become major areas of political conflict in Britain. At the same time, relations between central and local state have undergone a series of complex and confusing changes, so that the system of local administration and local policy-making in the mid-1980s was hardly recognizable as the system of ten years earlier. These changes have also formed part of a continuing political crisis between central and local government, a crisis that has become linked to deep-seated divergence over the form that society should take in the future and what it meant in the past.

Understanding this current political crisis lies at the heart of this book. But of course, there have always been strains between central and local states, especially so perhaps since electoral local government was established as one part of the state machinery in late nineteenth century Britain. This is almost the only centre of power outside Parliament itself that can claim legitimacy on the basis of universal suffrage and a popular vote. There have also been earlier crisis periods in central–local relations in Britain, most notably the 'Poplarism' period of the mid-1920s. Then a Conservative national government saw the local redistributive policies followed by some Labour councils as a kind of socialist movement in the making. These policies were initiated by the London Borough of Poplar, hence the term 'Poplarism'. Thirty councillors from the Borough were sent to prison in 1921, following their 'extravagant' payment of outdoor relief to the poor and their decision to only collect rates for local expenses. Like today, these earlier periods of crisis were intimately linked to political and economic issues outside local government itself. The present 'crisis of local government' is closely connected to the political dominance of the radical Right under three successive Thatcher governments from 1979. Its plan to 'rescue' British society and economy means controlling what local state institutions do and how they do it.

This is because the local state is not only a major provider of collective welfare services and a substantial spender of public money – both seen by the Thatcher governments as basically inimical to national regeneration – but also a site where experiences and expectations about how society works – or should work – are established through the provision of alternative services and facilities. Furthermore, local states do not just administer central policy in local areas. Local government in particular also represents local interests and views and has even had some autonomy in creating particular local policies. These views, interests and policies often diverge from the radical Right's project or may even be directly opposed to it. At the same time, for less politically powerful groups – of the traditional consensus as well as those representing the 'local socialism' of the New Left – the relative openness and autonomy of local government has been vital in establishing alternatives as well as in resisting the demands of a Conservative government. Hence the current political importance of local government and local state – or rather of what they do and who controls them.

Hence also the structure of the book. For it is our contention that the current crisis is the latest manifestation of contradictory sets of social processes. In order to understand the former we need to conceptually analyse the latter. Thus the first two chapters review existing accounts of local state behaviour and local–central relations for the light they throw on the contemporary conflict between local and central government in Britain – to which the rest of the book is devoted.

We aim throughout to provide a comprehensive analysis of the current crisis in local–central relations by placing events firmly in their wider political, social and economic frameworks. We do this in three ways. First we attempt to draw the mass of diverse legislative, administrative, financial and political changes since 1979 into a coherent statement showing how they have led to a major restructuring of local–central relations in Britain. In contrast most published work to date has detailed particular changes or events, or has been direct commentary or advocacy about current political issues.

Our second aim is to say why this restructuring has taken place, and how. To this end our survey of local–central relations since 1979 also refers the descriptive material to one view of the social origins of the crisis. It is clear that local–central relations are a hot political issue in the 1980s, but if we are to make sensible judgements we need to know why this issue arose in the first place and why it is so prominent in Britain today.

Our third objective follows on from this. In order to analyse the origins of the crisis one must show why specifically *local* state institutions developed in the first place. Furthermore, if – as we argue – local state institutions find their rationale in the fact that societies and nation-states have developed unevenly, so that there are specifically subnational or local variations in social structures and social relations, then we also need to seek the origins of this local specificity. Hence the more abstract and theoretical early chapters, and also the title of the book as a whole – The Local State and Uneven Development: Behind the Local Government Crisis – with its overall objective of relating changes in local–central state relations to underlying social causes.

To achieve this the book departs somewhat from more traditional approaches to local government. These have concentrated almost exclusively on the formal political machinery of institutions and their personnel (whether elected or appointed). Instead we seek to marry this political style of analysis to one that emphasizes social and spatial processes. In so doing, as will become clear throughout, we have drawn on and tried to integrate several (usually distinct) areas of analysis. Our ideas have come from recent academic debates in geography, urban sociology, political science, social history; as well as from journalistic and local political sources. Some readers, perhaps more used to traditional disciplinary boundaries, may find such an approach rather disparate and eclectic, but we feel that the very subject-matter of local government and local–central relations demands that we stand at the point where these approaches meet, for it is only by drawing on them all that we can hope to understand fully what actually lies behind the current crisis.

The Chapters

In chapter 1 we review existing approaches to local policy variation and local–central relations in Britain, first identifying local service variation as a crucial determinant of local–central tension. Put simply, if local government performed to a fairly uniform scale of acceptable (to the centre) service provision there would be less tension between the two levels, and less possibility of conflict and crisis developing. But policy autonomy is inherent in the very idea of local government, otherwise Britain would simply have non-elected local agencies of the central state (as indeed do many other capitalist countries). Given this importance we then look at other approaches to the idea of service variation and conclude that, in general, studies have been based too much on quantifiable variables, have focused too narrowly on political factors and have lacked any conceptual framework that could link local government to external social relations. This includes a noticeable reluctance to theorize the state as a whole, and to explore its wider role in society. Accordingly, the second part of the chapter reviews those theories that have attempted to specify the relation between the local and the central state, before we develop our own conceptualization of the local state and of its relation to the centre.

Chapter 2 looks at recent theories concerning the uneven development of society. This may seem a strange subject for a book on local government. As we point out in chapter 1, that these local agencies are elected is due to the particular social and historical processes underlying the emergence of representative democracy in capitalist countries such as Britain. But, that these local agencies *exist* at all is due to the need for states to manage the uneven development of society. Before we can properly understand the role of local government we need to examine the processes of uneven development which give it specificity. Having established that social and economic development is uneven, especially in capitalist society, we ask what difference these spatial variations might make to the ways in which social processes work. From this foundation we establish a rationale for distinguishing specifically local social processes, and develop this concept by referring the formation of local social processes more concretely to spatial divisions within society – spatial divisions of labour, of civil society and of imagined community. These combine in particular ways at the local level to produce the need for, and specification of, a spatial division of the state – the local state.

Chapters 3 to 7 turn to the more obvious public forms of the current local–central crisis – the mass of legislative, administrative and financial rearrangements that codify changing political relations between the two levels. Coverage concentrates on the period between May 1979 and the end of 1985, that is, the first term of the Conservative Government up to the May 1983 election and the period of the second Thatcher Government that culminated in the rate-capping and abolition legislation. This is the major period of legislative change. The threat of local state autonomy to the Government's plans to restructure British society led to various attempts to restrict and remove that autonomy. Nevertheless, events occurring in this key period of change also have connections with what went before, and we discuss these as appropriate. We begin chapter 3 by developing our ideas about why the central state should need to curb local autonomy in the particular political circumstances characterizing Britain in the first half of the 1980s. The rest of the chapter is concerned with the major changes in local government finance that have taken place during this period. We discuss in particular the 1980 Local Government, Planning and Land Act and the 1982 Local Government Finance Act. These set the guide-lines for the next few years of local–central conflict.

Financial control in this form, however, was not enough for the centre. Although Draconian, according to the standards of the time, in removing local autonomy, this centralization did not go as far as the Government desired. Some scope remained for local opposition, resistance and challenge to central policy. Chapter 4 looks at the attempts made to control detailed areas of policy after the general financial legislation failed. It illustrates these more specific central controls by examining attempts to restrict autonomy in the areas of local economic policy, housing and civil defence. First, legislation served to outflank local state autonomy in economic policy by creating new central government institutions at the local level. This was because local economic policy was emerging as an important part of local state action, partly of course, because the severe restructuring of the British economy since the mid-1970s had left many local areas in some considerable mess. How the economy works and for whom is also an area of some ideological significance and thus it became the focus for alternative policies from some highly visible left-wing local councils, as well as from the radical Right in Westminster. Local state involvement in the economy had largely been an *ad hoc* matter with little institutionalization of either local machinery or national legislation. Outflanking local government by creating new, centralized local institutions was thus an attractive and possible option.

On the other hand, housing policy was well entrenched as a key area of local action, and here the Government was forced to attack from another angle. The 1980 Housing Act set in motion detailed control over existing policy, although as we shall see, new institutions were also created to replace local governments. Finally, the chapter looks at the continuing threat to the Government represented by local autonomy over civil defence policy. Unlike housing, there is not much at stake here in terms of levels of council spending or provision. There seems, however, to be a lot at stake in terms of establishing the credibility of alternative political views. The threat of local autonomy lies just as much in this, as in resource allocation itself.

Chapter 5 examines the Government's response to this discovery. If centralization of local policy-making did not work then a logical conclusion would be to abolish it completely. This is what the Government tried to do in its abolition and rate-capping legislation. Before dealing with this directly, we look first at the prefiguring 'Scottish solution' – direct control over local government expenditure and rate taxation established in separate Scottish legislation in 1981 and 1982. The success of this system from the centre's point of view, coupled with continuing local resistance in England and Wales, encouraged attempts to do something similar over the whole country. Elements of the Scottish solution were introduced in the 1982 English legislation, but on the whole this attempt failed. In 1984, however, despite intense opposition from all sides, the potential for direct financial control over individual local authorities was established by the Rates Act, which enabled central government to set upper limits on local rate demands. It would therefore no longer be possible for local government to use local political support to stray too far from centrally preferred guide-lines – it would not have the money to implement alternative schemes. But just in case, those most troublesome local governments, the Greater London Council and the other Metropolitan Councils, were abolished completely in March 1986; the chapter ends with a history of the abolition saga.

Nonetheless, however final this legislation may have seemed at the time, especially to central government, it did not prove to be the end of the story. Chapter 6 details how, for the centre, the problem of local government remains – because the Government continually has to respond to local specificity, local actions and so also local challenges. Indeed, this is the source of the whole 'crisis', and hence the attempts to restructure local–central relations. Abolition itself, despite eventual legislative success, has been very much a political own-goal for the Government, while rate-capping produced the most concerted local challenge to central power, and even to legal power, that Britain had witnessed for some time. Moreover, the complete story of local–central relations since 1979 has pushed the whole issue of local government autonomy versus central control into the open and onto the very centre of the political stage. There is still some scope for local governments to act independently, and the Government is still tinkering with improved plans for further controls. We end chapter 6 by examining this 'trying again' legislation.

Chapter 7 details one key way in which the Government could overcome local opposition – removing policy-making to an appointed regional tier of the state, isolated both socially and spatially from popular local protest. First we chart the general history of regionalization – the transfer of executive powers and responsibilities from elected local government to non-elected regional authorities. The implications of this growth in the regional state level are substantial in terms of the access of different sections of the population to both material and political resources – regional bodies have been dominated by large private-sector interests and the professional–bureaucratic axis, with very little voice for alternative policies from the consumers. We then look in detail at how the Government effectively removed control of public passenger transport from the local to the regional level – in response to direct challenges over how this service should be provided by the large urban (and left-wing) authorities. But this move, to an existing non-elected regional level, did not go smoothly, and local response necessitated direct legislative controls even before transfer took place.

Chapter 8 concludes by re-examining the issues raised in the first two chapters in the light of empirical material which followed. Given the centralization of the local state system, what is the remaining status and role of local policy-making? Also, if local political autonomy has been removed, does this mean that local social processes operating around the local state are also removed – or do they just reappear in some other, perhaps more destabilizing, form?

1

Local Policy, Local State and Local Social Relations

1.1 Introduction: Issues and Context

Almost 150 years ago, a small column of troops made its way slowly yet deliberately towards the Lancashire textile town of Oldham. These soldiers were on their way to establish a barracks in the town, so allowing a permanent military presence without billeting. Why should this have been necessary? What had the people of Oldham done to deserve permanent military occupation? To put it simply, they had taken over or rendered impotent local state institutions; in many crucial respects the writ of central government did not run in Oldham. Local working-class control was effective between 1812 and 1847, with virtual working-class political hegemony in the 1820s and 1830s (See Foster, 1974, on which this account is based).

The working class in Oldham was able to conduct wage bargaining in combination and conduct organized union activities despite the illegality of most of these actions throughout the period. Similarly, the local police, vestry commissioners, Poor Law guardians and other local officials refused to co-operate with outside authorities, and were controlled by, or consisted of, the unenfranchised and illegally organized working class. Hence the law of the land did not always apply in Oldham – for instance, the New Poor Law of 1834 could not be implemented until 1847 – and this resulted in large part from the loss of central state control over local administration. The erection of the barracks was just one of central government's numerous attempts to restructure the mechanisms and institutions of state authority in its favour, in order to reduce local autonomy and impose the rules of a national, rather than a local, system of government.

A century and a half later, less than 35 miles from Oldham, we again find the central state intervening in affairs of local

administration. In the 1980s it is the City of Liverpool that is under
pressure as central government strove to regulate and control certain
aspects of local policy. The use of troops to impose the will of
central government was replaced by the threat of Whitehall
commissioners, the rulings of the Court of Appeal and disqualification and personal surcharge for elected members of the local
authority. Although the means may have changed, the ends involved
remain essentially the same – the limiting of local discretionary
powers to carry out policies with which Westminster fundamentally
disagrees. Although local government derives its powers and indeed
its very existence from central legislation, its actions have historically
been discretionary within certain centrally·imposed limits. As we
describe later in the contemporary case these limits have been
refined and tightened considerably (see chapters 3–7).

Of course, these events do not concern only Liverpool. As we
shall see, since 1979 almost all sectors of local government have in
one way or another been severely affected by central legislation.
Local government has re-emerged as an important area of political
debate and public interest, and has become headline news for the
media. But the current tensions and topicality of local–central
relations, and the events in Oldham 150 years ago, and not two
isolated 'freak' incidents. On the contrary, if we look beneath the
surface we quickly find what appears to be almost constant tension
since the beginnings of local electoral government in the 1830s (and
even earlier for that matter). It is our aim to provide an explanation
and understanding of the current crisis of local government through
reference to this seemingly enduring conflict.

Moreover, at certain points in history – for example the 1980s
and Oldham in the 1830s and 1840s – this conflict intensifies,
consensus breaks down and the issues erupt onto the public stage.
Two well-known examples in Britain are Poplarism in the 1920s –
a municipal socialist movement which caused the Cabinet to discuss
disenfranchisement for those on poor-relief – and the Clay Cross
saga in the early 1970s – when rebellious councillors were supported
by the local population in refusing to carry out central government
housing policy, even when the local councillors were removed and
a centrally appointed commissioner was sent in to implement the
legislation in their place (see Duncan and Goodwin, 1982b, for
more details on each case). Nor was it coincidental that both these
episodes – like others and perhaps like today's crisis – were
contemporaneous with, and indeed part of heightened periods of
sharp political conflict when consensus was breaking down. Poplarism was just one strand of the social ferment – the challenge over

who governed Britain sparked off by the First World War and the 1917 Russian Revolution – which led up to General Strike in 1926. Similarly, Clay Cross was just one aspect of the supposed 'ungovernability of Britain' in the early 1970s when a miners' strike – which the state forces of 'law and order' had been unable to contain – had helped to bring down the Conservative Government. Equally, both situations led to important moves to restore central control. The 1927 Audit Act to strengthen central control over local government actions, and the strengthening of police and emergency powers during the 1980s after the scare of 'ungovernability' are well-known examples. So too, both these historical precendents lost importance when the wider social conflict was stemmed.

Thus the present series of Conservative legislation should not be seen as a singular event, introduced as a response to the current economic crisis or to particular 'Thatcherite' ideology. Rather, recent action and events should be seen as only the latest stage in a long history of central government restructuring in local–central relations, although of course it constitutes a significant step in the process. As long ago as 1933 a leading commentator wrote. 'It is indisputable [that the introduction of the Block Grant in 1929 and the National Economy Act of 1931] ... betoken a sub-ordination of local autonomy to the dictates of the central power, which if pursued, will be the virtual end of local government,' (Robson, 1966, pp. 53–4). It is interesting to note that the language used is mirrored almost exactly by that of the current debate. Thus in 1980, at the very beginning of the latest round of legislation, Geoffrey Ripon, a former Conservative Minister for the Environment claimed that 'This Bill, and its financial provisions in particular ... constitute a threat to local democracy' (quoted in Cheetham, 1980). These two statements, although separated by half a century, share more than language. They show a common concern about the encroachment of central power over local democracy. As we shall see, this concern lies at the very heart of local–central government relations, expressed in a history that is connected by a woven thread of social and political processes back to Oldham and beyond.

For our purposes this thread becomes important around the middle of the nineteenth century. As we have seen, one central government response to the threat posed by places like Oldham was to reimpose control through the widespread use of nationally controlled troops and a new, non-locally run, police force. But perhaps more important than outright repression was the gradual process of political restructuring. According to Foster (1974), both ruling-class and working-class consciousness began to change in the direction of class compromise, articulated both locally and nationally, in the period of liberalization that started in the 1840s.

The attempt to accommodate the demands and advances of the working class though liberalization set in process the whole chain of events leading to social democracy. Middlemas (1979), who interprets modern British history as being essentially the problem of integrating working-class political and economic power and institutions, so as to avoid collapse, considers this compromise largely established by the 1920s, if substantially consolidated after 1945. One essential part of this process was political democracy for the working class. This was finally achieved for men in 1918 and women in 1933, although the majority of working-class men had the vote after 1884. Clearly it would have been nonsense if local government had been excluded from this settlement. Indeed the extension of the franchise at the local level pre-dated its national equivalent. However, just as sharing the central state with working-class political and economic institutions raised as many questions as it solved, so did sharing local government. The contradictions between central and local state institutions were reaffirmed in a different form, rather than overcome and it is with the attempted resolution of these contradictions that this book is centrally concerned.

It is not that representative democracy and elected local government in itself inevitably leads to local–central tensions. It is rather the case that this system laid local state power open to control by particular local interests. Immediately after the extension of the franchise and the establishment of representative local government in the last two decades of the nineteenth century, the institutions of the local state were particularly vulnerable to class-conscious working-class groups; for local electoral politics quickly became important to the growth and development of a labour movement denied power at the national level (witness Poplarism, and the rise of the 'little Moscows' in London, South Wales and Central Scotland – see Branson, 1979; MacIntyre, 1980). Of course, it is not only the working class that is able to gain from control of local state institutions. Bourgeois local states can equally well be set up and maintained, in which policy is determined not in the Miners' Lodge or in the Trades and Labour Club, as in the 'Red islands' or 'little Moscows', but in the Masonic Hall or the Chamber of Commerce. Similarly, local government autonomy may benefit different interest groups among the bourgeoisie, especially weaker sectional or regional interests – witness the way landowners and large farmers have often used control of County Councils to protect the landed interest against industrial and development interests. Moreover, as with any organization, local government has its own internal dynamics, and its structure and personnel will also affect local policy significantly.

But whoever has control, or influence, the key point is that local government, through being laid open to local interests, allows this to be expressed in terms of policy variation and different levels of service provision. Although restrained by central government and centrally imposed legal statutes, local government retains a degree of choice in its actions. Thus local government law is primarily concerned with powers rather than duties, and essentially establishes a legal framework within which local authorities are given discretionary powers to act (see Loughlin, 1986).

It is this framework that allows tension between local and central government. Each open conflict, from Oldham and Poplar through to Clay Cross and Tameside (when a Conservative borough successfully opposed the 1976 Labour Government's legislation on comprehensive education), has been built around the centre trying to impose its policies onto a reluctant local authority. The same is true today, as we shall see. Saunders (1984a, p. 30), has identified four distinct dimensions to this current tension. In the organizational dimension there is tension between centralized direction and local self-determination; in the economic dimension there is tension between economic and social priorities; in the political dimension there is tension between rational planning, as seen from the centre, and democratic accountability; and in the ideological dimension there is tension between social-citizenship rights and private-property rights. Each of these related tensions has produced its own particular problems, and central government has attempted to counter these in recent years by introducing an unprecedented volume of local government legislation in an effort to remould and tighten the framework. But despite a decade of tension and change in local–central relations, as the centre has tried to cope with these four dimensions of crisis, it remains true that discretionary powers hold sway over imposed duties. Hence the crisis continues and deepens.

We therefore agree with Stewart, when he writes:

> The local authority has much more than administrative discretion. It is not directly subordinate to departments of central government. The authority uses powers conferred on it by the national system of government but has the right to vary – within limits – its use of those powers. The degree of variation differs from service to service, but

in both the amount of resources devoted to services and in their form, there are important differences from one authority to another, *This variation is not accidental but inherent in the nature of local government. It derives from the exercise of local choice [which] marks local government off from local administration.*The possibility of variation marks the significance of local authorities in the government of communities. The local authority can express or can shape the particularity of the locality. (1983, p. 3; our emphasis)

Figures 1.1 and 1.2 show two contemporary examples of this 'local choice', and the resultant variation in local authority service delivery. The first shows variation in total (net) per capita expenditure for 1984/5 by the English and Welsh County Councils. This figure covers every expenditure undertaken by County Councils, including services like education, which are both statutory and subject to strong national direction, as well as many non-contentious and apparently standard services. We might expect, therefore, approximate uniformity in spending. Obviously this is not the case: for instance, the county with the lowest per capita expenditure (West Sussex) spends at a level amounting to only 63 per cent of the highest per capita spender (Cleveland). Indeed, only 18 of the 47 counties spend within ± 5 per cent of the average. But the distribution of these variations is not so surprising: by and large the variations on the map reflect what we know about variations in political control and in the social need for spending at the time. Figure 1.2 enlarges on this implication by illustrating the extreme variations in spending–rates that can emerge for a single issue of some political contention, in this case rate–fund contributions to the housing revenue account (that is, a local tax contribution to subsidize council housing). National policy (see chapter 4) is to minimize these transfers, and the means of achieving this has given many councils the possibility of making a profit out of council housing – thus reversing the whole tradition of council housing and subsidizing ratepayers from council house rents. As the map shows, this is what has happened in London. Nevertheless, five boroughs still maintain large rate–fund subsidises to council housing, with the most extreme case, Camden, being no less than 443 per cent above average. In all only 7 of the 32 London boroughs are even within ± 50 per cent of the average transfer.

Now, the origins of this local variation is another matter. It may partly reflect conscious political choices made at the local authority level (outside or inside the local authority itself). Partly it will just reflect existing patterns of need, or pre-existing decisions on delivery

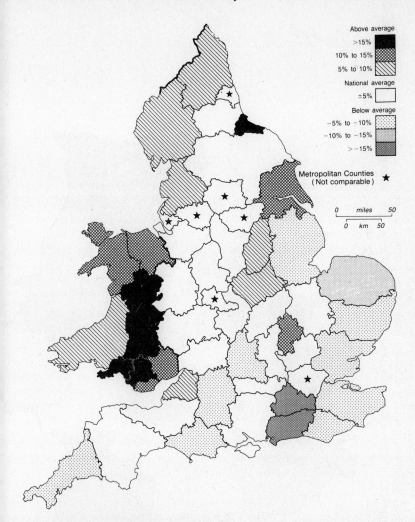

Figure 1.1 Variations in expenditure by County Councils: 1984/5
Source: CIPFA, financial, general and rating statistics

mode, service type and spending. Centrally imposed financial systems are also partly responsible for creating local variations. But whatever the cause, there is no doubt that there is considerable local authority variation in policy and service delivery and that this is connected to socially uneven development in one way or another.

Such 'local choice' – where it comes from, how it is shaped and the reaction it has brought from the centre – is our main concern, together with how and why a local authority can express *and* shape

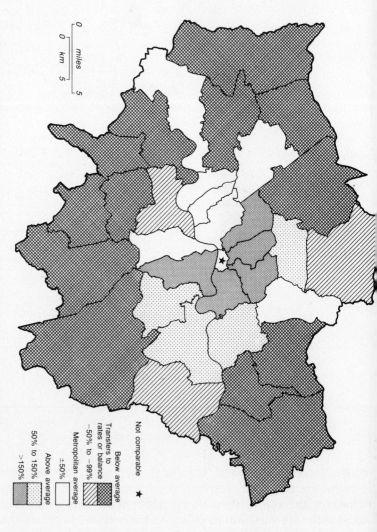

Figure 1.2 Variations in rate-fund spending on council housing, and profits made from council housing: London boroughs 1984/5
Source: CIPFA, financial, general and rating statistics

Not comparable ★

Below average
Transfers to
rates or balance
−50% to −99%

Metropolitan average
±50%

Above average
50% to 150%
>150%

0 ___ miles ___ 5
0 ___ km ___ 5

the 'particularity' of its locality. Only through a concern with these questions can we shift analysis to look behind the legislative surface of the local government crisis, and so tease out underlying social and historical causes.

The book thus attempts to reconcile a long-held conceptual and analytical division, which in our view has considerably impeded research in the fields of political and social geography, urban sociology and political science. On the one hand we have numerous geographical and statistically based studies of local policy variations, which all share a remarkable disregard for situating their analyses and results within a general theory of state activity. They are therefore unable to say very much about why the phenomena they describe so intimately have actually occurred. But on the other hand those accounts which address themselves analytically to providing such a general theory tend to ignore the existence and importance of local variation in state behaviour. These studies may be able to say why events happen, at least in a very general way, but they are notably deficient on the more specific questions of where and how they happen. We shall attempt to bring these two sides of analysis together, to link the social and the spatial, the abstract and the concrete, by relating a general theory of state development to the specificities of intergovernmental relations and the local social relations that inpinge upon them.

But having identified local control, local choice and service variation as crucial factors in explaining local–central tension we should first review previous attempts to explain variations in local state behaviour, before providing our own conceptual account of such variations and their inherent importance for understanding the long history of crises in local–central relations.

1.2 Understanding Local Policy

Why are there variations in local authority policies, not only between the lush Tory shires and the run-down Labour-controlled inner cities, but also between similar councils of the same political complexion? During elections, voters are often showered with literature claiming how much their particular council has spent on libraries, or on home helps, or on schools, compared with a neighbouring authority. (Since the level of rates has become a key political issue, purely financial claims have been replaced increasingly by statements about the number of books per head, or home helps per hundred pensioners, or teacher–pupil ratios!)

Whatever the measurement of variation between one authority and another, if we can understand why such differences exist we will have gone a long way towards understanding the current local government crisis. This is because the tensions between local and central government are ultimately derived from the latter trying to control the activities of the former. If we can understand how these activities come about, why they are being carried out, and how they vary from place to place, we can gain a sharper understanding of why the centre should want to control them.

There now exists a huge volume of literature concerned with variations in local authority service provision, which provides enough documentation for us to accept that these differences are widespread, significant and important socially and politically. In reviewing this work, as well as adding to it significantly, two of the leading writers in this field have recently confirmed that 'There is a very high level of variation in service provision' (Sharpe and Newton, 1984, p. 46), and they conclude that

> the claim that local authorities are little more than agents [of central government] has little support from either our data, or what may be reasonably deduced from what we know from other sources. . . . It is this conception of the centre, as having far more limits on its ability to impress its will on the localities than the centralization thesis admits, that, in our view emerges from the preceding discussion and analysis. (pp. 55–7)

We follow Sharpe and Newton's view that local discretion is sufficient to allow significant service variation; indeed we would claim that this is so significant that the centre responds by imposing controls to limit such discretion. The work on local policy variation that has lead us to this view is spread over the disciplines of social and political geography, urban sociology, history and political science and is as diverse and confusing as it is large. The brief review that follows attempts to cut a very broad swathe through this complex research field. Inevitably some approaches will be cropped slightly shorter than others, but this does provide an overview of an ever-increasing field of academic study.

IN SEARCH OF QUANTIFIABLE COMPARISONS

Much of the work concerned with explaining differences in local service provision has come to be known as 'output studies'. As the name implies, research concentrates on the local outputs of political processes and decisions, and attention is directed at defining, measuring and comparing policy variation. Output studies were initially developed in North America, not by political scientists but by economists. Their work centred on a concern with local public expenditure, and as early as the 1920s they had developed a methodology to quantify and compare the expenditure of the different states (see Dearlove, 1973, pp. 61–70; Pinch, 1985, pp. 60–3; Sharpe and Newton, 1984, pp. 8–19). Essentially this consisted of using multiple regression techniques to test the relationship between these expenditure levels and a number of external variables such as population density, income per capita, degree of urbanization and level of industrialization. It should be noted that political variables were conspicuous by their absence, so it is hardly surprising that these studies were able to claim that the major determinants of local expenditure were socio-economic rather than political.

But political scientists were equally guilty of the sin of omission. They focused almost exclusively on the internal political process and neglected to examine any external factors. They carried out quantitative research on elections, on voting behaviour, on parties and their leadership, on pressure groups and on legislative structures. In other words they looked at political 'inputs', at what went into the policy decision, and almost by default assumed that these were the main determinants of policy outcomes. Not surprisingly then, they claimed that political factors were the most important! But gradually, in the face of increasing pressure from the economists, who continued to claim that political factors were relatively unimportant in explaining policy variations, North American political scientists also began to undertake quantitative comparative analysis in an attempt to prove the link between political inputs and policy outputs. This link, however, proved difficult to find. As one influential study concluded:

> Differences in the policy choices of states with different types of political systems turn out to be largely a product of differing socio-economic levels rather than a direct product of political variables. Levels of urbanization, industrialization, income and education appear to be more influential in shaping policy outcome than political system characteristics. (Dye, 1966, p. 293)

Summing up the results of these early American studies Sharpe and Newton conclude that they showed that 'economic and social characteristics such as urbanization, population density, and, above all, per capita income were more strongly associated with expenditure levels than any other factors' (1984, p. 9).

Their use of the word 'association' is important, for it signifies that this approach, whatever its empirical sophistication, contains one major flaw. Statistical association does not in itself provide an explanation of how or why social processes occur. Dye recognized this in his early study when he wrote that there is 'a serious gap between the language of correlation and regression analysis and the language of explanation ... statistical associations can at best tell us only how close the association is between variations in economic development and variations in public policy outcomes' (1966, p. 24). Statistical analysis might be well help us identify an association between the social and economic characteristics of a city and its public policy, but this in no sense 'explains' that policy. At best we can note that some sort of relationship exists between the selected variables. But how, why and through what mechanisms political, social and economic forces are translated into policy outcomes remains a mystery. As Dearlove has noted of this type of research:

> On the surface it presents a great deal: a model with inputs, outputs, and feedback, and data that are rigorously quantified and manipulated by statistical techniques. But when it comes down to it, we really have learnt little of interest as a result of this work. Certain socio-economic conditions are associated with certain types of public bodies and certain crude political variables are less important than has been thought in affecting the nature of public policies. These findings point to a close relationship between certain socio-economic conditions and the form of public policies but they provide no clues as to how or why this relationship exists. (1973, pp. 69–70)

Even though Dye himself seemed to recognize the leap he was making between correlation and causation, he was still prepared to take this explanatory jump – dispite the fact that he lacked any theory of the actual linkages that cause different socio-economic conditions to be translated into policy variations. We shall see that he was not alone. The methodology and assumptions that lay at the heart of this North American research rapidly made their way across the Atlantic, intact and largely unchallenged. Dearlove's protestations were a lone exception, and at most British adaptations called for statistical refinement rather than rejection. There followed a number of studies that replicated their American progenitors in their statistical search for the quantifiable inputs that supposedly determined policy outputs. (For some of the best examples see Alt, 1971; Ashford et al., 1976; Barnett and Topham, 1977; Boaden, 1971; Danziger, 1976, 1978; Dawson, 1976; Foster et al., 1980;

King, 1973; Nicholson and Topham 1971, 1972, 1975; Sharpe and Newton, 1984.)

The bulk of this British work followed its North American counterpart in assuming that there will be correspondence between an areas' socio-economic environment and its policy outputs. Hence it has gained the description of the 'demographic approach', since the policy of a local authority is assumed to respond to its demographic composition. But no strict connection between socio-economic input and policy output is assumed and it is recognized that political factors will play a large role in determining the actual policy response. Thus political characteristics such as party control, size of majority and level of vote take their place in a long list of social, economic and political variables which are assumed to describe the local population. These independent variables are then tested against a set of dependent variables – usually income per capita spent on a particular service – in an effort to establish an association, or rather a statistical fit, between them. As with the earlier American studies this testing is usually done by means of correlation and regression analysis. In the words of Sharpe and Newton:

> A likely-looking set of independent variables is run against expenditure figures to see if anything statistically significant comes out. It is not too much to say that many of the studies of this kind are a trawling exercise in which as large a net with as fine a mesh as possible is thrown out and the catch then inspected for things of interest. (1984, p. 69)

Unfortunately for the demographic approach, little of interest has been caught, and even where something does turn up the results are often unreliable and confusing. In one of the earliest British studies, Alt (1971) concluded that 'Party control is by far the most important contributor to an explanation of variance in housing expenditure', although a few years later in a general review he wrote that 'The search for the impact of politics on expenditures is going to be a long and hard one' (1977, p. 91). Pinch (1978) used a similar approach in a study of different levels of housing provision by London boroughs and concluded that the political variable of Labour Party control was more important than needs or resources. Yet this directly contradicts an earlier finding by Minns (1974), which stated that in the context of London housing, political variables were relatively unimportant. Such differences are normal rather than exceptional in this type of study. A major review of comparative output research from many different countries was forced to conclude that 'the variables that have been found to possess strong predictive value are different for each [local authority] function, each country and each time. Rather than a comparative theory of performance, we seem to be laying the foundations for another monument to 'ad hockery' (Fried, 1975; quoted in Hoggart, 1986, p. 4). One of the very best and most comprehensive of all output studies, that by Danziger, had to conclude that 'The demographic approach provides a weak and generally unsatisfactory explanation for the variation in county borough resource allocation ... the demographic approach has minimum explanatory power for most allocation measures' (1978, p. 113).

This failure to explain can be traced directly to the methodology of the demographic approach, though some have tried to refine and improve the empirical techniques used (see Pinch, 1985, pp. 71–9). We would claim that no amount of statistical tinkering can alter the fundamental deficiencies of this approach, for while it is obvious that the use of more variables, especially of a political nature, would enhance coverage of the local political environment, it is difficult to see how this would improve matters. To put it simply, the results which come out depend totally on what data is put in. Furthermore, of necessity the method is limited to using data that is in a statistical form and so amenable to multivariate analysis. As an early American critique put is, 'While census bureau data are available for a variety of variables ... these data obviously are silent on such matters as the distribution of power and the attitudes of community elites' (Bonjean et al., 1971, p. 264). In other words there are important facets of the political system which, though undoubtedly affecting the policy process, cannot be measured in this formal, statistical way. Under the output approach these must be left out, and because they cannot be quantified they cannot appear anywhere in the 'explanation'.

Even if we could somehow quantify variables such as patronage, personality and power the model would still be left wanting, because of its assumptions that local policy reflects the objective socio-economic characteristics of local citizens. In practice, as we shall see, areas similar in terms of social and political conditions can produce very different policy results, since the manner in which political decision-makers respond to 'objective' conditions will be subject to a myriad of influences, values and judgements. Local governments, moreover, do not exist in an isolated world where they are linked only to their resident populations. The policies of a city may reflect wider influences, such as its role as a regional shopping centre, or as a tourist area, or as a place providing specialized public services such as museums and art galleries, or hospitals. In recognizing this, Sharpe and Newton have noted that local governments have functions to perform

> that may be only tenuously related to their own population characteristics, and that are derived from the fact that the jurisdictions they govern perform a specialised role as unitary entities within a wider economic system. . . . We must view cities, in short, as systems within systems of cities. The major deficiency of orthodox output studies is that in concentrating almost exclusively on the same battery of individual socio-economic characteristics they have not only assumed an automatic transmission process, but have also ignored the fact that government policy-making includes holistic functions. (1984, pp. 20–1)

Accordingly they have sought to replace 'orthodox' output studies with the 'unitary' approach, which attempts to relate policy to the role of the city as a whole within a wider system. Whilst this might be an improvement in moving the orthodox approach away from a narrow concentration on the socio-economic conditions of individuals, or groups of individuals, towards a more holistic view of an area it still cannot overcome the main deficiencies of the outputs approach. In identifying three kinds of city interests – its position in the urban hierarchy, its predominant economic function and its political control – they are simply replacing one group of independent variables with another. The same types of statistical tests are run and the results are just as limited, and although they claim (ibid., p. 206) that 'In our study we have rejected the transmission model and with it the orthodox input → black box → output view of the public policy-making process', what they have actually done is to replace one black box with another, albeit slightly more sophisticated.

Again, they can only claim that a city's expenditure is related, or associated, with its primary economic function, or its position in the urban hierarchy, or its political party control, or (as actually occurs) with an indeterminable mixture of all three. We have not overcome the transmission problem simply by introducing more sophisticated variables. We still need to know how, why and in what manner policy output is related to these three 'city interests'. As Wilson claimed of the original American demographic approach, 'That such characteristics are relevant is beyond much doubt, but how or why are they relevant?' (1968, p. 4).

Sharpe and Newton never really answer this question and remain stuck in the realm of statistical associations. This means effectively that they do not provide any insights into the political process itself, and they ignore wider notions about the distribution of political and social power, about the role played by the state in preserving this distribution and about the specific part played in this by the local state. Whilst they provide a thorough critique of previous output studies, they remain trapped within the very same methodological limitations.

This inadequacy is highlighted when Sharpe and Newton, two leading political scientists, turn to geographical concepts in an effort to overcome it. It is obvious that the study of variations in public policy has an explicitly geographical focus, but the use of geographical techniques has been largely confined to the concept of territorial justice (see Pinch, 1985, pp. 41–59, for a review). Sharpe and Newton recognize the importance of this focus, but unfortunately largely restrict its use to producing a taxonomy of British towns and cities that can be readily analysed statistically. We never get very far beyond the view that geography is important; how and why this is so is never answered. As Hoggart has recently pointed out 'The particular geographical attributes of localities might make it more attractive for certain packages of services to be provided, but geographical conditions only occasioned these service patterns, they did not cause them' (1986, p. 12).

Sharpe and Newton effectively reduce geography to just one more independent variable, when in fact uneven geographical development, in all its forms, is a key social process (see chapter 2). We will go on in that chapter to review and extend some recent geographical and sociological work which has developed insights as to how particular places develop specific social formations, and how the spatial constitution of society affects its political formations, especially at the local level. We feel that these insights are important in shifting research towards an examination of the social and political processes involved in policy formation, and the relationships within and between them. Unless we do this we remain stuck at the surface level of superficial empirical associations, which may turn out only to have a statistical rather than a social relation. Given the underlying principles of even the most refined demographic and unitary approaches we are forced to conclude that they can only hint at the real processes involved in any policy decision. At best they can only serve as a very rough guide as to the existence of particular relationships, and certainly cannot be viewed as the finished analytical product.

IN SEARCH OF A POLITICAL PROCESS

In contrast to output studies, the second major stream of research on British local government policy has concerned intensive case-studies of individual authorities, rather than extensive comparative work. This is no surprise, for this research arose partly from a sense of disquiet concerning output studies. Not only did these studies stress socio-environmental factors rather than political ones in accounting for the form of public policy, but they actually neglected to study the processes of policy-making at all. As Dearlove commented. 'What is noticeable . . . is not simply that government is given a small role in the policy process, but that it is not really made the subject of any serious research attention' (1973, p. 74).

In order to rectify this neglect, research turned towards the policy process itself, to the people who took the decisions and to the institutions in which they operated. It was argued that this approach was especially valid when analysing local government in British cities, where party politics was well developed and where one party often enjoyed extended control. In such a situation it was claimed that research was correct to concentrate on the internal political and administrative structures, since they would be subject to relatively weak and passive external pressures and thus allow only limited influence form outside groups. This was in contrast to the North American situation where research on external influences had only reflected their relative importance in a system of numerous, dispersed local government agencies (Pinch, 1985 and Short, 1982, both give simple descriptions of the North American case). So in Britain research came to concentrate on case-studies of the internal workings of particular institutions, and more specifically on the detailed processes of policy-making. This changed the research field considerably. Until the late 1960s according to Rhodes, 'The politics of local government was a lost world' (1975, p. 39), so endorsing the claim of Blondel and Hall who wrote at the time that 'We still know very little about what really happens in the council chamber and in the other seats or corridors of local power' (1967, p. 322). Such a view would be untenable today as the following decade witnessed a plethora of case-studies on both individual authorities and individual policies. (For excellent examples see, in chronological order, Jones, 1969, on Wolverhampton; Hampton, 1970, on Sheffield; Budge et al., 1972, on Glasgow; Davies, 1972, on Newcastle-upen-Tyne; Dennis, 1972, on Sunderland; Dearlove, 1973, on Kensington and Chelsea; Stacey et al., 1975, on Banbury;

Newton, 1976, on Birmingham; Young and Kramer, 1978, on London boroughs and the Greater London Council; Saunders, 1979, on Croydon; Simmie, 1981, on Oxford. For reviews see Rhodes, 1975; Jones, 1975; Gyford, 1976; Darke and Walker, 1977; Dunleavy, 1980; Goldsmith, 1981).

Some of these studies were stimulated by earlier American work on community power and political elites, which concentrated on interest groups and their relation to political power and decision-making. For example, Hunter's pioneering study of the community power structure in Atlanta (1953) identified the dominant 'elite' position of local business men in municipal government, whereas Dahl's seminal 'pluralist' work on New Haven (1961) pointed to a number of shifting alliances between different groups depending on the policy issue at hand. Following Hunter and stimulated by Dahl, American interest in the question of community power generated around 500 empirical case-studies (Saunders, 1979, p. 138), and inevitably British research, although rather more muted, began to respond to these questions. But by far the biggest influence on the emerging field of local political studies in Britain came through the work of Pahl and Rex in the 1960s, which directed attention towards the activities and values of key officials – the 'urban managers' who through their positions in local authorities, building societies, estate agencies and the like, could allocate scarce 'urban' resources. These studies have been termed the 'managerialist approach', and in Pahl's well-known expression centred on "Who gets the scarce resources and facilities? Who decides how to distribute or allocate these resources? Who decides who decides?' (1975, p. 185). In other words, research sought to identify the 'gatekeepers' of the urban system, who provided 'the independent variables of the subject' (ibid., p. 206, and see Saunders, 1979; Dunleavy, 1980; and Short, 1982, for reviews).

Urban managerialism gave a great impetus to British studies of local politics. It offered a way of shifting research from an emphasis on empirical variables to one that stressed the political processes involved and which concentrated on examining actual decision-making and the exercise of power. But the shift was only from one limited set of variables to another, for this work came to view the local political sphere, and those who worked within it, as autonomous – both from local social and political pressure and from wider constraints imposed by say, central government, or the need of companies to accumulate capital. Thus Mellor writes of Dennis's work on Sunderland, 'The professionals arbitrating over the future of the inner districts of the town were made to seem whimsically arbitrary and personally culpable' (1977, p. 14).

This concentration on the role of the individual manager has other crucial implications for those trying to understand the policies of local government. First, the actions of local government officials were juxtaposed with those of managers in the private sector. Urban managerialism fails to differentiate between the relative effects of say, estate agents and housing officials, or landlords and building society managers, in explaining local housing provision. This is more than just a case of arguing for different levels of power to be attributed to different sets of managers. There is also a qualitative difference between the roles of public managers and those in the private sector. Pahl has recognized this difficulty and in later work reformulated his thesis by limiting his application of the concept of urban manager to local state officials, assuming 'that control of access to local resources and facilities is held by the professional officers of the authority concerned' (1975, p. 270).

It is not enough, however, to simply identify the actions of these managers, however crucial they may be, in the distribution of scarce resources. For the very fact of scarcity itself is determined socially, and as Gray has noted 'The managerial approach, in concentrating on studying the allocation and distribution of scarce resources, fails to ask why resources are in scarce supply' (1976, p. 81). To ask why it is not simply a moral or political question, but a methodological one, which widens the field of research by linking the actions of managers to a much wider social and economic context. In other words, the state must be seen as more than just a collection of isolated individual managers.

But whatever its roots, whether in British urban managerialism of North American community power studies, this new flowering of empirical work usually addressed three key issues – albeit with different degrees of emphasis, (see Bassett and Short, 1980, p. 132). First, the community power studies in particular concerned local councillors themselves – their attitudes and perceptions, their organization and their relationship to their political party or grouping. Dearlove (1973) developed the concept of 'political ideology' to account for the outlooks and perceptions of councillors in the London Borough of Kensington and Chelsea, having traced their reactions and behaviour to a number of policy issues concerning housing and planning. Similarly, Young and Kramer (1978) use the notion of an 'assumptive world' to explain the actions of local politicians in Bromley, when resisting the development of overspill council housing from London. Whilst usually lacking these conceptual insights, the ubiquitous 'table of councillors' can be found at

the end of most studies, listing those representing the local
authority, or sitting on a particular committee, during the period
of research. Often their names are accompanied by data on age,
sex, occuption, years of service and even type of schooling – as if
these are the magical ingredients in accounting for how particular
policies come to be made. Although, as we have found in our own
work (for example, Goodwin, 1986a, 1986b), the values and interests
of councillors are important enough for policy outcomes, they are
far from the whole story. Furthermore, it is doubtful if these can
be deduced from a few personal details. Nevertheless, these details
are often subjected to minute scrutiny amongst a plethora of
research on the actions and behaviour of individual councillors.

A second strand in these case-studies attempts to trace the
relationship between these councillors and the officers employed
by the local authority to implement their decisions – to study, in
other words, the balance of power between appointed administrators
and elected representatives. Local government has well-developed
internal structures within which both officers and councillors act,
and it is more than likely that departmental or committee
considerations will affect policy, especially if party ideology is weak
or fractured. But not surprisingly, research on such issues has
produced conflicting results. Davies (1972) on Newcastle, and
Dennis (1972) on Sunderland, both show how council officials acted
almost independently over issues of urban redevelopment, their
actions being governed by planning ideology rather than political
ideology. This consisted largely of vague ideas about the 'nature of
a good society' – hence the title of Davies's book *The Evangelistic
Bureaucrat*. In contrast Saunders (1979) and Newton (1976), in
their studies of Croydon and Birmingham, both trace fairly close
relationships between high-level officers and leading councillors,
with each relying on the other during different stages of the policy-
making process. It seems safest to conclude that this symbiotic
relationship is the norm, but that it takes place under various
degrees of reliance, according to policy, place and circumstance.
Thus if Davies and Dennis had been studying other cities with
different political and administrative structures or different policies,
they would have found different results in the balance of power –
as would Saunders and Newton! As is the norm in social science,
yet one rarely acknowledged, what you find depends on where,
and when (and crucially how) you look.

Thirdly, these studies of the local political process are interested
in the role of external 'pressure groups' in the policy-making
process. Both the existence and influence of such groups have come

under scrutiny, for as many researchers have pointed out, there is no necessary relationship between these two factors. In Dearlove's words 'The rules of the game are the rules of access: they allow some groups to be involved and to be influential in the policy process gaining public policies which they favour, whilst denying others a part' (1973, p. 58). Those gaining access he labelled 'helpful' (p. 171). The most extensive British study on pressure groups, by Newton, found similar results. He identified over 400 organized groups active in Birmingham, but concluded that only a small minority were influential in policy terms – those that were 'established' (1976, p. 85-8), as long-standing organizations seeking only incremental change to existing policies. In contrast, both studies found 'unhelpful' or 'unreasonable' groups, whose suggestions for policy changes were invariably treated with suspicion and dismissal.

When taken as a whole, these studies, with their emphasis on councillors, officers and pressure groups, played a valuable role by shifting local government research away from the mechanistic search for empirical relationships between statistical variables, towards an understanding of the actual processes involved in policy-making. But unfortunately their desire to bring back the political to the centre of the research stage has to be seen as their one great limitation. For the political process is usually focused on to the exclusion of all else, often despite protestations to the contrary. Thus we have Dearlove writing that

> I accept the view that governments only have a relevance in the context of their wider social and economic environment, and it would be a retrograde step to study the activities of these structures as if they were in a vacuum. The question is not one of deciding whether or not we should study the impact of the environment on government, rather it is one of deciding how we should study and assess that impact, and what we should consider to be the relevant environment. (1973, p. 75)

Yet despite this awareness his work goes on to isolate 'councillor ideology' as the relative environment through which to study public policy. As we have seen, other case-studies identify other factors as being important in accounting for local political change. But whatever their conclusions, they will inevitably be limited to assessing factors within the local political process, since these are the only ones studied in the first place. It is our contention that local policy is created and influenced not just in the local political environment, but also through the social and economic environment and that research must be widened accordingly. Some studies of local policy-making are already beginning to point the way, and we shall briefly review these next.

It is worth noting that individual case-studies are not alone in suffering from a narrow emphasis on the political. In an eminently concise and comprehensible general study of the factors affecting local choice, Stewart (1983) calls on most of these local studies to build up an overall view of local government actions. But in so doing he too remains wedded to the notion of an essentially isolated political process. Stewart organizes his material in three sections – 'Boundaries and Context', 'Actors, Relationships and Settings' and 'The Limits of Organisational Choice'. In this way has examines the internal and external frameworks and organizations of local authorities in great detail, but unfortunately excludes almost everything else. Although he recognizes that 'The conditions of local government and its legal framework create shared characteristics for local government, but the working of local government is also deeply affected by its immediate environment' (p. 41), he is unable to follow through the implications of the dichotomy he has established. On the one hand he never analyses the 'immediate environment' of a local authority fully, restricting this to institutional, organizational and political variation, effectively ignoring social and economic differences, and on the other he never really conceptualizes what the 'conditions' and 'shared characteristics' of local government might be – aside from a common administrative framework. We are given vague notions that local government is an institution 'for maintenance and for ordering and for change' (p. 4), but no clues as to how these different (and sometimes contradictory) roles have developed historically, how they relate to each other, what their limits might be in a time of acute financial and political stress and how they are restructured and changed as at present. In common with all studies of local political processes Stewart lacks an adequate theorization of how these are linked to wider social, economic and political structures.

IN SEARCH OF A SOCIAL PROCESS

In the last decade or so the empirical scope of local political research has widened considerably. The almost exclusive concentration on the formal political process whether through intensive case-studies or extensive empirical surveys, has been increasingly challenged by accounts that take in crucial determinants outside this sphere. This challenge has come from a number of different directions – but interestingly political science has not been at the forefront. It has been left to other disciplines to shift the emphasis of research.

An early attack on the old orthodoxies was delivered by the so-called 'French school' of urban sociologists, who used the theoretical notions of collective consumption and urban social movements to develop an account of urban service provision and local planning (see Castells, 1977, 1978; Castells and Goddard, 1974; Pickvance, 1976). The most influential figure in a somewhat disparate 'school' has been Castells, who in his early work formulated a detailed critique of previous sociological approaches to an understanding of the urban system. His reformulation was woven around three key points; an argument that the urban is characterized not by any spatial or cultural boundary, but as the site of consumption processes involved in the reproduction of labour power; the idea that these consumption processes are increasingly provided by the state in a collectivized form; and the notion that state intervention and action in the urban system is influenced decisively by class struggle, expressed in the form of urban social movements.

But despite detailed empirical application in France, especially through the work of Castells, no major investigation of service provision using these ideas has been carried out in Britain. Instead, their influence derives from the way in which they broadened the scope of local political studies – empirically by investigating state intervention and urban development as part of wider processes of capital accumulation and class relations, and theoretically by linking local service provision to broader conceptual notions such as collective consumption.

Somewhat paradoxically, however, despite this widening of enquiry, the new urban sociology managed to impose limits on its own research. These arose mainly from an epistemological and methodological framework derived from Althusserian Marxism, and which insisted on viewing the urban system as an autonomous political (and ahistorical) entity. (See Bevan, 1980; Duncan, 1981; Foster, 1979; Harloe, 1979; Saunders, 1979; and Sayer, 1979, for extended critiques). Moreover, much of the French school's work has to be seen in the context of the political strategy of the French Communist Party, which was anxious to incorporate struggles over urban services into a larger oppositional alliance. The theoretical reasoning of Castells, which introduced ideas of urban social movements, provided the rationale whereby these new conflicts could indeed be claimed as part of a wider political movement. Although this combination of political and theoretical rigidity has hampered the development of the French school, its writings, when taken together, pushed urban political research into many new and interesting avenues which led to the exploration of social forces previously neglected by political science. As Short has put it:

> What we can develop . . . is the ways in which the local state provides the goods and services essential for the maintenance of capital accumulation, the relationship between provision of these goods and services in relation to the changing balance of social forces at the national, regional and local level, and the emergence or non-emergence of movements associated with protest mobilized around perceived crises and problems in the continued provision of certain goods and services. (1982, p. 170)

This exploration has been undertaken from a number of different perspectives in the decade since the first writings of the French school. One approach developed as a reaction to the 'urban sociological' tradition of Castells and others and their assumption of an autonomous urban politics based on issues of consumption. Instead this approach stressed the importance of production and relations of production, in understanding the urban question.

Most relevant here has been the work on housing production (Ball, 1978, 1982, 1983; Direct Labour Collective, 1978, 1980; Dickens et al., 1985) and on land ownership and land supply (Massey and Catelano, 1978; Murray, 1977, 1978). So, for instance, the problems of providing housing, including the political problems of local authority provision, are seen to stem from the problems of production. The British house-building industry in particular is notorious for its low rates of labour productivity and technical backwardness, and this prevents the provision of a ready supply of good-standard, low-cost homes. This means that it hardly matters what the distributional policies of local or central government are (increased rent subsidy or mortgage tax relief for instance). If enough good, cheap houses can't be built in the first place, the political problems of housing provision will persist. Hence the succession of 'technical fixes', such as high-rise housing. In this case it was apparently not possible to reform the structure of the construction industry, or to give city councils better access to suburban building land. Rather, the 'fix' of subsidizing high-rise building would, it was hoped, reduce the shortage of public-sector dwellings. But without better and more productive building, all that was constructed was another form of inner-city slum. In a similar vein, Massey and Catelano have emphasized how the social relations of land ownership have important effects on what is built, where it is built and how it is consumed, since land ownership means different things to different categories of owners. For the landed aristocracy, land ownership is a means to social status and political power and short-term economic return is less important than it is for the property developer or building company. It may well be against the interests of the landed aristocracy to develop land for housing, for this may destroy the very social situation on which their status and power depends. But the property developer exists to make profits by developing. These sorts of social relationships are clearly vital to understanding both central and local authority policies like housing provision or planning, but they are hardly ever included in traditional analysis.

As with much academic work developed as a response to previous approaches, the pendulum of this production approach has perhaps swung too far, and stresses economic relations at the expense of political ones. But this type of work, totally absent from traditional political science, does have important implications for understanding local service provision. First, it highlights the importance of integrating the economic and political sides of service provision. For example Dunleavy's (1981) excellent description of the development of high-rise housing in Britain shows how local housing provision can no longer be understood as purely 'politics'. The nature of the house-building industry and the incomes of consumers are vital components. But nor, on the other hand, can the problems of the British construction industry be seen as purely 'economics'. Low labour productivity has political origins and is maintained politically. Secondly, this production-centred approach has been important in introducing Marxist economic concepts into empirical urban research, and thus providing a bridge with notions of collective consumption and social reproduction.

Another reaction to the impact of French urban sociology is to deny the significance of local social movements. Dunleavy (1980, 1981), for instance, developed the idea that local political institutions are little more than cogs in a much larger political machine. He develops this idea after noting that 'Within broad limits the decentralized authorities implementing policies have moved in step with a precision that cries out for explanation' (1980, p. 98). Such similar policy development, he implies, demands an explanation in non-local terms, and he seeks his own explanation by examining three key areas of non-local policy determination. These are: policy formulation within the welfare state as a whole; the involvement of large private firms in urban development and public provision; and professionalism at both the local and the national level. He concludes that:

> The three non-local sources of urban policy change discussed here –
> central–local relations in the welfare state apparatus, the professions
> and the corporate economy – are in my view amongst the most
> important areas that need to be included within the scope of urban
> political analysis. (1980, pp. 131–1)

Although this wider conceptual and empirical framework is important, Dunleavy has perhaps overstressed these non-local factors in
accounting for local service provision – after all they are mediated
by local processes, and the translation of national forces into local
outputs is always contingent upon these. So, for instance, different
local authorities can mediate and translate these non-local forces
in dramatically different ways, as the example of local authority
housing provision shows (Dickens et al., 1985; see also section
2.5). Dunleavy's 'non-local forces' may well be important, but we
still need to investigate how they are related to and integrated with
those social processes operating locally around the institutions of
local government. Only then will we move closer to understanding
the social forces involved in determining service provision and
variation.

Our own studies of local authority employment policy (Goodwin,
1986a, 1986b), and of housing policy (Dickens et al., 1985; Goodwin,
1984), both attempt to take account of local factors as well as those
operating on a wider scale, and are also conscious of the links
between economic processes and political ones. In each instance
we found these linkages and relationships to be crucial. For example,
the form of local authority housing provision in rural Norfolk could
not be understood without reference to the particular nature of
farming in this part of East Anglia, and how this in turn led to a
certain type of social structure, village development, land ownership,
unionization, wage level and political conflict; all important in
determining the type and amount of council housing provided.
Similarly, in Sheffield the strength and traditions of the labour
movement, coupled with its early and continued occupation of the
council chamber, led to a sustained commitment to provide council
housing. Yet this commitment was shaped and fashioned by a
number of other local processes. These included the nature of land
ownership in Sheffield, the condition of the local economy, the role
of local authority officers (especially architects), and the political
forces operating in and around the local Labour and Communist
Parties.

But these studies also showed that we cannot just provide a litany
of local factors, both economic and political, and indicated the ways

in which these interlink with, and are constrained by, wider social forces. National housing policy, for instance (as with any central legislation) provided the limits within which both local authorities had to work. In Sheffield the beginning and end of its industrialized high-rise programme can be traced to national government Acts, as can the large-scale building of the 1920s in Norfolk. Our research also showed how wider economic factors helped to shape local service provision. For instance, the restructuring and nationalization of the post-war steel industry affected Sheffield's housing needs directly, as did the severe agricultural depression of the 1930s in Norfolk. It remains, however, for these wider forces to be interpreted locally. Councils in rural Norfolk used national legislation to the full and built a high proportion of public housing. But other – ostensibly similar – agricultural areas did not, and Sheffield built a higher percentage of council housing than any other similar industrial city.

The same picture merges from our research on local economic policy, which has recently developed into an area of contentious political debate (Duncan and Goodwin, 1985a, 1985b; and see section 2.5). Once again local economic factors were highly significant in determining the formulation and implementation of local economic policy and its variation from one authority to another. Sheffield, the first local authority in the country to set up and develop an entirely new employment department, did so partly as a response to the rapid recession in steel and heavy engineering that hit the city at the end of the 1970s, and the Greater London Council (GLC) has made no secret of the fact that it developed its economic policy after London lost 250,000 jobs between 1978 and 1982. But economic forces only operate within and around specific social and political conditions. For instance, within the GLC area the neighbouring riverside London Boroughs of Southwark and Tower Hamlets pursued totally distinct policies, determined largely by local political considerations, despite the fact that both were very severely affected by the closure of London's upstream docks and the decline of associated port industries. In Sheffield, the initial responses of the local authority in the economic field were deeply affected by the political influence of the city's steel and engineering trade unions, which urged policies to fight large-scale closures in the private sector. These initiatives have now been replaced by policies designed to combat privatization and unemployment within the City Council's own work-force, partly a reflection of the increasing local political influence of the white-collar unions (see Goodwin, 1986a). Again, of course, national economic and political factors provided the context and the limits within which these local authorities operated. The point is not to give any a priori causal primacy to either the local or the national, or the economic or political, in accounting for local authority actions. These will only be understood through an account that relates and interlinks the key constructs of social activity, both historical and contemporary (see section 1.3 and chapter 2).

Much of the early work that attempted to integrate economic and socio-political perspectives came from the Marxist-inspired school of urban social history. For instance, Stedman-Jones, in *Outcast London* (1971), was only able to understand the political and ideological shifts leading to state intervention in social reproduction at the end of the nineteenth century (in housing, for example), in relation to the economic development of Victorian London, with its huge casual labour-market. These early shifts were also important in establishing a new form of central–local government relations, with local authorities being ceded more power to intervene directly in their local areas. Other historical work on local political change has followed a similar pattern. Foster's (1974) work on Oldham (compared with Northampton and South Shields), which explored the whole process of liberalization during the nineteenth century; Neale's research on local political groups in Bath (1981); and Smith's (1986) recent book on nineteenth century municipal education policy in Sheffield and Birmingham; have all succeeded precisely because they explored the interconnections between socio-economic change and local political activity.

Other work by social scientists has recently begun to consider similar sorts of connections with specific reference to local government. We believe this gives a better understanding of local political activity than does the rather static and limited work of traditional political science. Material that has given us insights into the social relations operating around local government in particular places is international and extremely varied, and most of it is drawn from outside traditional political science; it comes from historians, geographers, planners and sociologists. This work includes Byrne (1980a, 1980b, 1982) on the emergence of different housing policies in the context of various local social structures; Clavel (1986) on urban politics in the United States; Cooke (1985a) on a comparison of how the 'radical regions' of South Wales, Emilia and Provence have emerged; Danemark et al. (1985) on variations in local housing and land policy in Sweden; Francis and Smith (1980) on a history of the South Wales miners' union; Jaggi et al. (1977) on 'Red' Bologna; Lojkine (1985) on conflicts over housing provision and public services in several French cities; MacIntyre (1980) on the politics of the 'little Moscows' of South Wales and Central Scotland; Mark-Lawson et al. (1985) on welfare provision, gender relations at work and inter-war politics in the Lancashire towns of Lancaster, Nelson and Preston; and Melling (1980) on housing policy in several British cities. What binds it together is a concern to examine real mechanisms and processes that produce particular events and situations, and to do this by integrating economic and political analysis.

Although at first sight this temporal and spatially specific research may seem to have little to connect it to local government in the 1980s, its methodological and theoretical insights are important to our argument. Not only does this work succeed in demonstrating empirically the links between economic, social and political change (and thus also the links between these and local government policy-making), but also it highlights the importance of social consciousness in creating such change. As these detailed historical studies show, not only do the specificities of local situations influence the actual outcome of more general processes, but those general processes are themselves created by conscious, active individuals. In a similar way, political and ideological shifts reflect how people engage actively in social relations, including class relations. In this way the 'bottom-up' perspective of these locally referrent studies can be seen as both an empirical and conceptual advance on the purely 'top-down' world of given structures and institutions. To put it simply, neither structures nor events just happen. This does not mean that these structures do not exist – just that it is insufficient to explain particular local outcomes by reference to structures alone. This perspective is even more of an advance on those studies where there are neither actors nor structures – just atomistic and abstracted statistical variables.

This has two further implications for our understanding of local government change. One is that particular political events and outcomes are inextricably bound up in historical and spatial specificities; we cannot hope to simply derive real history and geography from general theory – least of all in explaining current events – nor can we leave explanation in a spatial or timeless void. Secondly, if social relations are created and carried through by active individuals (whether operating on their own or as part of a wider group) we must consider just how people do this, and why their understandings, referrals and actions are 'unevenly developed'. We will follow through the implications of this in chapter 2. But first we must carry out another brief review. For the institutions

and actions of local government do not float in some social void –
even if, as we shall see, they are often studied in a theoretical one.
They are firmly established as part and parcel of a much wider
political and institutional machinery, that of the capitalist state as
a whole. Before we move on to look at the crucial processes of
uneven development, and at the effects they have had on local
government, we must situate our study in a conceptual framework
which allows us to appreciate and understand the relationships
between the local and the central state.

1.3   Understanding the Local State

One strong theme to emerge from many recent studies of local
politics is that the actions of local government cannot be understood
except in relation to the centre. We have already noted how the
work of the French school of urban sociology introduced notions
of state monopoly capitalism into the research field, and how
Dunleavy developed his own discussion of the 'national local
government system'. In each instance the focus of attention was of
necessity shifted from a narrow concentration on local government
alone. Other recent research has confirmed the importance of this
shift. The Community Development Projects (CDP) on urban
poverty, initially funded by the Home Office, concluded that the
problems and policies of urban authorities could only be understood
with explicit reference to a wider social and economic context, say
the policies of central government, or investment decisions of
multinational companies, or price fluctuations of basic commodities
– thus challenging the dominant, locally based, 'cycle of deprivation'
theory which attributed pockets of deprivation largely to the
characteristics of the people who lived there. The CDP research
(for example, 1976, 1977) also confirmed the importance of
differences in local action and political activity between different
local authorities. The problem is to examine the different levels of
national changes and local actions in combination, taking into
account how the latter translate and mediate the former.

Although this interaction has been traced in historical studies,
this is not so much the case in studies of the post-war period, and
least of all for current events. One of our aims is to help correct
this imbalance.

The extensive nature of recent change in central–local relations
has generated a whole crop of work on the legislative, administrative
and financial mechanisms through which central government has

attempted to extend its influence at the local level, and we do not seek to replicate this material (see for example, Burgess and Travers 1980; Jones, 1980; Newton and Karran, 1985). The key problem is not documentation but conceptualization. We are seeking a conceptual framework through which to understand and analyse, not just describe, recent developments in central-local relations. A review of the literature on these relations, beginning with the theories dominant in traditional political science, precedes the development of our own conceptual framework.

INSTITUTIONS AND ORGANIZATIONS

For a long time research and debate on central–local relations has centred on the rather static dicthotomy between 'agency' and 'partnership' (see Rhodes, 1980a, 1980b, for reviews). The agency model sees local government as simply the local arm of central departments, whilst the partnership model argues that local government has more autonomy, developed in an equal relationship of co-operating partners. Rhodes points out that the conventional wisdom of this debate (that there has been a shift from partnership to agency) has merely produced conventional critique (which demonstrates a continuing degree of discretion at the local level). He criticizes both views for failing to go beyond the rather limited parameters of agency versus partnership, arguing that both 'perpetuate the myths that central–local relations are limited to questions of financial dependence and of detailed controls', and claiming that in each case 'there is no explicit framework of analysis' (1980b, p 291).

Rhodes provides his own 'framework of analysis' through turning to the sociological literature on organizational theory, and develops three central questions for research on central–local relations (see Rhodes, 1983, for a review of both his own work and of the critiques it has attracted). These questions concern the degrees of power enjoyed by different government agencies in relation to each other; the extent to which their relationship is governed by particular 'rules of the game'; and whether there is any bias that routinely limits and channels organizational conflict and bargaining between them. Research addressed to these points would thus focus on the ways in which national and subnational agencies of government articulate and bargain with each other through a whole chain of individual, professional and institutional contacts.

This focus represents a great shift forward from the agency–partnership debates, and takes us into the complex world of real power relations, yet it remains aimed at only one aspect of intergovernmental relations. The organizational problem, although undeniably important, is only one dimension among several that need to be examined, and leaves many other key questions unasked – let alone answered – questions about the stakes that the various institutions are bargaining over; about the origin and maintenance of the ideology that pervades the 'rules of the game'; even about the development of the institutions themselves and why and how they work as they do. Rhodes attempts to defend his focus by pointing out that 'At the time when the framework was devised, the theoretical literature on central–local relations was distinctly limited. The form of any particular theory was less important, therefore, than the need to stimulate theorising' (1983, p. 42). This may well be true, but it does not make his theory sufficient for our purposes. To attempt to explain the current state of central–local relations through a focus on institutions and their problems of organization, would be to look only at the tip of the iceberg oblivious of the issues that have made intergovernmental relations problematic in the first place. After all, there is no given reason why these relations *should* be problematic. To find out why they are we need to look at the economic, political and ideological problems that are expressed in and mediated through the 'problem of local government'.

ENTER THE LOCAL STATE

In recent years some researchers have approached central–local relations from the perspective of the 'local state'. The term itself immediately suggests a focus wider than the narrow concentration on the institutions and organizations of local governement, and this work has indeed attempted to relate the question of intergovernmental conflict to a broader socio-economic context. The term originated in Cynthia Cockburn's study of the London Borough of Lambeth in her book *The Local State* (1977). It was not only the terminology that was new. In addition to her excellent empirical study of changing local government practices in Lambeth, Cockburn also presented a theoretical account based on the writings of Marx and his latter-day interpreters Althusser and Poulantzas. According to this view, local government (with similar local institutions) becomes the 'local state' as 'part of a whole'; where the whole – the capitalist state – is a relatively autonomous instrument of class domination, thus allowing it to manage social and economic reproduction above the competing demands of different fractions of capital but in the interests of capital 'as a whole'. The local state plays its part in this process of reproduction through the detailed management of families and institutions locally, and so differs institutionally – but not socially – from the nation-state. This new theoretical initiative was most important in condensing, and placing on a new conceptual stage, the mass of research and political action that had focused on local (community) politics since the mid-1960s.

Because of its innovative theoretical importance and its continued influence on radical approaches to local government, Cockburn's work needs to be considered further (see Duncan and Goodwin, 1982a, for a more detailed review). Cockburn begins by giving primacy to class relations as a cause of historical change. On the one hand, 'Local councils don't spring from ancient rights of self-government but are, and under capitalism always have been, an aspect of national government which is part of the state', (1977, p. 2). But on the other hand, 'This book begins with a different point of view about political change, that it stems from the working class', (ibid.). So far, so good; local government is not, it seems, to be reduced to a given function or role or set of institutions, but rather, contradictory processes are located in local government, reflecting the fluid changes within class relations – a view with which we are in sympathy. How then do we bring these two themes together in the concept of the local state? The answer in Cockburn's case is that we do not, since she is constantly frustrated by her concept of the state: the capitalist state is viewed functionally as a given thing, a pre-existing instrument possessed by the capitalist class, rather than as a historically emerging, changing and contradictory class relation. The local state then, is not differentiated from the national state in terms of process, only in terms of functions that happen to be carried out locally. In this respect Cockburn's account confuses historical generalization with abstract analyses of process.

To take the latter point first, Cockburn uses Poulantzas and Althusserian theory to update Marx's views on the state, to include social reproduction as an important concern of the state and ideology as an important dimension of domination. But in essence Marx's descriptive generalization of the nineteenth-century liberal state – without universal suffrage, parliamentary working-class parties or labour movement involvement – is fossilized and projected forward in time as a universal model. In using an update of the 'executive of the bourgeoisie' model of state behaviour Cockburn then has to treat local governments similarly, and thus, 'They are, and under capitalism have always been, subject to central government' (p. 46). But as we stressed earlier, the local–central state system has been subject to conflict continuously – and at times is in crisis as at present – ever since its inception during the latter half of the nineteenth century. In fact, in stark opposition to Cockburn's account, local government is no static or simple instrument of capital; if it were, why bother with all the political tension and uncertainty (which we will document later) in the latest attempt to reduce local autonomy? Why indeed allow local state institutions, which incorporate a somewhat troublesome electoral and autonomous element, at all?

Cockburn thus reduces two contradictory social processes of the local state – that it is simultaneously agent and obstacle for the national state – to those of a one-way agent. Not only does this ignore a whole aspect of local state activity – that which opposes the centre – but it also reduces social relations between active human agents to purely functional operations. This results from the search for a universal model of a thing – the capitalist state – which can be applied to all places at all times using one 'model' of activity as the basis of understanding. This line of reasoning is thus misleading, historically and conceptually. Instead we should seek those essential social processes that are institutionalized in governmental forms, but which are expressed differently both historically and spatially. Thus, despite here innovative theoretical reasoning and excellent empirical account of Lambeth Borough Council, in the end Cockburn's work is of limited use to us.

The only other explicit attempt to provide a theoretical account of the local state in capitalist society is by Saunders (1979, 1981, 1984a, 1986) and in conjuction with Cawson (1983). Although many others have worked with implicit theories of the local state, they have made no distinctions between national and local states. Concepts developed for the former are simply transferred to the local level as if the processes operating on the two levels were interchangeable. This begs the question of why the term and hence the concept of the local state is used at all. Cawson and Saunders overcome this problem by developing a 'dualistic' theory of politics, the 'dual state thesis'. This view argues that distinct political processes operate on each level and hence (although this seems a *non sequitur*) that two different political theories are necessary to make sense of them. State intervention at the central level is supposed to take place mainly in relation to the process of production, and it proceeds through a policy process of corporatist mediation addressed to the principle of private property and the need to maintain the profitability of capitalist enterprises. At the local level state activity is supposedly directed towards consumption processes, where policies are developed through a plurality of competitive political struggles, which address themselves to the principles of social rights and social needs. Those interests mobilized at the centre are formed primarily around production – the organized class interests of industrial and finance capital, the professions and organized labour – whilst at the local level mobilization usually cuts across class lines to be formed on the basis of specific and locally based consumption sectors – for example council tenants, parents of under-fives and so on.

This work has been of vital importance in highlighting the specificity of the local level, and in arguing for a conceptualization of the local state that is based primarily on its 'uniqueness' and on its separation from the centre. Its latest manifestation presents a useful analytical framework for cataloguing the differential dimensions along which local–central relations are organized, and the tensions that result (Saunders, 1984a). But for us the approach is still fraught with problems.

A major difficulty with the dual state thesis is that it rests on an a priori allocation of functions between national and local states, and that these functions are then assumed to produce specific political processes. The national state is identified with production, and is therefore a corporate state of mediation and co-option. The local state, on the other hand, is concerned with consumption issues and so becomes a pluralist state of conflicting interests. The trouble is that there seems little historical rationale or evidence for such rigid divisions between the types of functions and types of politics characterizing local and national states. Furthermore, the dual state thesis assumes that this functional division between local and national state levels goes on to *cause* or produce different politics. Again, it is not clear why this should be so and the historical record does not lend much support to this view. To begin with, there are severe difficulties in constructing categories round a dichotomy – that between production and consumption – which has little purchase on real state activities. As Saunders himself has written, 'Since most state policies will involve some relevance for both production and consumption, it can be difficult to disentangle the two and to distinguish empirically between primarily-production orientated and primarily-consumption orientated interventions', (1986, p. 44). For instance, any taxonomy of local state activity would have to place road development, education and housing as contributing to private production and capital accumulation (as indeed Saunders does: 1979, pp. 147-8). Yet as Dunleavy shows, roads, education and housing currently account for 65 per cent of local authority spending

(1984, p. 54). There are many other instances in which the central
state is responsible for areas of consumption and the local for
productive activities, and we could also show how these allocations
have changed historically and continue to do so, making a distinction
based on functions difficult to maintain. Indeed, the historical
emergence of the local state in Britain, as a set of institutions, was
characterized by its support for production and capital accumulation.
As Dunleavy has pointed out 'In the period up to 1914', only just
over a third of allocatable expenditure by local authorities could
be classified as social consumption (on generous criteria) (1984, p.
76).

Similarly, although this is less well researched empirically, there
seems as little evidence of any firm segregation of political processes
by the geographical scale of state institutions. This would be taking
spatial determinism a little too far and certainly plenty of
countervailing examples can be found. So corporatist politics is
sometimes marked in local state behaviour (see, for instance,
Simmie, 1985, on land-use planning or King, 1985, on local economic
initiatives). Cawson (1985) even distinguishes a whole category of
'local corporatism'. Similarly, pluralist and class-based conflicts are
not at all unknown in national states. As with the supposed
dichotomy between production and consumption, it is more the
case that corporatist and conflictual behaviour are related within
institutions and their actions (see, for instance, Middlemass's 1979
account of the development of corporatist politics in the British
national state, precisely as a means of institutionalizing class
conflict). Also, as we might expect, the dominant political mode
in any situation is not so much a matter of spatial scale but of what
actors are involved over what issues. Ironically enough, in a study
of corporatism at the *local* state level, Saunders makes very much
the same point: 'Our conclusion, therefore, is that the development
of corporatist forms in urban service provision is primarily a function
of the type of service in question, i.e., whether or not it has direct
implications for major producer interests in society (1985d, p. 172).
The level of state institution involved will of course affect this, and
the dual state thesis is correct to pick this up (where, for instance,
unions and large employers may negotiate through national state
machinery rather than local state machinery, and this may well
affect the sort of politics pursued in this case). But the dual state
thesis is surely incorrect to elevate this contingent factor to a
fundamental political distinction.

Saunders partly deflects criticism of this sort by putting forward
the dual state thesis as an 'ideal type' i.e. that it is a research

strategy rather than an account of reality, its use is 'to develop an analytical framework which can help to suggest which questions to pose' where the thesis 'can be evaluated analytically but not empirically' (Saunders, 1982, p. 58; see also 1986). Even if we accept this, it remains a moot point how useful an analytical framework can be which has an untenable base. The dual state thesis may be a place to start (as Saunders suggests). If, however corporatist bargaining over production in the national state and pluralist conflict over consumption in the local state, are *not* typical tendencies, or do not reflect some social logic, then perhaps the 'thesis' is not something to continue with. Saunders claims that this 'ideal type' methodology is adopted because

> the social world is a very complex place which cannot be known in its totality, in which case we proceed by developing partial understandings of aspects of that world and gradually build up a picture of how the different 'parts' affect each other. . . . It also follows that knowledge of the interrelation of the parts will be derived, not from a priori theory, but from empirical research in different places at different times. (1984b, p. 20)

This is precisely our point. To render the social world intelligible one must of necessity divide it up for study. But where and how is the divide drawn? It makes no sense to separate a central world of corporatist bargaining concerned with production issues from a local world of competing politics around matters of consumption. Instead we will explore a more process-oriented and historical approach, based on the notion of unevenly developed social relations.

SOCIAL RELATIONS AND THE LOCAL STATE

Although a decade has elapsed since the publication of Cockburn's book, the usage and application of the concept of the 'local state' remains rather uncertain. The term itself could refer equally to 'autonomous local state' or to 'local institution of the central state', and both meanings are present in the literature. Confusion is not confined to the semantic level, but also results from conflicting and imprecise ideas of the status of the concept in relation to historical events and the theoretical interpretations of the capitalist state as a whole. Consequently it is difficult to apply the concept to empirical research, except in a very general way that denotes an area and approach for research – an overall political economy of local state institutions as a whole (rather than, say, the organizational details of local government). As we have seen, traditional pluralist and positivist policy analysis is much narrower in this respect – it rarely speaks of the capitalist state, still less does it overtly see the nature of the state as being part of the problem. Our contention is that more use can be made of the concept 'local state' than just to denote a radical methodological approach, or an area of social and political research interest. Indeed, the concept is vital to a full understanding of the current crisis of local–central relations.

But to use the concept constructively, it must be related to overall accounts of social relations and social change. Studies have often treated the local state (at least implicitly) as a static thing, more a collection of physical institutions than a process of social relations. Rather than concentrating on descriptions of things or structures that are essentially outcomes of social processes, it may be more useful to focus on the causal processes themselves. It should then be possible to *explain* the nature of state actions and changes therein, rather than just describe them. State forms and actions can then be linked to changing relations between groups of people instead of being left as socially inexplicable orginizational forms or bundles of given functions. Just as the capitalist state is a historically formed social relation, so are state institutions at the local level. We should not expect given and unchanging local state forms although this is what the dual state thesis and Cockburn's structuralist thesis both imply. Instead, local-level state institutions are constantly being restructured, as at present, and these changes are linked to changes in state relations as a whole and to changes in the overall form of capitalist social relations (see Duncan and Goodwin, 1980, 1982a, 1982b).

A successful theory then, should be able to relate historical differences and changes in state behaviour to those social processes crucial in causing such specific situations. Also, if these crucial processes are different for national and subnational state institutions, then we can talk about a 'theory of the local state'. To do this we need to perform two linked conceptual tasks. First, we need to indicate the nature of those social relations institutionalized in the capitalist state; why are relations of gender and production, and other social relations taking place outside the state in workplaces, households and communities, not sufficient for the reproduction of society in advanced capitalism? Why must there be states? Secondly, given that some of the social relations of capitalist society do partly take place in state institutions, we must clarify whether and why these have a local dimension. That is, do local social transactions take place in local state institutions, specific to local areas and autonomous from those taking place in the national state?

Perhaps the essential preliminary idea is that capitalist states have developed historically as one part of the social relations between subordinate and dominant classes. They did not suddenly appear from the sky as an autonomous entity standing above society in order to regulate the squabbles of competing capitals, nor were states just called into being by dominant classes as a convenient tool for the subordination of others. Capitalist states may indeed have these functions (amongst others), but by definition dominant class behaviour, and indeed its very existence, rests upon its relationship with subordinate classes. National and local states were formed historically as part of this relationship and its development.

In order to disentangle ideas of the state as a 'thing', and as a social relation, the CSE State Group (1979) has used the distinction between 'state form' and 'state apparatus'. The latter refers to a set of physical institutions (such as water boards or District Councils), the former to the social relations expressed through them (such as those between dominant and subordinate classes). Most accounts muddle the two and consequently analysis is confused. In contrast the CSE State Group is able to make the crucial point that the importance of the state lies not so much in what it does (the functions that particular institutions carry out) but how it does it (the power relations between social groups as mediated by these activities). In those capitalist states with representative, electoral democracy (franchise states), crucial social and economic differences and relations between social groups – like those of classes and gender – are transformed into the legal relations of supposedly individual and equal citizens. Franchise states formally separate a political world from an already existing social and economic one (hence the paradoxical validity of the appeal to 'keep politics out of it', even, on occasions, out of electoral state institutions). But this supposition of atomistic equality in fact takes place in a situation where collective inequalities are paramount. For instance, as the women's movement has spent some time and effort arguing, female citizenship is not actually equal to male citizenship (see Mackenzie and Rose, 1983, Ruggie, 1984 for accounts). The assumption of atomistic equality rests upon real inequalities and so, perversely, confirms them. In other words a major role of capitalist state institutions becomes one of interpreting social relations. This abstraction of political relations from class relations is specific to the capitalist state and Marx (like many others) saw the artificial separation of the state from society occurring finally in an undisguised way with the French Revolution and the birth of 'the citizen'. With this event 'The class distinctions in civil society became merely social differences in private life, of no significance in political life. This accomplished the separation of political life and civil society' (Marx, 1975, p. 146). Class relations are thus broken down, individualized and absorbed into artificial legal relations of equal citizens – although since the world is not actually made up of these equal citizens, the real distribution of power is replicated as the state acts out artificial equality. To quote Marx again contrasting the modern alienation of the state with the traditional alienation of religion, 'Just as Christians are equal in heaven though unequal on earth, the individual members of the people become equal in the heaven of their political world, though unequal in their earthly existence in society' (ibid.).

Thus, as one form of the relation between capital and labour, capitalist states act to transmute class relations (and other social relations like those between genders, for that matter) into the supposedly equal legal relations of individual citizenship. Hence the way people and state authorities talk about 'the national interest', or 'the public', when these collectivities hardly exist in reality. It is this transmutation of real social relations into artificial legal relations which is the 'state form' of the capital–labour relation. It parallels the 'wage form' of the capital–labour relation – developed in that other central capitalist institution, the firm. Here the class relation between capitalist and labourer is transmuted into the supposedly equal and legal contractual relations of employer and employee. Neither transmutation is, however, necessarily secure or given. People have to work hard to maintain both, and equally people strive against them. For instance, some people work to support the discipline of the 'free market', others act for trade-union organizations. Similarly, some state institutions see the unemployed as individual pathological citizens while others (for example, some Labour local authorities) seek to build collective organizations of the unemployed to help combat the social causes and results of unemployment. Moreover, these artificial relations also have to be maintained in the face of other everyday practices which suggest that class relations and other collective social relations are a basic part of society. In addition even if everyday practices are transmuted meaningfully, periodic events like the strike, or the heavily policed demonstration, or involvement in explicit consciousness-raising activity, can disturb this. Class, gender and race can be attractive – and threatening – ways for people to organize and view society. Social democracy is one compromise position in this conflict where organized labour has an institutional place qualifying both wage form and state form although, in Britain, this compromise is now under threat. To be successful therefore, this threat must involve changing social relations in the state, as well as those elsewhere in society. This interpretive role is therefore not fixed; how this role is performed and with what results remains a matter of social dispute.

But where exactly does the local state fit in? To put it very briefly, social relations including class relations are just that – relational between people and formed socially. This means that they will be unevenly developed, over space, in time, even for the same person in different situations (see chapter 2.) Class relations, gender roles and political cultures are not the same in, say, Sheffield as in Camden, and are quite different again in Croydon or Cheltenham. The crucial point is that social relations are unevenly developed, hence on the one hand a need for different policies in different places and, on the other hand, a need for local state institutions to formulate and implement these variable policies. Local state institutions are rooted in the heterogeneity of local social relations, where central states have difficulty in dealing with this differentiation. But, as we have suggested, this development of local states is a double-edged sword. For uneven development means that social groups are also spatially constituted and differentiated, with variable local strengths and importance (see chapter 2). Such locally constituted groups can then use these local state institutions to further their own interests, perhaps even in opposition to centrally dominant interests.

The double-edge sword may seem a little blunt. It is, however, sharpened up considerably with the development of representative democracy and universal franchise. For now the extra leverage local state institutions give locally constituted groups is not only available, but it is legitimized and even expected. The second structural role of local states is this 'representational role'. It is important because, although locally-constituted groups may be marginal or subordinate in national terms, local state institutions allow them local legitimacy and access to state power. The City of London, well represented in the institutions of the British nation-state, hardly needs local state support. But for trade unionists or farmers, without such guaranteed access to the centre and with important local bases of support, local state institutions can seem vital. The local institutions they control will be important in administering, implementing, qualifying or even opposing central decisions. The centre will attempt to neutralize the influences of local interests in local states, while at the same time having to support local states in order to intervene in locally differentiated social and natural systems. In this way the 'interpretive' and 'representational' roles of the local state can coalesce, if in a rather contradictory way. This representational role lies beneath the 'constitutional' issue of local democracy that has been raised recently as part of the local–central debate. Very few people live on constitutions alone. More important are the interests best served by any constitutional balance, and how these will be affected by its change. For instance, farmers and landowners can maintain a cheap local labour force via their domination of many rural local governments, through the provision of a stock of council housing. (Indicatively, an amendment to the 1980 Housing Act sponsored by the Country Landowners' Association and the National Farmers' Union allowed restrictive covenants on council house sales in national parks, Areas of Outstanding National Beauty, or designated Rural Areas). Similarly the provision of cheap and often good-quality council housing by Labour authorities was an essential component in the development and maintenance of local cultures of labourism. Both these interests – relatively minor on the national stage, but often very important locally – are fundamentally threatened by the changing balance of local–central relations which we will chart later. Thus the underlying processes of local government must be examined before we can fully appreciate what interests are being damaged by its change. It is not enough simply to assert that it is a 'good thing' in its own right (see, for instance, Jones and Stewart, 1983).

Moreover, the impact of this representational role has been increased since the mid-1960s by the rise of locally based community politics and action groups. These are partly a reaction to the changing social geography of Britain. As a result of large-scale economic and social restructuring, areas have become more differentiated, with some rapidly entering a period of steep economic and social decline. There is thus a greater need for specifically local actions and responses. But crucially, as new local coalitions grow to promote these responses, so the need for those centrally strong interests to curtail their power becomes more pressing. This conflict lies at the heart of the problem of local government, and it is a constant structural possibility. (Note that 'constant' does not mean 'inevitable', simply that generative mechanisms are always there to be activated.) The possibility of conflict does not arise because the local state performs particular social and economic policy functions for example, providing non-profit rented housing, or subsidized nursery places, although these are very important for other reasons.

It is clear that there is no given need for housing provision, education, police, social welfare or anything else that is managed by the state, to be mixed up in a local electoral system based on universal franchise. In many capitalist countries this is not the case and an equal or greater part of capitalist history, Britain included, has been without such a system. Indeed many state functions fluctuate to and from the local electoral orbit. It is thus not its functions that give the local state its specificity, but the contradiction inherent in its representational and interpretive roles, a contradiction that is activated and sustained through the uneven spatial development of social relations.

1.4 Concluding Comments

The next chapter will go on to analyse this crucial social process of uneven development in more detail, and to give empirical examples of the ways in which it affects the local state. For the moment we must add some concluding comments to our discussion of alternative approaches to analysing local policy and local–central relations.

We first showed the historical nature of the current local government crisis and pointed to differential local service provision, in opposition to central wishes, as the common factor in each conflict. Most traditional theories attempting to explain such provision were based too narrowly on quantifiable variables and positivist methodology, and more recent accounts which eschewed this approach in favour of more process-orientated studies concentrated too much on political factors in isolation from other social forces. Outside political science, studies of local political change that linked economic, political and social events provided excellent descriptive accounts of local politics, but could only give a base for understanding the relationship between national and local states. This approach was then linked to a theorization of the capitalist state and its role in society.

Studies attempting to situate an analysis of central–local relations in a wider analytical framework had an inadequate historical conceptualization of state action and were unable to specify the crucial determinants of local, as opposed to national, state action. A brief account of our development of the concept of the 'local state' stressed the role of uneven social development. This highlights the importance of linking a spatial analysis to a social one; in disciplinary terms of linking geographical concepts to those already developed in political and sociological theory. Sharpe and Newton (1984) flirted with such a link in their work on local service variation, but were unable to develop it fully because of their essential reliance on a positivist framework which insisted on uneven development as just another quantifiable variable. We will now attempt to establish this link through a more substantive analysis of uneven development, before moving on to apply this to an understanding of the most recent 'local government crisis'.

2
Uneven Development and the Local State

2.1 Introduction: Aims and Outline

The last chapter showed that variations in local state policy can be important and pointed out that peculiarly local social relations may be significant in helping to shape these variations. This chapter goes on to discuss where this local peculiarity comes from, primarily through a focus on uneven development in capitalist society. It is in capitalist society that uneven development is most mature and most dynamic. It is also in capitalist societies that states and state institutions are particularly well developed.

These two tendencies are not unrelated. State institutions are invaluable in the organization and management of the increasingly large-scale, differentiated and changing societies typical of capitalism. But this very differentiation complicates such management, and one response is to use specifically local state institutions to deal with specifically local situations. In other words, without the uneven development of societies there would be little need for local – that is subnational – institutions in the first place. Of course, that other major institution of capitalist society – the firm – also plays a part in managing, as well as creating, uneven development. And, for the very same reasons, firms too must have their local management centres. Indeed, take away the firm, as in socialist countries, and state institutions gain even more social prominence.

This conclusion is given a further twist by the development of representative democracy with periodic universal franchise. This emerged at the end of the nineteenth century, although even in the Western democracies it was not well established until after 1945. For again, national representation cannot always deal adequately with local differentiation, and so local electoral politics was clearly a necessary part of representative democracy. But adding a democratic or popular element to some local state institutions also strengthens and legitimizes the role of representing local interests *to* the centre. This may then increasingly contradict the role of dealing with local situations *for* the centre. As Miliband pointed out in his seminal work *The State in Capitalist Society* (1969), local state became both obstacle and agent for the national state.

Although Miliband's insight has largely been neglected since then, his assertion seems quite appealing in the context of Britain in the 1980s where local–central state relations are clearly a hot political issue. Abolition of the Greater London Council (GLC) and Metropolitan County Councils, rate-capping, court cases enforcing central decisions over local governments and vice versa, rival publicity campaigns, a mass of complex legislation seen as 'the death of local democracy' – all this and more makes the crisis obvious enough. But if we are to understand *where* this crisis comes from, we must begin by answering the question of why have a local state level at all? For clearly, without a local state level there could hardly be a local–central crisis. It is this simple but nonetheless crucial fact that most theorizations of the local state – and even more accounts of the current crisis in Britain – have neglected.

We will tackle the linkage between uneven social development and local states in four stages. First, in section 2.2, we ask what difference space makes to social processes; while spatial patterns are not causative in a generative sense these contingent effects can be crucial to how events and changes actually occur in practice. Section 2.3 examines how the social processes of capitalism themselves are uneven; not only do spatial differences make a difference to social processes, but the social processes of capitalism themselves create a highly developed spatial differentiation. Section 2.4 unpacks the notion of uneven development in conceptual terms, distinguishing between spatial divisions of labour and spatial divisions of civil society and suggesting how these divisions give rationale to spatial divisions of the state – the local state. Finally in section 2.5 we draw on empirical research to show how these three major components of society are related in practice, and to show the importance of uneven development to the actions of the local state.

2.2 The Difference that Space Makes

THE SOCIAL IMPORTANCE OF SPATIAL VARIATION

The argument in this section is primarily an abstract one, so it is as well to begin with some examples of the difference that space makes in practice. On a global level, the variations and opposing trajectories between First and Third Worlds, and between countries within these 'worlds' are so obvious that they scarcely need comment. Think, for instance, of the physical, social and economic differences between Sudan, Mexico, Bangladesh, Sweden and Japan. The fact that capitalism as a world system and the natural world of physical and biological processes are both so clearly uneven directly supports our arrangement that 'space makes a difference'. Looked at this way, the 'spatial amnesia' of economics, sociology and other social sciences, which commonly see social processes existing on the head of a pin without any spatial variation, appears rather misleading. This is why, in the context of empirical research, these disciplines often (although usually implicitly) wrongly identify 'society' or 'economy' with the nation-state – as in 'British society' or 'the British economy'. For empirical research must perfoce recognize spatial and temporal specificity. However, this sort of recognition is equally misleading for there is no reason why spatial variation should be completely encapsulated by nation-states, however important these may still be in institutionalizing social practices. Supranational differences (for example, First versus Third World, European Economic Community [EEC] versus Latin America) and subnational differences (Wallonia versus Flanders, Brixton versus Sutton) may also be significant – perhaps increasingly so as the nation-state becomes less important as a unit of economic management and even as a unit of political organization.

The importance of subnational variations is obvious on a day to day practical level even if various social science accounts ignore this fact. Access to jobs and housing are two of the major material conditions of existence in Britain, yet how, with what success, and even if these conditions are achieved at all varies widely between different regions and areas. In the Rhondda Valley of South Wales 13 per cent of houses lack basic amenities, compared with only 1 per cent or less in most suburban areas of South-east England. Over 60 per cent of housing in much of urban Scotland is council housing, compared with less than 15 per cent in many small towns in the South of England. As many as 25 per cent of adult males are registered unemployed in part of London Docklands, compared with only 5 per cent in Winchester. Similarly, and indicatively with partially correlating patterns, phenomena perhaps more open to individual control vary just as much. In Camden 10.3 per cent of households have a single parent, and only 48.6 per cent follow the supposedly 'normal', structure of two parents and children, while in Bracknell these figures are 5.8 per cent and 77.6 per cent respectively. Likewise, rates of participation in industrial disputes vary widely across the country – they can be up to three times higher in Scotland than in the South-west of England.

To some researchers, however, spatial differences like these are little more than deviations from the norm and as such are of little interest. Some even treat these 'deviations' as being somehow less real than the norm. Yet it is, of course, the theoretical norm or the national average that is the statistical fiction – the average household size of 2.56 people can never exist. Nor do these researchers explain why they take national figures as the norm. Are these not merely 'local' deviations in an international socio-economic system, as multinational corporations know well? In fact, these researchers are using an implicit theory which gives some sort of 'national state social system' considerable autonomy, and this may be a mistake. Irrespective of how important national states may or may not be as institutions, it remains that differences at a national level can just be local variations on another scale, or they may just be fictional aggregates of local differences.

So local and national variations from statistical averages or theoretical norms can be significant, but the importance of spatial differences goes much further than that. Not only are they often co-variant but also, as this suggests, they frequently seem influential in a causative sense. For instance, the percentage of council housing in any local authority is not just a reflection of variations in income distribution or earlier inadequate housing. It is also a reflection of the strength of local political action to provide such housing, and sometimes this factor may well be quite crucial. What is more, this strength will co-vary with other social factors like strength of union organization, or the need for farmers and landowners to maintain a low-waged labour force. Thus our own work on housing provision in Britain showed how abnormally high rates of council housing in Labour-controlled Sheffield and Conservative-controlled Norfolk alike could be traced to locally generated action developing from locally specific social structures (Dickens et al., 1985). Other work draws similar conclusions. For just one, quite instructive example, see Mark-Lawson et al. 1985 on local variations in women's political action and the provision of municipal welfare. In both cases significant variations in social action were not just some pre-ordained, passive mapping of national policy, determined by national actors or international forces. Rather, local policies were absolutely crucial. These were formed consciously and actively at the local level, but in turn did not simply reflect the different political balances in the various towns. It was more a matter of what these balances meant in relation to locally-formed consciousness and possibilities for action. So for instance people's experiences of paid work and gender relations in Nelson meant that Labour Party policy there was different from Labour Party policy in Preston.

Even more indicative are the few records of those times when masses of people made their own choices. Miller (1977, 1978), Johnston (1983) and Warde (1985) have shown that, even if class identification is weakening as a basis for individual voting behaviour in Britain, paradoxically it is becoming stronger at a constituency level. They postulate some sort of 'neighbourhood effect' of local interaction dominated by specific political cultures in different places to account for this. Voting variations are not simply reducible to variations in social characteristics, but also depend on how these variations add up to something more, and this more seems to be a locality-based 'neighbourhood effect' that is socially active. Variations in strike polls and strike action, which by their nature often minimize class and occupational differences, tell a similar story. In Tyneside and Liverpool as many as 95 per cent of teachers belonging to the National Union of Teachers voted to go on strike in March 1985, compared with a low of 59 per cent in Surrey. Similarly in July 1985, 84 per cent of members of the Association of Professional, Executive, Clerical and Computer Staff (APEX) in Wales and 83 per cent in Scotland voted to continue with their political fund in support of the Labour Party, compared with only 66 per cent in the Midlands. Or how should we explain the quite different reactions of face-working coal-miners doing very similar jobs, in equally secure pits, in Yorkshire and Nottinghamshire during the 1984/5 coal dispute? The former stayed on strike for almost a year, much to the surprise of a nationally focused establishment who were forced to rediscover the power of 'community spirit' (see *Financial Times*, 23, 24 July 1984). The latter, just 50 miles away, were equally opposed to strike action (see figure 2.1). Whether this contrast reflects long political-cultural histories (as some analysts believe, see Rees 1986), or just on-the-spot differences in group pressures and actions, or a mixture of both, it cannot be denied that what became a variation of momentous political impact is rooted in 'locality'.

Nor do things end there, for people are not only influenced by their contexts but are also aware of them and act partly on that basis. Managers of multinational firms make decisions reflecting what they see as significant local differences in labour forces (Massey, 1984). Equally 'local people' (sic) can act according to some idea of what their 'local area' is or should be, even if this is

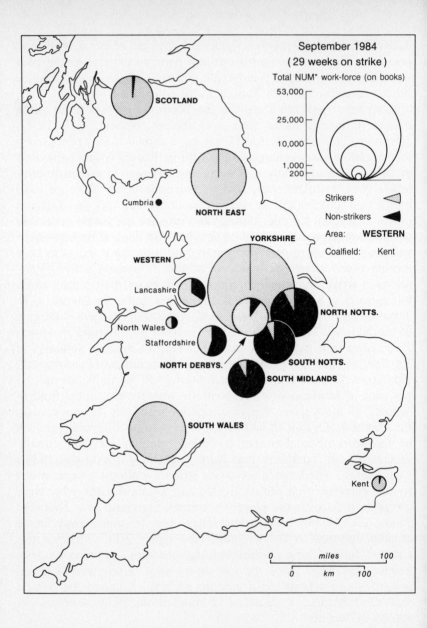

Figure 2.1 The 1984/5 coal industry dispute: strikers and non-strikers by area

Sources: The Guardian (28 September 1984) and National Coal Board Area Offices (21 October 1984)

Note: * National Union of Mineworkers

just as much an 'imagined community' of localism as anything real in material, social or economic terms (cf. B. Anderson, 1983, on nationalism). In effect they see 'their' local area as a specific locality even if they do not use the term. So the few hundred inhabitants of Allerdales in Northumberland campaigned successfully, both to gain control of their own defunct school building and to keep out a planned ski-centre, all – apparently – on the basis of what sort of place they thought Allerdales was and ought to be (Strathern, 1984).

These examples demonstrate that a varied mixture of local differences, locally centred action and locally referent consciousness can be socially significant. It is this combination that researchers have tried to capture with the terms 'region', *'pays de vie'*, 'community', 'local social system' and 'locality'. There is certainly something there even if most of these concepts have led researchers in the wrong direction. Sure enough, space makes a difference – but these research traditions have nearly always gone to the other extreme and ended up in a cul-de-sac where space is seen as determining social behaviour. This spatial determinism, it is now agreed, is just as bad as ignoring space altogether. (See Saunders (1985a) for urban sociology; Sack (1980) for geography, and Duncan 1988 for 'locality research'). Our first task must be to try and establish how spatial arrangements actually do make a differencee to social processes, to find some credible position between ignoring space and reifying space.

SPACE AS A CONTINGENT EFFECT

Space makes a difference to how social processes work. Yet it is equally clear that spatial processes do not operate in some way independently of social process, and that consequently spatial patterns and areas cannot be analysed in isolation. Spatial patterns are not autonomous, nor does space determine social organization and activity. Similarly, it is incorrect to talk as though there were interdependencies between different spatial patterns in themselves. It is social objects that interact, not the spatial patterns they form. This is the conclusion to a thoroughgoing debate in both geography and urban sociology (Sack, 1980; Saunders, 1981, 1985e; Sayer, 1982, 1985a; Urry, 1981a, 1985). The notorious 'spatial fetishism' once so common in those subjects is now ruled out.

But despite this conclusion, research can slip back all too easily into this 'spatial fetishism'. This is because spatial arrangements clearly do make a difference (as we saw earlier) and because 'space' or the 'spatial' is also an appealing common-sense or shorthand way of signifying what we might otherwise have to call 'the contingent effect of the uneven development of social processes'. Quite often, however, the shorthand can take over, as is notorious in urban ecology and indeed in the whole concept of the 'urban' (as in 'urban society', the 'urban way of life', 'urban policy', etc.). The hidden supposition is that particular spatial arrangements, in this case the distinction between urban and rural areas, have some independent causal power. This is not the case, and by speaking of 'the urban' we are really talking about social relations like access to housing, racial discrimination or the costs of traffic congestion, or even natural processes like the physical effects of pollution. Unfortunately, calling these 'urban' only confuses the issue. In reviewing this fetishistic tendency in urban sociology, Saunders (1985e), uses the interesting example of the 1981 inner-city riots in Britain. Even though they did take place during long, warm summer evenings in inner cities, it would be a great mistake, he says, to try to find the causes of these riots in this spatial and temporal dimension. They were caused by social factors like racism, unemployment and policing practice. These factors were not 'spatial' or 'urban' in origin even if they clearly had a spatial and indeed urban setting. Rather, this setting made a difference to exactly how these factors worked and either facilitated or inhibited rioting as one response to them.

One way of dealing with the differences that space makes is simply to deny that spatial arrangements have any significance at all. This has traditionally been the view of most of sociology and economics, which have treated societies and economies as though they exist without a spatial dimension. In so far as spatial patterns were admitted, they were usually just a matter of minor and limited deviations from spaceless (and usually also timeless) social phenomena. Such a view was conveniently confirmed by the opposite extreme of geography and urban sociology, where the autonomy of the spatial was, equally incorrectly, the prime explanatory dimension. This situation led to an easy all-or-nothing academic division of labour where neither approach could properly capture the spatial dimensions of societies.

In traditional economics and sociology, this 'fallacy of composition' has three results. First, societies and human activity necessarily involve passing through – and hence changing in – time and space. Both are temporally and spatially specific. Neglecting this fact is serious, quite possibly crippling, if we seek to produce explanations of any concrete, real-world problems (which is, after all, the supposed function of social science!). The 'inner-city problem' in Britain is a good example. At one level this is clearly a result of changes in the international division of labour and labour processes. But, equally clearly, national (British) and local (city-level) histories, cultures and social forms have their own significance in specifying such processes and mediating them in particular ways (see for example, Massey, 1984 on the changing geography of manufacturing in Britain). This first problem of ignoring spatial variation is in some ways akin to the problem of the average, which never exists in reality.

Ironically, when researchers use their economic or social abstractions in a concrete way, and this inevitably means in specific places, they find all sorts of qualifications and particularities. Perhaps, some researchers conclude, class or the new international division of labour, or whatever abstraction it is, do not exist. Or if they do exist this is only as abstract concepts that cannot by themselves say much about real-world situations. This is the second problem of approaches that deny spatial differences; how can they account for all the detailed real-world variations that clearly exist? Finally, if the effects of spatial variation were to be specified we find that theories developed in their absence are sometimes inapplicable even at this abstract level. The classic example is of those economic models that imply perfect competition, although this is quite impossible in a spatial world like the one we live in.

Interestingly, some apparently non-traditional theories have ended up in a similar position, again partly because of an over-reaction against spatial determinism. The new urban sociology of Castells is one example. Criticizing the spatial fetishism of urban sociology, Castells (in *The Urban Question*, 1977) and others concluded that space is not something that exists outside society, rather it is something produced by society. So far, so good, but then – as Sayer (1985a) points out – comes the *non sequitur* that the spatial is therefore entirely social. While we can agree that the spatial is indeed *constituted* partly by the social (for we should not forget the natural world) this does not mean it cannot be simply *reduced* to these constituents.

This brief discussion of disciplinary approaches confirms our previous conclusion that both extremes concerning space *vis-á-vis* society should be rejected. First, space *per se* has no general effects, nor is it some sort of empty container separate from social and natural objects. But on the other hand, spatial arrangements do make a difference to how social processes work, even though much of mainstream economics and sociology ignores the fact. This conclusion leaves us in a less comfortable middle position. It also leaves us with the question of *how*, precisely, space, or at least spatial arrangements, make a difference.

The logic of our argument so far is that of the relativist position on space. This view denies that space is an object or substance, in the sense that objects are made up of various materials. Rather, space can only exist as a relation between objects (such as planets, cities or people), which do have substance. Without these objects, there is no spatial relation – and hence no independent space can exist. Spatial patterns cannot, therefore, have independent effects. This means that we reject the opposing concept of absolute space, according to which space does exist independently of objects and where it can have its own effects. Hence in our view concepts like the 'friction of distance' in quantitative geography are untenable.

The logic of our argument so far, however, also modifies this relativist position in one important way. For, even though space is created by natural and social objects, it does *not* follow that the effects of these spatial relations can simply be reduced to the causal powers of these objects. This was the mistake Castells made. Having been constituted by objects, spatial relations may then affect how, if and in what ways these objects then relate (see Sayer, 1985a; Urry, 1985, for reviews).

Making a distinction between causal processes and contingent effects permits further specification of how space actually makes a difference. This distinction has been of particular importance to the realist account of scientific explanation (Sayer, 1984). Urry (1981a) summarizes this position. Space in itself has no general effect, and hence no autonomous causal powers. Rather space

> only has effect because the social objects in question possess particular characteristics, namely, different causal powers. Such powers may or may not manifest themselves in empirical events – whether they do or not depends upon the relationship in time–space established with other objects. (Urry, 1981a, p. 458)

Spatial relations are, therefore, contingent where effects stem not from these relations but from the internal structure of social objects possessing causal powers. However, contingent spatial relations are crucial (among other contingencies) to whether and how such powers are realized.

Sayer (1985a, 1985b) reaches similar conclusions, again basing his argument on the realist philosophy of science. Rejecting the concept of an autonomous absolute space, but also opposing the complete reduction of spatial effects to its social (or natural) constituents, he concludes:

> Space makes a difference, but only in terms of the particular causal powers and liabilities constituting it. Conversely, what kind of effects are produced by causal mechanisms depends *inter alia* on the form of the conditions in which they are situated. (1985a, 52)

Sayer takes the implications of this conclusion further by drawing a distinction between abstract and concrete research. Abstract research, according to Sayer, 'is concerned with structures (sets of internally or necessarily related objects or practices) and with the causal powers and liabilities necessarily possessed by objects in virtue of their nature' (ibid., p. 53). But because it is contingent whether and how these are exercised, concrete research is needed to determine the actual effects of the causal powers.

Now, because spatial effects are contingent, abstract social theory need pay little attention to them (and indeed Marx, Weber, Durkheim, etc., did not do so in in this theoretical sense, see Saunders, 1981, 1985a). This is not to say that such theories can be developed without recognizing this contingency effect, however. They must, says Sayer, recognize that all matter *has* spatial extension and hence that processes do not take place in a void, and that no two objects can occupy the same relative place at the same time. Hence our earlier comments on the inapplicability of economic models which, by neglecting this fact, are able to assume perfect competition. But while social theory must be spatial in this basic sense, such theories have neither to concern themselves overmuch with spatial effects nor, indeed, can they say much about them.

The situation is quite different with concrete research, where it is the interrelation between structural mechanisms and contingent effects that is crucial. This is certainly the case for the research objects of social science – people and society. For it is rarely, if ever, possibloe to remove or standardize contingent effects in social science as it is in the controlled experiment of natural science. The research objects of social science must perforce remain 'open systems' (see Sayer, 1984 chapter 4). This remains the case despite the existence of various quasi-experimental methods used in social science, notably statistical standardization and comparative analysis, which attempt to circumnavigate openness and contingency. While useful in particular circumstances, neither can create closed systems out of open ones and misapprehension on this point has been one cause of low explanatory power in social science research. Spatial patterns form one such contingent effect and this is why space matters. Indeed, and this is one strand of our argument, space matters so much that local state institutions have been developed to deal with it (even if they then help to create more spatial problems). We will return to this issue later in the chapter.

We can often fool ourselves that social processes are *not* constituted contingently in space and time (in the context of social theory that is, we would be most unlikely to assume this in everyday life). This theoretical blind spot can develop from the false – or at least misleading – distinction often made between general processes and local processes, between macro and micro. Supposedly general processes, for example capital accumulation, class conflict or deindustrialization, are commonly but incorrectly seen as being aspatial. It is as though these processes somehow floated above the real world in some spaceless realm. Rather, they are constituted from the start in countless places and are only general in the sense that their spatial dimensions are not those of a single place. It is on this spatial constitution that spatial contingency effects take effect. In area X, for instance, the general processes of deindustrialization and gender-role definition might interact in a specific way, different from the way they might interact – if at all – in areas A and B. In one area paid employment might be 'feminized', in another women workers might be laid off, in a third female employment opportunities might increase in one sector as they decrease in another, and so on.

This artificial distinction between general and local emerges from a conflation of our mental processes of abstraction with what actually happens in reality. Thus we may *mentally* abstract theories of the state, say, from the places where real states are created and reproduced. This abstraction can be useful enough for theoretical analysis, which is after all a vital part of any research. We may then more easily talk about the social relations of citizenship or class without getting too involved in the very particular histories and contexts of, say, Swedish local authorities. But we should not be fooled by our own abstractions into imagining that processes can actually exist in an abstract way, and hence without spatial relations. States, for instance, can only exist concretely and hence enmeshed in all manner of contingent relations including spatial ones. This confusion has been a particular obstacle to the attempt to provide theories of the local state – where it is precisely the fact of uneven development in space and in society that underlies their existence.

LOCAL PROCESSES – DERIVATIVE OR CAUSAL?

The conclusion so far is that nearly all processes and forms will be differentiated spatially, and hence most processes and forms will also have some sort of 'local' expression. 'Local' should be interpreted elastically here: for instance, in a discussion of world development, particular nation-states or even groups of states like the EEC, can be seen as 'local' constitutions of global processes just as much as areas within nation-states can be considered 'local'.

This conclusion can reintroduce the dilemmas we started with, however. First we should resist the temptation to reify 'the local' or 'the region'. For it is apparent that these can be just as much a statistical aggregate as 'national' (although perhaps on a more sensitive spatial scale). Nor are there local or regional social systems as such – rather there are people, households, firms, state institutions and so on. People, acting individually or in collective situations, carry out social acts and so respond to and reproduce structures through their agencies. Local descriptions of these activities will aggregate and conflate in just the same way as a national description does – but arguably for most processes at a less aggregated level.

Secondly, in recognizing that general processes are in fact always constituted spatially, how far does this mean that causation, or causal power, is constituted locally? In some ways this is a hypothetical question, in the sense that general processes only exist in our minds as an abstraction. One way out of this difficulty is to make a distinction between contingent local variations and causal local processes. The former refers to the contingent effects of spatial patterns; the latter to the local specificity of generative social relations. The social basis for the former should by now be clear enough, but we can also imagine that some generative social relations (that is, they cause changes to happen rather than merely affecting contingently how change occurs), may be locally specific. This seems logical enough, because as we know, societies are unevenly developed. This uneven development is not just a matter of forms and outcomes (for example, certain industries locate in certain areas) but also of social mechanisms themselves. In some places, for instance, capitalist social relations will not be fully developed, or may be developed in some very particular ways, or may be partly decomposed.

Two contrasting examples of the development of spatial variations in contemporary Britain may make this distinction clearer. The first example, of contingent local variation, is the relationship between the 'M4 corridor' – a region of relative prosperity founded on high-tech industries strung out along the M4 motorway between London and Bristol – and London's Heathrow Airport. The emergence of the M4 corridor owes something to the fact that Heathrow lies at one end of it. But Heathrow did not in itself cause the development of high-tech industry in Britain and its particular requirements for various sorts of labour supply as well as infrastructural backing like airports, motorways and government defence laboratories. Nor did the social relations of creating and staffing an airport underlie the development of high-tech industry. Without Heathrow, or if London's major airport had been sited elsewhere, this high-tech growth would most probably still have happened – although perhaps in that case the corridor would have been somewhere else, up the M11 motorway to Cambridge and Stanstead Airport for instance. The importance of Heathrow was to affect, contingently, where high-tech growth took place; it did not cause it.

In contrast, causal local processes are those locally specific relations that are socially generative. Our example is the building of council housing in 'red islands' of labour movement local political hegemony. Sheffield is the sort of place we have in mind here. For a long period much more council housing was built than the average for British local authorities or even the average for large northern towns. Exceptionally, much of this housing was built using local authority direct labour and hence in a non-commodity form (see Dickens et al., 1985, chapter 5). This local outcome was not, however, just a result of spatial contingency effects – where, for example, more council housing was built because there was already more substandard housing in Sheffield. Rather, more was built because of the specific social relations existing there. A class-conscious and organized local political movement dominated the major local organ of state power – local government – and conciously used this power to build council housing which they saw as important to their political project. For the same reason, direct labour was often used to do the building. In other words, the causal social mechanisms were locally specific. Variation was not just a matter of the contingent effects of spatial patterns on some invariant and universal (or at least national) mechanism. Many other similar examples can be found (see, for instance, Murgatroyd et al., 1985, on the significance of 'localities' for social and economic processes). Figures 2.2 and 2.3 summarize the distinction between contingent local variation and causal local processes for the example of subnational differences in the provision of council housing. Note that we do *not* claim, by virtue of this argument, that these locally

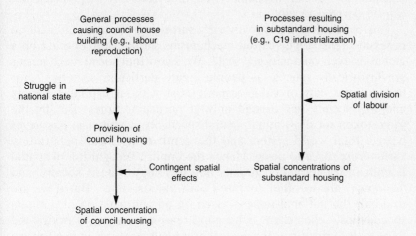

Figure 2.2 Contingent local variation: the case of council housing

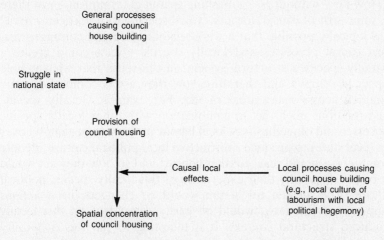

Figure 2.3 Causal local variation: the case of council housing

produced mechanisms were the only causal mechanisms involved or even the most important. For example, national legislation and national politics were crucial in allowing Sheffield's labour movement to act the way it did – as the collapse of council house building in the city since 1980 testifies only too well.

Local variation therefore, is not only a matter of the contingent effects of spatial arrangements. There may also be local causal mechanisms. Social mechanisms are not necessarily universal, but can be derived locally.

This conclusion is not really very surprising. There is after all no necessary reason why causal mechanisms should only operate on a global or even on a national scale. We know that social mechanisms are historically specific as people create particular societies – for instance the 'law of value' cannot exist without capitalist society and this society has existed only at particular times. But by the same token we must admit spatial specificity. Capitalism has never been a total world system and the depth of its social penetration varies from place to place. Hence the implicit recognition of spatial bounds in traditional economics and sociology, where 'society' and 'economy' are so often confused with 'nation-state'. But if we are to admit the national scale – based on an appreciation of national specificities – then there is no good reason to reject, a priori, the local scale. Of course, this logical argument does not in itself prove the existence or importance of local causal mechanisms in any situation – this still has to be demonstrated empirically.

How far – without re-establishing spatial determinism – can there be some sort of causal 'locality effect' specific to a particular area? It is logically possible that a whole gamut of spatial contingencies, local causal processes and locally specific effects could create a spatially specified structural system, in the sense that what people expect to happen and therefore how they act is comprehensively moulded across many areas of life. For example, locally specific class relations might act in combination with other locally specific processes and outcomes (say local labour movement hegemony over the local state) to produce a distinctive local political culture. People monitor, learn and react to their context and so how they act would be partly shaped by their experience of this locally specific political culture. The agenda for action would be changed; *what* actions happen, not just how, would be partly dependent on this locally produced structural context. It is tempting to call this a 'locality effect'. Two provisos follow, however. First, this criterion for the existence of 'locality effects' is a fairly demanding one. It is not something we would expect to happen often. For instance, the evidence for autonomous local political cultures in Britain (as opposed to local variations in political culture) is fairly weak (see Savage, 1987). Secondly, the existence of such locality effects should never be assumed simply because significant local variations exist.

We have now developed a three-stage hierarchy of how space makes a difference to social process. The first two elements in this hierarchy are based on the distinction between contingent and necessary relations, namely

1   'contingent local variation' (where spatial contingency affects how social mechanisms operate in practice), and
2   'causal local variation', (where the social mechanisms themselves are locally derived).

Finally, we argue that a third level

3   'locality effects', could occur (where a bundle of complementary and locally derived processes and outcomes produce some sort of local social system).

This is likely to be a rather rare occurrence.

We will return to this combination of spatial effects, in empirical terms, in sections 2.4 and 2.5. Before this, however, a considerable complication has to be dealt with. For not only does space make a difference in this essentially contingent way, but the social and economic processes of development – especially those of capitalist development – actively create spatial differences. We will deal with this considerable 'complication' in the next section.

2.3   Uneven Development and the Geography of Capitalism

The last section established how spatial relations made an important difference to how social processes work. However, in carrying through that argument we inevitably become aware that social processes are unevenly developed *in themselves*. Local variation is then built into the very nature of societies and their social mechanisms. This is particularly true of capitalism, for uneven development is a structurally based feature of its economic and social functioning, and in a capitalist world this will be the prime determinant of geographies at every scale, local as well as global. We need only think of the dramatic restructuring of geographic space over the last decade or so – deindustrialization, regional crisis, the inner-city problem, urban deconcentration, gentrification, the rise of newly industrializing countries, the further emmiseration of those Third World countries already worst off, sun-belts versus rust-belts and frost-belts. These processes are not separate, but are symptoms of capitalism as an unevenly developing system. If we can unravel something of the logic of this restructuring of space, we will then be in a much better position to understand how local differences are created. This is an essential preliminary for any discussion of the role played by local states in capitalist society.

Such a task – the construction of a theory of space relations under capitalism — is a stiff one. Things are made even more difficult because of all the complications of pre-existing social orders, of natural geographies and of those other social processes outside the strict causal remit of capitalist development. Fortunately, two excellent attempts at doing just this have recently been published: Smith's (1984) comprehensive treatment in his book *Uneven Development* and Harvey's (1985a) brilliant essay 'The Geopolitics of Capitalism' (based on Harvey, 1982). Much of our discussion is based on these accounts.

CAPITALISM AS UNEVEN DEVELOPMENT

Capitalism does not just develop unevenly because of pre-existing social and natural variation, nor because of the influence of contingent spatial effects. Uneven development is not, therefore, simply that the types and quantities of socio-economic activities vary from place to place so that there will be imbalances between them. Rather, uneven development refers to the uneven *process* of development that derives from the particular characters of capitalism. Indeed, uneven development in space and time is central to the processes of capitalist production and social reproduction. Development in one place and time is causally linked to underdevelopment elsewhere, development in one area of life is causally linked with underdevelopment in another, and the conditions that both create lead to further uneven development. In this way geographies can be seen as a systematic expression of the very constitution and structure of capitalism. And both state and local states have been developed in response to the production of these social geographies.

What then, is the logic of uneven development? According to Smith this consists of the opposed but simultaneous tendencies towards the differentiation and equalization of the levels and conditions of production. Both tendencies are inherent in the way capitalism works as an economic and social process.

Differentiation is a consequence of the division of labour and direction of investment where different amounts of surplus can be produced for the same expenditure of labour. At first this is dependent on spatial differentiation in natural endowments and pre-capitalist development. To take the classic example, the early industrialization of Pennine Lancashire and West Yorkshire in the eighteenth century depended on the concentration of domestic textile workers there, workers who were not organized in guilds and were surrounded by sites suitable for water-powered factories and, later, coal-fired steam engines. Very soon, however, this pre-existing profitability surface is largely overlaid by qualitative and quantitative differences in social organization and infrastructure. So, for example, it was the development of canals, railways, factories, skilled labour, market knowledge, inter-plant linkages, etc., which underlay the further rise of the Pennine textile industries and – equally – saw the demise of earlier cloth-making centres elsewhere, in East Anglia and the West Country. At the same time Britain's growing political power was used to undermine foreign competitors, such as Ireland and India, primarily through erecting tariff barriers and preferential trading. Only later, when technical superiority was assured, was free trade imposed, and with the same objective. This social development largely replaces natural conditions in producing a shifting surface of relative 'fertility' in producing surplus value. Now, of course, the North of England is largely worked out as far as profit via textile production goes. Smith (1984) shows in detail how these changing divisions of labour, and hence changing geographies, are established through the changing balances between economic departments (for example agricultural, production goods, consumption goods), industrial sectors, and firms as individual property units. In the latter case, for instance, the concentration and centralization of capital leads to rearrangements in spatial relations as well as in ownership and organization.

But at the same time pressures exist for the equalization of the conditions of production and in the development of productive forces. Through the competitive process in a world-wide system of circulation the processes of investment, aimed at improving labour productivity and hence market survival, generalize the conditions that once led to polarized development. Capital is simultaneously withdrawn from worked-out developed areas and reinvested in underdeveloped areas where the conditions for extracting surplus have improved. Far Eastern textile producers can now beat the North of England at its own game although, as this example suggests, such equalization is unlikely to be even – for the processes of differentiation go on unabated.

The upshot of all this is that capital is constantly invested in creating environments – the productive, infrastructural and reproductive facilities (factories, roads and houses for example) necessary to produce surplus value and expand the basis of successful capitalism. But equally, capital is continually withdrawn from its built environment so that it can move elsewhere and take advantage of conditions now allowing higher profit rates. The created environment is then a mosaic at every stage of development – parts are being built, others are at every stage of devalorization (where its value gradually decays), and some elements are abandoned remnants of fixed capital now rendered valueless. The transition from canal to rail to motorway and the consequent geographical rearrangements of economic activity is perhaps the best-known example of this 'see-saw' development, although such processes also affect whole places or economic sectors. Crises are a particularly effective way of achieving rapid capital transfers, quickly devaluing old fixed capital and old places and so allowing new sectors – and places – to take off. Such crises may affect only particular sectors and small areas (like the collapse of steel-making in some erstwhile steel towns all across Western Europe and North America), or they may affect whole departments and countries (the deindustrialization of Britain perhaps) or even the whole world, with global depression.

There is, however, another twist to this process of uneven development and that is the factor of space. As Harvey points out, 'The aim and objective of those engaged in the circulation of capital must be, after all, to command surplus labour *time* and convert it into profit within the *socially-necessary turnover time*' (1985a, pp. 144–5). From the standpoint of capital, space is in the first instance a barrier to be overcome, something that inflates turnover time. This standpoint echoes Marx's famous aphorism that capitalism perpetually strives to 'annihilate space with time'. Transport technology, electronic and physical communications are among the major means of achieving this annihilation. But, and here lies the rub, this objective can only be achieved through the production of fixed and immobile spatial configurations – a railway network with conurbations and industrial centres, for instance – and of course this system becomes part and parcel of one stage in the creation of an environment. Spatial organization and the creation of geography is necessary to overcome space and outflank geography. Furthermore, the creation of new improved spatial organization (a motorway network with small town and suburban production sites perhaps) means the abandonment of at least parts of the old. The annihilation of space also creates space.

We should not imagine that people are left passive as 'capitalism' creates and destroys geographies around them. It is, of course, people who create and run these social and economic processes even if they do not do so in freedom from others, or in conditions of their own choosing, and with the nightmare of the past always bearing down on them. People are able to monitor and learn from their experiences and may attempt to change and control them. One way in which people do this is the attempt – a doomed attempt according to Smith – to find a 'spatial fix'; to establish some sort of geographical stability within which they can work and live even as they work against it. Fixed capital and hard-won spatial configurations, social as well as physical, should not be abandoned or destroyed as soon as they are created. State intervention in the social economy – fixing exchange rates, labour laws, housing subsidies, welfare systems, internal security, etc. – is one major means of establishing this fix.

The need for a spatial fix interacts with an in-built tendency to produce what Harvey (1985a) calls the 'structured coherence' of production and consumption over given spaces. Processes and infrastructures, both social and physical, combine to produce a particular space currently suitable for a specific mix of surplus value production. Forms and technologies of production, inter-industry linkages, patterns of labour supply and demand, physical and social infrastructures, patterns of life and consumption, all these interact to produce this coherence. On one scale this structured coherence may exist as that space within which capital can circulate without the limits of profit being threatened by the cost and time of movement. This suggests some sort of regional socio-economic unit, for example the West Midlands in Britain based (until recently) on a close interlinkage of firms and labour around metal-making, engineering and vehicle production. (This 'regional unit' could of course be a nation-state.) On a smaller scale, structured coherence may exist as the space within which labour power can be substituted on a daily basis, that is a local labour-market defined by commuting patterns. So within the West Midlands, specific labour-markets exist with particular characterizations of labour supply. Needless to say, this essentially capitalist rationale can be reinforced by the development of regional and local cultures and consciousness. And these cultures (although Harvey does not develop this point) will be partly formed by social practices and relations autonomous to the logic of capital.

In Britain, South Wales is perhaps the most comprehensively studied example. Created economically for coal and metal export, the resultant class structures, combined with cultural experiences both at work and outside it, led to the development of a 'radical region' (Cooke, 1985a, b). Interestingly, even though the economic rationale for this particular regional coherence has all but disappeared, to some extent the radical region still persists. The social practices and institutions created in the context of a regional economy of coal and steel may outlive the latter's dissolution. And, we may note, local states have been one means by which this regional reproduction is assured (Cooke, 1983). We will return to this uneven development in civil society later in this section.

By 1985 the regional economy of the West Midlands was in tatters, and was rapidly becoming one of Britain's highest unemployment areas – although some firms continued to do well by diversifying into other sectors outside the region. Similarly, employment in South Wales now centres on services and branch plant-assembly while two new regions seem to be emerging – the south and east of South Wales as down-market extensions of the M4 electronics corridor and the erstwhile coal-mining valleys as a labour reserve. As these examples show, structured coherence is both undermined and transformed by the processes of uneven development. Changes in labour processes and capitalist organiz- ation (for example, deskilling combined with the rise of multination- als) both permit command over progressively larger spaces and alter what capital requires – and hence how particular places rank in the profitability surface (see Massey, 1984, for an analysis of these changing 'spatial divisions of labour' in Britain). Technological developments weaken the spatial contraints over production and increasingly 'annihilate space with time' At the same time, internal processes threaten coherence, as when labour becomes redundant and is pushed out or when capital leaves when labour becomes more organized. International divisions of labour dominate local or regional divisions. Local consciousness is transformed to capitalist consumerism. The spatial fix is both porous and unstable.

How, then, has structured, spatially specific coherence survived? Harvey provides one answer, a version of a now-familiar paradox. If each form of mobile capital, each improvement in the capacity to annihilate space with time, is to function, each also requires a relatively fixed and secured socio-spatial infrastructure. Even that superlative symbol of capital mobility, the international money market, requires a well-organized telecommunications system, substantial support from territorially organized legal, financial and state institutions, specialised office space and suitable living space for its high-paid workers. Currently, both the built environment of the City of London and large residential zones of the South-East of England are being restructured as part of the spatial coherence needed for this capital mobility to function. Ironically enough, the City of London partly survives as a world financial centre because its spatial position straddles time zones. At the other end of the spectrum labour power is relatively immobile in the short term, while a similar paradox operates. For capitalist development as a whole, the free and rapid movement of labour appears necessary, but for individual workplaces a stable, reliable work-force is equally necessary – possibly with the support of reproduction services in education, health, welfare and so on. The former requires spatial fluidity, the latter spatial stability. Harvey summarizes this with the aphorism 'The ability to overcome space is predicated on the production of space' (1985a, p. 149). Note also Harvey's shorthand here: by 'space' Harvey actually means 'the uneven development of social relations'. The discussion of spatial patterns easily leads to the reification of space.

Another answer would stress how people must work to create and maintain these spatial fixes, to contest their insecurity and porosity. At the same time, the actions of others undermine structured coherence. A major mechanism for doing both these things is the state. The subdivision of the world into 200 or more nation-states, several supranational state systems like the EEC, and a multiplicity of subnational states, reflects in part the desire to defend fixed capital and organize social capital.

Just as this desire for stability means, among other things, a spatial fix, so states are fundamental to the organization and indeed the very concept of territoriality. Different levels of the state, as well as particular state institutions, may refer most to different scales of spatial fix – international economic organization, national political organization, local labour-market organization. This does not mean that state institutions only respond to the uneven development of capitalism and to economic processes in particular. Quite the opposite, for in organizing spatial fixes states must intervene between capitalist production and civil society, (that is, households, communities and voluntary social life). So state policy must be interested in the development of civil society.

Equally, states are useful in dismantling old fixes in favour of new ones. Dominant groups at the centre may see their best interests served by breaking up state cemented spatial fixes. The activities of the nineteenth-century bourgeoisie in creating free trade is a well worked example (e.g. Hobsbawm, 1975): the 'opening up' of Britain to the market – in personal life just as much as in the economy – since the Conservative government came to power in 1979 is just a current example. Interestingly for our argument, this attempt to move from a supposedly outmoded spatial fix has led to central–local conflict. Because for other social groups, not so well represented in the national state in Whitehall but influential locally, the question was more how to defend or revitalize existing spatial fixes. Various left-wing local governments in Britain attempted to 'restructure for labour' or at least to defend labour, using local economic policies aimed at regenerating dissolving spatial fixes. Typically, these policies attempted to keep a manufacturing base in the older industrial conurbations just as central government was making their position all the worse. This is also one explanation for the need for central states to control local government more directly – as the current case shows all too well (see chapters 4 and 5).

State power, wielded through a variety of institutions with various levels of competence and spatial responsibility, is one means of creating and maintaining spatial fixes. We might even say an essential means, for states are fundamental to the organization and indeed to the very idea of territoriality. Furthermore, different social groups will have different ideas over what sort of spatial fix is best for them, and these groups will also have different access to various sorts and level of state institution.

UNEVEN DEVELOPMENT, NATURE AND CIVIL SOCIETY

As examples like local government economic policy or the creation of the South Wales as a radical region suggest, uneven development cannot be seen purely and simply as a matter of capitalist production – however central and wide-reaching this might be. Natural processes retain their own autonomy, even if they way that these processes work out is mediated by social practices. Desertification and acid rain are classic examples, where climatic and biochemical processes are given particular results in particular places by political economy. Similarly, not all social processes derive from the capital–labour relation; far from it, even if most interlink with capitalism and are often deeply permeated by it or even subordinated to it. The practices of civil society – relations of kinship, gender, household, or the 'imagined communities' of locality or nation – these too are generated by mechanisms pre-dating capitalism and to an extent surviving it. Indeed, the mechanisms of patriarchy and ethnicity are sometimes given equal weight in accounts of social action.

This point is of considerable importance in our discussion of the development of states, including local states. Rather than existing as a mere reflection of the uneven development of capital, states stand in a complex mediating position between capital, civil society and nature. The basic idea is that capitalism needs both civil society and nature to exist; it depends on the first to supply labour power and consumer demand, and on the latter to provide raw materials and a waste bin. Production could not take place without nature, and without civil society neither production nor valorization would be possible. It is the Achilles' heel of capitalism that it does not create either nature or civil society. Raw materials are produced and waste materials are dispersed by geophysical and biological processes (even if their value and use is socially mediated); workers and consumers are produced in families and communities. The development of capitalist states is one means by which capitalists and other dominant groups attempts to regulate and intervene in these autonomous systems, an intervention which becomes all the more pressing as both civil society and nature are overlooked by capital's demands. As these systems are spatially constituted and differentiated, it is necessary for state systems to respond with the development of local states.

While the physical mechanisms of the natural world may be invariant, they are also constituted contingently in space and time – and in the context of social systems. The practices of civil society are also constituted contingently, in the context of nature, of each other and of world capitalism. For example, gender divisions of labour in simpler gatherer–hunter or agrarian societies owe much to the cultural interpretation and organization of labour, and the types of labour done in turn owe much to the uneven development of nature. The same principle holds in capitalist societies, except that now the uneven development of capitalism overlays natural unevenness. Thus, recent research on the geography of manufacturing in Britain has pointed to the importance of female labour reserves in accounting for the dramatic locational changes that have occurred since the 1950s (Massey, 1984). But the uneven development of these reserves was not simply a matter of the level and nature of pre-existing economic activity. It was also a result of the uneven and changing nature of gender roles in families.

The practices of civil society are not only constituted contingently and are hence mapped out unevenly. They are also, like the processes of capitalist development, uneven in themselves and so create differentiation. (Although arguably uneven development in civil society is not so powerfully self-reinforcing). This is because social relations are just what the term suggests – relational between people, (although this is often forgotten). They are developed actively in practice, they may change in their nature and they may undevelop. Ironically enough, Marx's aphorism about the annihilation of space by time was apparently taken from a poem by Alexander Pope about love and lovers:

> Ye Gods! annihilate but space and time,
> And make two lovers happy.

Marx of course, gave a whole new meaning by changing 'space and time' to 'space by time' (see Smith, 1984, p. 170–1).

As we have seen, the processes of uneven development in capitalism paradoxically lead to a structured coherence in social activities in space and time, and people try to build on these coherences by creating 'spatial fixes' of nation, region or locality. The same thing happens through the uneven development of nature and civil society. Reinforcing sets of natural processes and cultural practices can coalesce to produce on the one hand, spatially organized ecological systems and, on the other, particular ways of living in particular places. Neither sort of coherence is likely, in the late twentieth century, to be independent from capitalist development but, paradoxically, this gives good reasons for state institutions to get all the more involved in these spatially constituted systems.

Cooke (1985b) develops just such an argument in explaining the emergence of South Wales as a 'radical region'. He bases his explanation partly on Gramsci's ideas of why some class practices are dominant, some subordinate and how this varies historically and spatially. According to Gramsci, social action is not just a matter of economic agency and of the social rationality based upon economic position. It is also a question of specific and spatially varied social relations concerning the production and maintenance of social ideologies and expectations. These variable cultural practices – and Gramsci stressed the role of intellectuals (where Catholic priests in the South of Italy play this role just as much as middle managers in North Italian cities) – provide the means by which social constraints and opportunities are communicated and reinforced. These spatially distinctive sets of hegemonic practices and ideas then provide the basis for the formation of regional power blocks of interests, which in turn systematically reproduce themselves and hence also maintain the uneven development of the economy. In Italy during the 1920s, according to Gramsci, the uneven relationship between a northern power block of industrialists and workers, and a southern one of *rentiers* and peasantry was disturbed by the emergence of a radical rural proletariat in Central Italy. This disruption to the 'spatial fix' in both economics and politics produced the conditions in which fascism could develop.

While approving this focus on the spatially uneven nature of social relations, Cooke argues that Gramsci nevertheless under-emphasizes the importance of work practices. These may be crucial to whether individuals take up the idea of acting collectively, and if they do whether they act in a deferential or combative way. Thus, in South Wales the relatively autonomous and egalitarian work practices of coal miners encouraged a combative and collective outlook (where the more hierarchical and paternalistic work practices of coal miners in North-east England had the opposite effect). These practices in one sense depend on the uneven development of the economy – the development of coal-mining was clearly necessary to their emergence, but they cannot be reduced to this economic sphere. The precise way coal-mining was developed in South Wales (relatively late when mass working-class trade unionism was developing and on a large scale), the nature and practices of the particular capitalists involved (who wanted to break unions rather than incorporate them), the inherited social practices and traditions of South and West Wales (that stressed Welsh resistance to an English upper class), the development of a specific set of labour intellectuals and labour institutions in the trade unions – all these interacted to produce a sum greater than the parts, a structured coherence in the uneven development of civil society. Again, this coherence is porous and unstable, but again one way of managing, controlling, destabilizing or maintaining it is through using state institutions. This brings us back to local–central state conflict, for different interests will be able to gain access to different state institutions at different levels and will set about managing, controlling, destabilizing or maintaining.

STATES AND UNEVEN DEVELOPMENT

In this section we have tried to establish two things. First of all the processes of change are uneven, especially the processes of capitalist development. Processes are constituted in a spatially specific, contingent way and uneven development is also an inbuilt feature of social change. Societies will therefore show considerable differentiation and variation both between one another and internally, and this will be expressed spatially. Nonetheless this is a paradoxical outcome, for these same processes of change also create the conditions for structured coherence, and this is also expressed spatially. Secondly, we have suggested that state institutions play a major role in people's attempts to organise and control uneven development – to institutionalise structural coherence as a 'spatial fix' or, if need be, to manage the transition between spatial configurations and the development of new fixes.

The nation-state has been the most important means of intervening in the process of uneven development, in the attempt to control and organize social and spatial charge. Indeed, the history of capitalism is also the history of nation-states, so much so that commentators often identify nation-state wrongly with 'society'. But just as this identification is misleading so states have developed on other spatial levels. This is because processes of uneven development in the economy, in nature and in civil society also operate at levels relatively inaccessible to nation-states. There is no given reason whatsoever why variation should be confined to national state boundaries – quite the opposite. We should not be taken in by those old-fashioned altases which print each country in its own separate, quite uniform, colour. The circulation of money-capital and commodities now operates on a global scale, but the processes of extracting surplus value or ensuring daily labour production take place on a workplace, household or labour-market scale. Hence the development on the one hand of supernational state institutions like the General Agreement on Tariffs and Trade (GATT), the EEC and the Organization of Petroleum Exporting Countries (OPEC), and on the other the emergence of local states institution. (These may be subnational agencies of national government – like water boards – just as much as electoral local government.) It may even be the case that nation-states are becoming less important, as production shifts increasingly onto a global scale and military competition operates more on a continental level. Nation-states may increasingly be left as the 'local states' of an international system, concerned mainly with internal social regulation. Certainly, however strongly institutionalized nation-states may be, in principle their boundaries and coherence are just as porous and unstable as any other spatial fix.

This conclusion opens one way into the current crisis of local–central relations in Britain. State systems need to be developed at a local, subnational level if dominant groups are to confront fully the problems of the uneven development of societies and of nature. If this subnational response is to make any sense, then this local level must have some sort of autonomy in implementing policy or even in formulating it. The precise way of providing water-supply in South Wales or managing labour reproduction in the old Durham coalfield cannot be wholly reduced to national guide-lines and procedures. At the very least these must be adapted if local conditions are to be taken adequately into account. But this local autonomy will, by the same token, become a hostage to fortune. The uneven development of societies also means that class structures and other social relations are constituted spatially, sometimes in rather specific ways. Social groups and interests dominant locally may well be different from those dominant nationally or inter-nationally and which make national and supernational state policy. Local groups may even be hostile or recalcitrant. They will often seek to influence local state policy to their advantage; this is after all a social prize within their grasp – and hence local–central state conflict results. To repeat Miliband (1969), local states become both agent and obstacle for national states. Add to this universal franchise and elected local government, where local groups have a right to local representation and particular locally derived policies become legitimate – and local–central conflict becomes almost inevitable.

So far, so good – but it is one thing to assert these linkages between the uneven development of societies and local–central state conflict; it is quite another to show how this works in practice. In order to do so two further tasks remain. First of all we should unpack our rather general conclusions about states and uneven development, to provide some sort of middle-range conceptualisation which can link these abstractions to actual outcomes in particular places. This is the idea of 'spatial divisions of society' and we expand on this in the next section. Secondly, we still need to demonstrate how these spatial divisions of society affect the actions of the local state. This is dealt with in section 2.5.

2.4 The Spatial Divisions of Society

The development of states is part and parcel of uneven development, and local sub-national state institutions develop as part of the unevenness of local, sub-national development. How can we translate this rather general conclusion into more concrete terms, and so provide a basis for empirical analysis of local states. One starting-point is Urry's (1981b) *Anatomy of Capitalist Societies*.

Urry identifies three spheres of social relations in capitalist society – capitalist production, state authority and civil society. The first is based on the wage relation and commodity production; the second is based on the 'state form' of citizenship in the context of a centralized monopoly of legal power and ultimately legitimate violence within a given territory. The third sphere, civil society, is

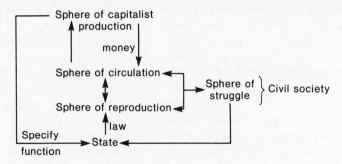

Figure 2.4 The anatomy of capitalist societies
Source: Adapted from Urry (1981b), p. 116, reproduced by kind permission of
Macmillan, London and Basingstoke

more nebulous and consists to an extent of all those social relations
left outside (and indeed historically pre-dating) the other two. In
modern capitalist societies, however, the core function left to civil
society is that of 'people production' in both an economic and social
sense, and the core relations are those of the family and gender.

It is important that these spheres of social relations should not
be imagined as separate levels or objects, still less as base and
superstructure. Rather, they are conceptualizations of sets of social
actions, and it is most appropriate to visualize interacting circuits
of social relations. For instance, commodity exchanges of labour
and products clearly link civil society to capitalist production, and
take place in both spheres. Similarly, the formation and activities
of interest groups like political parties takes place in civil society,
but no analysis of state behaviour can afford to ignore this.
Furthermore, because of the way production is organized, capitalist
societies are subject to continual change, so the extent of these
spheres and the relations between them is constantly changing. In
his book Urry describes how these three spheres typically operate
and how they link together. (Figure 2.4 summarises this discussion).

Now, for our purposes the important point is that this anatomy
of capitalist society is developed as though it existed without a
spatial dimension. We know that this is not the case, and that the
processes going on within and between the spheres are in fact
constituted spatially (and Urry has developed this point at length,
for example, 1981a). It is this spatial constitution – with all its
contingent effects – that creates local variations in the first place.
How can these spatial constitutions be conceptualized?

The same essential problem emerged earlier in the context of the
Marxist reformulation of industrial location theory and the changing

industrial geography of Britain (for example, Massey, 1977, 1979, 1984). The crucial causal dynamic was the law of value and consequently pressures for industrial restructuring. This restructuring was subsequently mapped out concretely as locational changes in industry. Massey formalized this spatial constitution of a general economic process as the 'spatial division of labour'. The economic and occupational structure of any local area can be seen as the product of a whole succession of roles played by that area within the spatial division of labour. In this way different occupational groups and economic activities will have particular geographical distributions. And, because 'space makes a difference' these particular spatial divisions of labour will then affect how industrial restructuring can happen in practice (see Massey, 1984, for a review).

The same treatment can be applied to the other spheres of capitalist society. Work on 'the local state' is in fact distinguishing a 'spatial division of the state' (see section 2.5 and Duncan and Goodwin, 1982b; Cooke, 1983). Many of the same arguments apply for civil society. The concept starts from the observation that in capitalist societies there is a diverse realm of social practices outside the realm of relations of capitalist production and also outside the realm of the state form. But this civil society is highly differentiated and the differentiation is constituted spatially. Hence we can distinguish 'spatial divisions of civil society'. Although clearly interacting with spatial divisions of labour and the state, the spatial divisions of civil society partly find their origin elsewhere and are in this way constituted autonomously. Indeed, local civil society developed in association with a particular spatial division of labour can outlive the dissolution of the latter. This is what Cooke (1985b) claims has happened in South Wales, for instance. There are very few coal-miners and steel-workers left, but we can still speak of a radical region based on the organizations built by coal-miners and steel-workers in the past.

Following on from this perhaps we should add a fourth sphere to capitalist societies, an imagined sphere of social relations. So where B. Anderson (1983) talks about the 'imagined communities' of nation-states (where there is no real community of social interaction between most compatriots – the world market is in fact far more concrete), we can see a 'spatial division of imagined community'; that is, people's own beliefs in locality even where actual local social interactions are unimportant. Finally, Urry's distinction between the 'vertical' organization of civil society (where the diverse social relations and groupings of civil society are predominantly class-specific), and 'horizontal' organization (where the opposite is the case), provides something of a starting-point for understanding how these spatial divisions knit together, and how they might be analysed.

This 'spatial divisions' solution does not, of course, answer the problem of working out how general processes are concretely constituted in practice. What this scheme does is to simplify the explanatory task of establishing the causal group to be examined, including the spatial dimensions if appropriate. The notion of a spatial division of labour, and spatial divisions of the state, of civil society and of imagined community allows us better to conceptualize what this spatial dimension consists of.

2.5 Spatial Divisions and Local State Activity

It should be emphasized that there cannot be theoretical answers to empirical questions. There is no necessary one-to-one connection between a certain kind of uneven development and a certain kind of state activity. We cannot predict that a predominantly industrial town, or a heavily agricultural region, or a city with a long labourist tradition will give rise to a particular type of local state action, as the mechanisms that transmit socio-spatial inputs into political outputs are complex and varied. Thus we cannot tabulate the connections between an industrial division of labour, say, and local service provision, or those between horizontal civil society and local government activity. What we can do, however, is to use recent empirical research to indicate the kinds of processes involved in these linkages and the types of mechanisms that help transmit them from one sphere of social activity to another.

When trying to account for the existence of exceptional forms of local politics it is tempting to see the local economy as the crucial factor. For it is apparent that work plays a crucial role in constructing and defining local political attitudes, while the spatial division of labour has allocated both work and workers in a particular geographical way. The Left especially has been ready to link radicalism at work to radicalism in local politics, and to claim that radical class-consciousness is an inevitable result. Hence Skinner and Langdon (1974) state at the beginning of their account of Clay Cross Council's refusal to implement the Conservative Government's 1971 Housing Finance Act, 'As the history of Clay Cross is tied up so inextricably with the mining industry, it is not so surprising to find that the development of political awareness there came through the growth of trade union militancy in the pits', (1974 p. 14). Many other examples spring readily to mind. These include 'Red Clydeside' during and immediately after the First World War based on the organizations of Glasgow's shipbuilding and engineering workers and the scene of a series of strikes and demonstrations that contributed to fundamental changes in national housing policy; the 'little Moscows' of inter-war Britain, built on the Durham, Fife and South Wales coalfields, whose councils gave their streets names like Engels Terrace, Marx Terrace and Lenin Terrace; Poplar Council, whose councillors went to prison in the 1920s for defying central government, dependent upon support from the areas' dock and transport workers; Sheffield, which owes its position as the 'capital of the Republic of South Yorkshire' to the industrial strength of its skilled steel-workers; and the Vale of Leven Council, called 'Little Russia' or the 'Scottish Poplar' in 1923 when it paid the poor more generously than national guidelines permitted, based on its close-knit community of textile workers (see Damer, 1980, Smith, 1982, Goodwin, 1986, MacIntyre, 1980, Branson, 1979).

Yet we must resist the assumption that a particular spatial division of labour will lead to particular forms of local consciousness and hence local state policies. For a start there are as many non-radical coal, engineering and (particularly) textile areas as there are radical ones. Or to take the opposite example, farmworkers are often taken as the epitome of the British deferential worker, bowing and scraping to the local gentry. However, while this might be true enough over large parts of Britain, in some areas such as East Anglia they have in fact provided some of the foremost episodes of labour struggle (see Howkins 1985, Dickens et al., 1985, ch. 5). In such cases this was partly because of the influence of a pre-existing culture of religious radicalism in the region, buttressed by the effects of a particular history of subordinate-dominant class relationships in turn reinforced by everyday experiences in large working-class villages and large work gangs. The basic point that emerges is that the effects of spatially distinct patterns of production will always be combined with, and mediated through, spatially distinct social practices arising in local civil society and sustained culturally through an 'imagined community'.

Thus, after stressing the importance of the mining work-force in producing a local 'political awareness' in Clay Cross, Skinner and Langdon point out that it was not until the 1950s that this industrial militancy was channelled into life outside the pits. Only in 1948 had nationalization ended the industrial and political control of the town by the paternalistic Jackson family, and 'also brought to an end the feelings of a 'family' community which the Jacksons had striven so hard to foster' (1976, p. 15). The moribund local Labour Party was revived in the late 1950s and neatly filled the political space vacated by the decline of the Jackson family. From 1959 until local government reorganization in 1974 it won every seat it contested on Clay Cross Council, a political dominance that provided the base for implementing radical policies and challenging central government. But as Skinner and Langdon make clear it was a base built on the social relations of the community as well as those of the workplace. Only when the former were changed could those generated in the latter be transformed into political control and action. In other coal-mining villages different cultural and political processes had different effects. In many Nottinghamshire pit villages, for instance, paternalism was replicated successfully after nationalization in 1948, leading to a 'moderate' political culture in both pits and council chambers (see Rees, 1986). This was to be of crucial importance to the course of the 1984–5 coal-miners' strike in Britain, when the majority of the Nottinghamshire miners continued to work.

The importance of this combination between particular spatial divisions of labour, civil society and imagined communities in producing a particular spatial division of the state with distinctive local policies, is also highlighted by several other studies. In 'Red Clydeside' it was apparently the class-consciousness and organization of skilled engineering workers which led to a local proto-revolutionary situation in industrial Scotland between 1914 and 1919, and which was critical in setting the guidelines for national housing policy for the next 50 years. But recent in-depth research has shown that it was women – excluded from skilled work in production – that were crucial to the success of this radical movement. It was the Glasgow Women's Housing Association which organized many of the housing actions, while it was apparently women who got men out of the shipyards and armaments factories for the momentous demonstrations and strikes in the autumn of 1915. For working-class Clydesiders had a family history of struggles against landlords, many being evicted from the smallholdings in Ireland or the Scottish Highlands and forced to migrate, while the suffragette movement had given women a political organization and leadership (Damer, 1980, Melling, 1980).

We have already noted how Cooke (1985b) explains the existence of a 'radical region' in coal-producing South Wales through the interaction of specific work-based practices with particular cultural, linguistic, religious and political practices developed in civil society.

Extending this work to examine the development of radical regions in France and Italy, Cooke (1985a) stressed the importance of social relations that sustain specific cultural practices and ideologies in the production and maintenance of a radical local politics. Thus a particular form of property ownership in Provence, enabled individual peasant proprietors to be unusually independent. Reinforced by the spatial concentration of settlements and the ability of women to find some economic autonomy, this led to 'the unique blend of personal, commercial and political openness which is referred to as Provence "sociability" – 'a communal, democratic spirit' (Cooke, 1985a, p. 33). Importantly, this 'spirit' was transferred from agrarian to industrial production. Similar processes were at work in Emilia-Romagna in Italy, where the early development of capitalist agriculture led to the formation of a class-conscious rural proletariat. When the share-croppers were pushed into the inter-war armaments factories and later into modern industrial plants, they took this radical collective, political consciousness with them — and again Cooke points to the importance of the spatial concentration of the population in sustaining such consciousness. Similarly MacIntyre points out in his study of three 'little Moscows', that 'The community ... made sense to those who lived in the little Moscows. The great majority of the inhabitants of Mardy, Lumphinnans and the Vale of Leven believed that they were members of communities, and this belief played no small part in shaping their behaviour' (1980, p. 176).

The effects of this same combination of spatial divisions of labour, civil society and imagined community is no less evident today. In Britain, many of the local government challenges to the last two Conservative national administrations (1979–87) have come from places where manufacturing employment has collapsed and where, as a consequence, the labour organizations of the male working class have been in decline. This has been especially marked in London, where the radicalism of the 'new urban left' (see Gyford, 1985) has been based on a coalition between white-collar unions, with their active membership overwhelmingly state employees often in the local state itself, and 'civil' organizations built up outside work to represent various disadvantaged groups, particularly women, blacks and sexual minorities. As Ken Livingstone, leader of the now abolished Greater London Council put it:

> I am in favour of coalition. I don't believe that society can be transformed solely by the male white working class. But the coalition we need is one which includes skilled and unskilled workers,

unemployed young and old, women, black people as well as the
sexually oppressed minorities. (Quoted in Tariq Ali, 1984, back
cover).

This 'new urban left' coalition was able to use local state
institutions – especially local government – to directly challenge the
national Conservative government and to implement a whole range
of alternative policies. National government had to strike back by
progressively reducing the political autonomy of electoral local
government, and removing its powers to non-elected local state
institutions insulated from these locally-based coalitions. This whole
conflict is well symbolized by the rise of the Greater London
Council as a centre of alternatives to Thatcherism and its eventual
abolition, if only because it became a polarized media event in this
case. Chapters 4–7 will look at this in more detail. The point here
is that coalitions of the new urban left are based around diverse
groups in local civil society just as much as around those at work.

In stressing the importance of civil society in accounting for
variations in local state behaviour, we should resist the temptation
to go from one extreme to another. It is rather how these social
relations combine with those formed at work which are important.
For instance, the rise of the new urban left in the Labour Party
has generally been based on an influx of young professional workers
as the urban economy has changed from manufacturing to service
provision. The growth of female employment in this sector has
been especially important, forming a basis for the development of
feminist consciousness and women's organizations. In turn this has
played a major role in forming oppositional political cultures at the
local level.

It is important to remember that these wider processes of
economic change, class and gender role restructuring do not
inevitably create particular local policies. They are spatially
constituted and mediated in quite particular ways. Our current
research into local government women's initiatives (Women's
Committees etc.) shows that only a small minority of councils (less
than 10%) have experimented in this way; for those councils
controlled by the Labour Party, this percentage still only reaches
25%. Even when implemented, there is considerable variation in
the status and backing for women's initiatives. Some are largely
symbolic or even tokenistic, while others are able to press through
meaningful policy changes and to wield some political clout (see
Halford, 1987). This variation seems to relate not only to the
varying patterns of economic change and gender-role structuring,

nor even to the varying density of feminist organization. It is more a matter of the interaction of variations. For instance, the continuing strength of male-dominated workplace organizations can determine how much organizational and political space is available. Hence in Camden, in Inner London, women's groups are politically influential and women's initiatives have been pursued with some vigour. By contrast in Sheffield, until recently Britain's 'steel city', the new urban left coalition depends on maintaining the political organization originally built up by social and economically central, skilled and male workers. In this situation women's initiatives can only develop slowly and fitfully.

A recent pioneering study of variations in interwar welfare provision shows very well how it is this local combination of relations which is the crucial issue, not the simple presence or absence of structural categories (Mark-Lawson et al., 1985). The three Lancashire factory towns of Lancaster, Preston and Nelson – all within 40 miles of one another – were apparently very similar economically and socially. But while Nelson had a well-developed municipal welfare provision, Preston's was more tokenistic and in Lancaster it was virtually non-existent. Why were they so different? At first sight this could be put down to differences in political control and orientation. In Lancaster the local Labour Party was both relatively weak and had little interest in municipal welfare. In Preston, although the Labour Party was dominant in local politics, there was still a relative lack of interest in welfare provision. Only in Nelson was the Labour Party both locally dominant with welfare provision as a major platform.

This answer, of course, only begs the same question – why the difference between Preston and Nelson? It was organized women who were most interested in welfare services, and true enough in Lancaster there was virtually no women's political activity. But in Preston, without much welfare provision, there was an active women's movement, it was just that it did not have much political success, whereas in Nelson women were crucial in setting Labour Party agendas. The difference appears to result not just from how far women participate in the labour force, but in the precise gender relations experienced in doing the work. So in Lancaster, relatively few women worked outside the home, and those that did were mostly employed in paternalistic, small service workplaces. We would not expect an active or influential women's movement. In both Nelson and Preston a high percentage of women worked in the cotton mills, and in both cases this appeared to give the basis for active women's movements inside the Labour Party. However, in terms of gender relations the meaning of this same work varied significantly between the two towns, and this seems to be the key for explaining differences in the political success of organized women. In Nelson women worked alongside men in similar positions for similar wages. In Preston most men worked in higher-paid jobs in other industries, and the few that worked in the cotton mills with the women were mainly foremen, controlling the female labour, or young men still hoping for a better job elsewhere. It was these differences in the relative status and subordination of men and women in paid work which seem to have been the crucial factor behind the relative success of women's political mobilization, and hence in turn behind local variations in welfare provision in the three towns.

We cannot, therefore, read policy variations from economic or social categorizations. (Nor should we forget the importance of national policy changes and the national state. For instance the nationalization of health and welfare services in Britain in 1947 made the welfare variations between Lancaster, Preston and Nelson insignificant). The locally based influences on policy formulation and implementation are very much relational and actively formed in the context of particular places – that is in the context of particular combinations of spatial constitutions. This means that rapid changes can occur as people's social experiences and relations change, and according to how they monitor and respond to this fact. How local states interpret and represent is by no means a constant.

We should also emphasize that local states will not be passive in this process. Political groups controlling local state institutions will not simply respond to the changing local environment. The very nature of these institutions means that they will be involved in the management and interpretation of their local constitutions of society. In the current form of the local state this means involvement in the provision of homes and schools, of welfare services and cultural facilities and in the planning and regulation of physical development generally. In carrying out these activities those dominant in the institutions of the local state will have regard to their own 'spatial fix' – attempting to ensure continued support amongst local people. In a recent study of changing local politics on Clydeside, Savage (1987) has indicated how council policies have been affected significantly by the Labour Party's need to sustain support in the face of severe industrial decline. He concludes that 'Local political parties are not the passive reflection of their environment. They are not the simple embodiment of "traditions" or of "political cultures".... Radicalism is an inherently unstable quality always threatening to dissolve itself' (1987, pp. 18–19). Central government is apt to promote this dissolution through measures designed to reduce local autonomy (see chapters 3–5).

Our final example, drawing on our own research on the formulation of local government economic policy, shows up this dialectic between civil society, workplace organization and local politics quite well. Each case study, the London Boroughs of Southwark and Tower Hamlets and the City of Sheffield (see Goodwin, 1986a, 1986b), has an early history of radicalism. Sheffield's goes as far back as the late eighteenth century; the old Borough of Poplar, home of 'Poplarism', is now part of Tower Hamlets; and Southwark contains the former Borough of Bermondsey, renowned for its inter-war provision of welfare services and housing. Each has recently suffered from ostensibly similar types of industrial decline, leading to long-scale manufacturing job losses and a new place in the spatial division of labour based on the service sector. How were these political traditions and current economic realities combined in each area, and how did these particular combinations affect local government policy-making?

In each case the spatial division of labour operating in the area, and the way in which it changed, was of vital importance in understanding policy formulation – and not just because we were considering economic policies. The influence of the local economy was felt through much of civil society, at home and in the community and was thus exerted over a whole range of council activities. After all, it was the dominance of the labour movement, based on its industrial strength, that led to the early control of these councils by the Labour Party and to the early implementation of radical policies. But as we shall see, this similar labour movement hegemony developed in three different directions as a result of the influence of other local social relations.

In Sheffield a political structure was developed which closely linked representatives of the city's labour movement to its borough politics. It is usual when a council is controlled by the Labour Party for council policy to be monitored and influenced by Party committees. In Sheffield until 1973, the influence of the industrial labour movement was channelled through delegates from the city's Trades and Labour Council. Seven of these were sent to each meeting of the City Council's Labour Group (all the Labour councillors), and the chairman (never a woman) and secretary also sat on the Labour Group executive – the most powerful internal policy-making body. In return, two members of the Labour Group were nominated to the executive of the Trades and Labour Council, and several other councillors would be present as delegates from constituent organizations. This tightly knit framework of liaison between the three sections of the Sheffield labour movement – Labour Council, Labour Party and trades unions – helped unite its political and industrial wings. Following local government reorganization the national Labour Party set up new local monitoring committees, District Labour Parties, to coincide with the new District Councils. Despite being ordered to disband its Trades and Labour Council, Sheffield continued to elect direct union delegates to its District Labour Party, who could be influential in determining council policy.

This influence was felt particularly in industrial and economic policy. In May 1981 Sheffield City Council set up the country's first Employment Committee, serviced directly by its own council department. This policy initiative was part of much broader policy changes set in motion by a new Labour leadership, elected to control the council in May 1980. Many of the leading figures were young left-wing councillors with professional jobs, part of a new breed of local politicians promoted by an increasingly radical local Labour Party to take up positions held previously by older more right-wing councillors who had close links with the steel and engineering unions (see Goodwin, 1986a, for more detail on these processes).

The first years of the 1980s also witnessed dramatic changes in Sheffield's economy. Severe unemployment followed redundancy and closure. Councillors who had grown up and learnt their politics in a labour movement founded upon the dominance of Sheffield's skilled workers in the steel and engineering industries, now had to formulate a response as this dominance quite literally crumbled to the ground. Committees and forums were set up inside the council, and in the Trades Council and Labour Party. Together they formulated the idea of a new Employment Department to co-ordinate all the council's efforts to tackle the economic crisis in the city. But this involved much more than supporting private-sector employment as is the norm with local authority economic initiatives (see Cochrane, 1983, for a review of traditional policies). In Sheffield the task was also one of political regeneration and recomposition – to help rebuild a labour movement devastated by economic decline – and, we might add, to preserve the authority's 'spatial fix' by rebuilding its own support. In the words of the Employment Department's first co-ordinator:

> The more serious weakness in the trades unions' failure to defend jobs, is their lack of political perspective on de-industrialation and restructuring. So the more positive way of interpreting the role of Labour councils in the employment field is that they help to 'repoliticise' the issue by showing the link between the economic and the social . . . part of the challenge for us in the local authority is to try to reintroduce some political perspective. (Alcock et al., 1984, p. 83)

The role of employment policy in Sheffield then combines an economic function with a political one. As David Blunkett, the leader of the council told us in an interview in 1983, Sheffield council had set up the Employment Committee and Department because they wanted it to 'act in a political manner' and that its function was 'political mobilization not just a social service'. But reconciling these two functions proved difficult and has caused a significant shift in employment policy.

In its initial year the new Employment Department spent a great deal of time and energy intervening in the private sector to save jobs. This was partly as a result of policies inherited from the previous council, but was also because the council 'had to be seen to be doing something'. 'We had to wave the banner', in the words of a council officer employed in the department (interview with authors, 1983). The most obvious place for this waving was in the private sector, where many of Sheffield's traditional jobs and skills were being lost. The 'imagined community' of a vibrant, important and expanding city, controlled by the organized, skilled male working class and built on the strength of its steel and cutlery industries long outlived their dissolution. The council was responding as much to this as to real economic changes. But this strategy was faced with firms that were going under for 'good reasons' – ultimately leading to market failure – and would need considerable investment of time and money even to have a chance of recovery. How could a new economic strategy be based on failing capitalist firms? A crucial breaking-point came in 1983. The Labour Group first took a decision to support a small steel firm and save around 60 jobs, but later withdrew its support leaving the firm to collapse. This reverse, made after economic and legal advice from council officers, provoked a huge split in the labour movement. As the Secretary of the Labour Party told us 'It's the only time in recent years that the terrific tolerance has broken down.' The split was between those who wanted to intervene politically to support members of the skilled manual working class and those who wanted to act on more economic grounds and thus not intervene in a losing financial battle. A council officer encapsulated the dilemma neatly when he told us that 'It was crazy to support Manganese Steel in economic terms, but the councillors felt a political need to deliver.' More cynically another officer saw the initial decision as merely a 'political gesture to traditional support' (all interviews with the authors, 1983).

It is indicative of the particular social relations existing in Sheffield, and the strength of feeling that they generated, that this gesture had to be made. It is, however, perhaps more significant that in the end the political gesture was overturned in favour of more pragmatic financial reasoning. That such reasoning – 'betrayal by middle-class bureaucrats acting like bankers' in the words of two leaders of the traditional wing of the labour movement – won the day is indicative of broader changes in Sheffield society. The former political coalition which directed policies and support towards the skilled working class in the private sector of metals and engineering has begun to dissolve. In its place the councillors now find an amalgam of interest groups, some class based, some not, some based on production issues, others concerned with matters of consumption. The older organic links between the council, the Labour Party and the trade unions have been replaced by a much wider constituency and coalition. Local government policies have changed as a result. Employment policy has now switched to concentrate on the public sector – more specifically saving and creating jobs within the council's own work-force in the face of the public expenditure cuts, the threatened privatization of services and rate-capping. This is not only a result of pragmatic concerns, but also makes political sense. For white-collar and public-sector unions have become increasingly dominant in the local political culture, and the largest single union branch in the city, with the largest delegation to the Trades and Labour Council is the National and Local Government Officer's Association (NALGO), representing nearly 7,000 of the Council's own work-force. In a sense then, the move to the public sector represents a return to base; but a new base built on the changing economy and society of Sheffield and its region, and one that results in different local state policies.

The two London dockland Boroughs of Southwark and Tower Hamlets, facing each other across the Thames immediately below Tower Bridge, have also suffered similar economic trajectories. In each a port-related economy fostered a proletarian culture and labourist political tradition similar to that produced by the steel and engineering industries in Sheffield. Again, both have suffered from huge job losses in these traditional sectors over the past 20 years. But the response of the dockland local authorities in London to these events has differed from that which we have just outlined in Sheffield, and crucially for our argument they have differed significantly from one another.

The communities of the docks, socially and physically close-knit, produced an intimate link between economy and civil society. Workplace issues also dominated local politics, hence in part the radicalism of the two riverside Boroughs of Poplar and Bermondsey in the inter-war period. As in Sheffield the Labour Party built up a solid and unshakeable local political rule, but in docklands its almost automatic election victories were, in time, built more on apathy than enthusiasm. The link between local council, local Labour Party and local trade unions was never established in such an interlocked way as it was in Sheffield. When the docks were shifted downstream to Tilbury, and the port-related industries began to decline, the local Labour Party was left purely as an electoral machine with no real influence in civil society generally – a process exacerbated by the 1965 reorganization of local government in London which amalgamated the old boroughs into larger administrative units. Replacement organizations linking a changing civil society to the local state were not developed. Policy-making in the new Boroughs of Tower Hamlets and Southwark was left very much in the hands of a few leading councillors, and even the Labour Party's involvement was more nominal than actual. A recent study of local politics in Southwark commented that the Labour Party there 'was a close knit cabal run by three or four families and held together by powerful Roman Catholic influences' (Goss, 1983, p. 47).

The continued loss of both industry and population from London's docklands left these political 'cabals' further isolated and open to challenge. In place of the former unified homogeneous social and political structures there arose 'a division between the "old politics" of the traditional labour movement structures representing the manual workers and long established communities, and the "new politics" of the articulate, radical middle class representing both their own interests and those of excluded groups' (ibid., p. 84). But although the challenge came from the 'new politics', because of the rigidity of an ossified Labour Party it was channelled and articulated through community action groups. It was here that the new organizations of civil society were created. This meant that council policy remained largely untouched. In the economic and industrial fields this continued to run along traditional lines of supporting and attracting private capital in the hope that this would bring development and jobs.

In Southwark, however, this policy was changed following the election of a new Borough Council leadership in 1982. Over two-thirds of the Labour Group had never held office before and many of the old 'cabal' members had been rejected by their Labour Party branches. Economic and development issues played a key role in this process. As one leading Labour Party member told us 'The move of the docks fetched on political decisions' (interview with authors, 1983). Thus, those who had been opposing a Labour local authority for 10 years now found themselves occupying positions as 'honorary planning advisors', as the local community groups were drawn into consultation with the council. As a result local government policy has changed. Criteria for giving permission for new industrial and commercial development has switched from private gain to public accountability, designed 'to ensure what land remains is developed to provide the homes and jobs the local community needs' (North Southwark Community Development Group, 1983).

Across the river no such change has taken place. In Tower Hamlets local political activity around economic issues has remained external to the Borough Council. As a thesis on local politics in Poplar concludes, 'The local action groups have replaced the Labour Party as the chief expression and instrument of class solidarity and collective action. Moreover they are much more representative of the community than the local Labour Party' (Cole, 1983, p. 340). This was confirmed to us by the leader of one such group, who said 'The council have been the main enemy. People look to organizations like ours because the Labour Party is seen as separate from the real fighting situation' (interview with authors, 1983). So separate in fact, that Labour lost control of Tower Hamlets for the first time ever in May 1986, to the Liberal Party. Until then local political activity in civil society was firmly fixed around tenants' organizations and community groups and the dominance of the 'old politics' went unchallenged at a party political level. Similar economic change has thus lead to divergent political outcomes in neighbouring local authorities – confirmation of the way in which the influence of a particular spatial division of labour is mediated by civil society.

We can see from even this brief description the kinds of linkages involved in policy formulation at the local level. Different policy areas will, of course, involve different sections of local society; tenants' associations in housing issues, nursery groups in childcare policies, women's groups in equal opportunities policies and so on. These relationships will overlap neighbouring councils and coalesce – we can hardly expect social processes to refer continuously to local authority boundaries! Crucial external influences enter from the national and international stages (for example, closure of docks and steel plants in the face of international competition). Our point is that these more general processes can only be realized in particular places, and that whether they spread beyond administrative boundaries or not their effects can be traced in local state action.

For these wider processes will be constituted in particular ways to produce a whole set of interlocking social relationships that will influence local policy-making, although in what ways this happens is always a contingent matter to be determined empirically. It is these complex and heterogeneous relationships that result in the local state pursuing policies which the centre finds inappropriate. As Cooke puts it, 'Within the general social relations of production under capitalism (and other sets of social relations SSD/MG) it is likely that certain spatially specific social cleavages, alliances or antagonisms will underpin regional radicalism' (1985a, p. 32). Moreover, the likelihood of these spatially specific social cleavages producing conflict with the centre is heightened during particular social episodes. The recent crisis of local government is an example – the ideas and wishes of a radical right-wing government trying to restructure British society in its own image have been challenged and questioned by antagonistic local governments. It is to this crisis that we now turn, and its details will fill the pages of our next five chapters. We will begin with a brief review of the social, economic and political background that has made this conflict and tension especially likely, if not almost inevitable, at the current juncture.

3

Centralizing the Local Government System I

Finance

3.1 Restructuring Britain and the Threat of Local Autonomy

Since the mid 1970s, and especially since the accession to national power of a radical right-wing government in 1979, local government and its relations to central government have emerged as leading political issues. This is not just something for professional politicians or academic specialists; local government has become front-page material. The right-wing popular press can sell copy through sensationalist headlines about Red Ted, Red Ken (or whoever was the foremost local government bogyman of the time) and the dangers of 'municipal Marxism' or 'socialism on the rates'. At one time 'Red Ken' (Ken Livingstone, leader of the Greater London Council (GLC), which was abolished by the Conservative central government in 1986) was voted the most popular man in Britain, after the Pope, by listeners of BBC's 'Today' programme. This interest is mirrored, and also exaggerated, by the more earnest reports in the left-wing press on local socialism, town-hall feminism and popular planning. Even those shadowy local state institutions outside the orbit of officially public electoral politics, like police authorities, water boards and health authorities, now share some of this attention. Above all, there is a clear, continuing and at times quite dramatic tension between central and local government – complex and Draconian legislation is introduced, opposed, removed and repeated, ministries and local governments battle it out in the courts, publicity campaigns are mounted and participants strive for propaganda coups. Furthermore, this conflict often cuts across party lines or becomes part of internal party divisions such as those between left and right in the Labour Party, or 'the Wets' versus 'the Thatcherites' in the Conservative Party.

This is a remarkable change of fortune. As one commentator put it recently 'In the 1960s the study of local government had a wholly justified reputation for stultifying boredom, and this was apparently confirmed in the resounding apathy which greeted the debate about local government reorganization leading up to the 1972 Local Government Act (Cochrane, 1983, p. 285). In contrast, the 1980 and 1982 Local Government Acts, and to an even greater extent rate-capping, the abolition of the metropolitan counties and the imposition of a poll tax, have stimulated wide interest and intense debate; the boredom of political consensus has evaporated. Where local government used to be little more than a means of keeping worthy but dull party stalwarts out of harm's way, it now seems as if 'the local state' (an interesting renaming in itself) is a magnet and a testing-ground for new ideas and new politics – and new careers. Hence also its suitability as a personalized media event. What makes this all the more remarkable is that almost everyone agrees that the powers of local government and of other local state institutions have in fact *declined* considerably over the last two decades particularly since 1979. The balance of power has actually shifted markedly towards central government. How is this paradox to be explained?

The starting-point is the deterioration of Britain's position in the world-wide division of labour and, even more starkly, of particular places within Britain. This overwhelming fact of British life has been only too well charted to need repeating here (See Glyn and Harrison, 1980; Jessop, 1980; Gamble, 1981; Fine and Harris, 1985, for Britain in general; Fothergill and Gudgin, 1982; Massey, 1984; Townsend, 1983, for Britain's changing economic geography). The point is, however, that this experience of uneven development is not simply a purely economic process, nor is it one that people accept passively.

In some ways British politics, as well as the policies of local areas, can be seen in terms of how people react to this uneven development. What is the best way of stemming decline, or even better, or regenerating the economy? Perhaps it is possible to shift Britain or a particular area to a new, more secure place in the world-wide division of labour. Different responses have different costs and benefits for different groups of people. For instance, accepting the role of Britain being a reserve of flexible labour for multinationals also means accepting less secure and less satisfying manual jobs. On the other hand, the attempt to develop high value-added production in strategic sectors and industries, with a view to creating more secure and more satisfying jobs, will mean controlling the flow of capital and hence, in the short run, lower profits for financial institutions. Concomitantly, these plans have spatial implications. Can past spatial fixes, with all their valuable human and physical infrastructures, be preserved or even transformed to a new stage, or should they be allowed or even encouraged to decay?

So the Labour-controlled GLC, until its abolition by Conservative national government in 1986, was committed to a policy of 'restructuring for labour' in the attempt to preserve London as a manufacturing centre. On the other hand, central government's own local state in London, the London Docklands Development Corporation (LDDC) sees the existing social culture of the docklands as an obstacle to progress, something to be removed in order to allow proper room for the market to recreate geography in its image (see Goodwin, 1986b, 1988). In a slightly bizarre way, these two rival scenarios even came into direct conflict; the GLC sponsored community platforms to fight the LDDC's development proposals for the area (see Klausner, 1985).

In other words, as this example shows, Britain's economic crisis is deeply political. The broad political consensus existing since 1945, where a compromise between the organizations of labour and capital were supposed to deliver profits on the one hand, with high wages and good welfare on the other, is widely seen to have failed. (Compare with Sweden for a relative success story, Korpi, 1978.) The two major political parties, Conservative and Labour, shared both political power and this broad consensus over a mixed economy with a welfare state. But, as the economic and political bases for this consensus have weakened, more radical alternatives have been seen to be necessary and political polarization has deepened. The Labour Party has turned increasingly to ideas of democratic socialism, where popular state intervention would be used to regulate and control capital, whereas the Conservative Party – under a zealous New Right leadership – has become committed to a market-ruled society working for capital. Ironically enough, the erstwhile political consensus is best preserved in the formation of a new party, the Social Democratic Party, founded in 1981. Other groups have thrown up more radical versions of society, from no-growth and 'ecological' scenarios to visions of a non-hierarchical and non-exploitative feminist world.

But, at least in the short run, the most important of these visions of how British society should be is the New Right view. For, in Britain's increasingly 'elective dictatorship' the crucial political institution is the prime ministership. The Prime Minister dominates executive power within the state, represented by the Cabinet–ministerial–Whitehall nexus. Given electoral victory once every four or five years and a working majority in the House of Commons, this concentration of state power appears practically uaccountable to both voters and even elected representatives. This is not to say that prime ministers can do what they will – their power is always relative and not all social power resides with the executive side of the central state. Hence, for instance, the half-hearted opposition to some of the Conservative Government's proposals by the House of Lords and parts of the Civil Service, while industrialists and financiers continue to make crucial social decisions quite outside the state. But while the office of prime minister in Britain is not yet equivalent to that of an elected monarch it remains the single most powerful site of state power – and since 1979 this site has been captured by one particular interpretation of New Right ideology, personified by Margaret Thatcher.

Perhaps the central tenet of this 'Thatcherite' view of the world is the belief that free markets are both most economically efficient and socially just, and that Britain's economy has deteriorated because free markets – in labour as well as in goods – have not been allowed to operate (see *Economist*, 27 May, 1978, for of the Ridley Plan, which set out Conservative Plans for attacking public sector trade unions; Hall and Jacques, 1983). State regulations, unions, welfare services – all these are seen as obstacles to a just and efficient society. There are two serious problems for this view, however. Free markets have to be created and people need to be convinced that this is the best way. Both operations are fraught with difficulties. It is doubtful if, in the realities of societies and economies, free markets can exist; certainly the very process of trying to create them seems to depend on a high level of state regulation and intervention. Similarly, given a choice, it seems unlikely that real people will ever opt for social and economic insecurity however purifying this might be. So capitalists like cartels, monopolies and state subsidies just as much as individuals appreciate a free health service. So as well as removing obstacles directly it is also necessary to create an appropriate social context of beliefs and attitudes – the 'new Victorianism' of self-help, commercial values and the traditional family.

So to have a chance of success, the Conservative Government's plans to 'rescue' (as it sees it) British society and to regenerate its economy depend on a paradox. The purifying winds of market efficiency depend on state action to remove obstacles and to create the appropriate social context of the new Victorianism. This immediately places the local state at the centre of the political stage. For local state institutions, and elected local government in particular, both embody these obstacles in practice and provide the means for overcoming them.

First, local state institutions are a major provider of public services. These services are allocated collectively, sometimes even on criteria of social need. They are also funded collectively. As such they offer protection against markets, insulate individuals from the need to depend on the traditional family and militate against the cut and thrust of commercial rationality. Secondly, local authorities bear a major responsibility for 'crowding out' (as the dogma goes) private enterprise; resources and effort are absorbed by a supposedly parasitic and non-productive public sector. Thirdly, local state bodies are major public spenders where the Government's strategy of monetarism requires reductions in public spending. Monetarism, as an economic dogma, fits in well with the Thatcherite strategy. The supposed need for controlling public-sector borrowing has been reinterpreted as strict controls over public-sector spending on welfare or nationalized industries (the massive state expenditures on defence, the police force, farming or owner-occupation are apparently exempt). This economic principle potentially reopens whole areas of social life to market forces where once they were comparatively insulated from them.

Fourthly, local state institutions are not only important in a strict material sense, as providers of goods and services and as spenders of money. They also embody important ideological and political roles. As we discussed in chapter 1, a fundamental role of capitalist states lies in the presentation and interpretation of the social relations. Is this a class society? Is the market natural or socially produced? Can local political action be effective? Should the state provide services for need? Can we achieve results by organizing on this basis? Because social relations are unevenly developed over space, local states become important to this interpretation. As the Conservative plan of action concerns attitudes and expectations just as much as material policies, this role of local state institutions becomes vitally important. Hence the threat posed by women's committees or enterprise boards, eliciting a political response apparently far out of proportion to their significance as spenders and policy-makers. For these bodies actively interpreted society in a way directly opposed to the Thatcherite scenario.

This takes us directly to the last obstacle presented by local states – their representational role. Electoral local government in particular does not only represent locally the social interests dominant *at* the centre. It also represents local interests *to* the centre. These local interests may be marginal or subordinate in national terms, or even opposed to the nationally dominant interests. At the national level it is large financial and industrial interests, represented by the City of London, that pull most weight (cf. Jessop, 1980; Leys, 1983). The coalition of interests supporting the governing political party will also have favoured access to executive state power. At the level of the local state, however, other interests excluded permanently or partially from this favoured access to national state power may dominate. In some authorities it is local trade unionists, large landowners or professionals who call the tune. These local state executives are not only charged with implementing locally the decisions reached in central government, decisions they may not like, but they also have an ability to create their own local policies. This follows from the autonomy of operation necessary to allow local states to carry out the function of responding to local variation, an autonomy legitimized by local electoral politics. So for instance, the provision of cheap, good-quality council housing has often been an essential element in maintaining local cultures of labourism in those areas where local labour movements have achieved political hegemony. Yet this political culture, its practices and its policies are inimical to the New Right Thatcherite version of how society should work.

Local state intsitutions are one important sphere of social life where the truth of the Thatcherite slogan 'TINA' ('There is no alternative') can be established. Similarly, TINA must be implemented in the local state if this view is to succeed – but at the same time it is a site where the old values and practices of social democratic consensus are well established. Furthermore, excluded from direct access to central state power, the autonomy of the local state becomes of prime importance to those groups attempting to establish that there *is* an alternative, for this is where concrete practices opposing TINA can be established. This is why it has often been said that the 'Socialist Republic' of South Yorkshire, Sheffield City Council and the GLC, as well as other radical left local governments, have done more to oppose Thatcherism and show possible alternatives than the official and apparently impotent parliamentary opposition.

For all these reasons, the local state and especially electoral local government is both obstacle and threat to the Conservative Government's plans for restructuring British society. This threat, fuelled by local state autonomy, is not just a matter of what local governments do (provide cheap public transport, for instance) but also how they do it (give oppositional groups a voice). There is also the substantial complication that not all local state institutions provide the same sort of threat. A low-spending Conservative-ruled shire might only be an obstacle in terms of overall controls, while the GLC, for instance, was also an acute embarrassment in terms of policies and social visions. The problem remains of how to deal with this multi-factored and varied threat while at the same time retaining a viable system of local administration (chapters 4-6 record how the Conservative Government attempted to deal with this problem). Elected local government, with its legitimized financial and political autonomy, lay at the forefront of this problem.

3.2   Centralizing Local Government Finance

PRE-1980: GOLDEN AGE, ECONOMIC CRISIS AND
IDEOLOGICAL ATTACK

Before 1980, electoral local governments in Britain set their own local spending levels and their own local taxation levels through the 'rates', or local property tax. Prior to 1975, this political and financial autonomy was left largely outside central government's remit. Of course Britain is a unitary state where Parliament is the sovereign executive body, so local autonomy has always been subject to central direction. On the one hand, national government set down minimum standards and hence minimum spending levels, for those locally run services deemed in some way crucial for the political and economic system. All children up to a certain age, for instance, should be in full-time education. On the other hand, upper limits were set on total local government spending, including non-elected local authorities, as part of national economic policy. Since the 1960s these limits were co-ordinated and set in constant prices by the annual Public Expenditure Survey Committee (PESC) although allowances were made for inflation.

Setting these limits was not, however, a purely monetary calculation; PESC levels were arrived at by considering the real value of services – the first question was how many teachers, miles of road, houses, etc., should be provided and then how much this would cost and what could be afforded. Furthermore, both upper and lower limits were flexible and had considerable leeway, especially at the level of individual authorities. It was difficult to determine what a minimum spending level really amounted to, so despite the activities of government inspectors and central ministries, actual spending levels – on education per pupil, say – varied substantially between authorities. Similarly, total expenditure often exceeded PESC targets. This was despite a strong element of 'He who pays the piper sets the tune', as central government was providing grants to cover over 60 per cent of local government spending by the 1970s, with rates accounting only for about 25 per cent or less. This was because the discipline of central grant allocation could be ouflanked by local political decisions to raise more rates and spend accordingly. Control via grant allocation was also eroded from within – not only were PESC levels set in volume terms, a hostage to inflation, but grants also were calculated according to past expenditure levels so that high-spending authorities attracted larger grants with which they could then increase spending. Finally, as part of central control over public-sector borrowing (which the Treasury was coming to see as a central economic manipulator) local governments needed central permission to borrow in order to finance capital spending. Again this was a loose constraint. Sometimes it was regarded as a Keynesian instrument (i.e., to encourage spending) as much as a restrictive one, and in any case it was still open to local governments to finance capital spending through the rates.

Within these broad, centrally imposed constraints, the convention was that each elected local government unit could set its own tax level and, using central government grants in addition to its own resources, could determine its own particular mix and balance of local spending according to local political and social circumstances. This did not mean, however, spending on whatever local government wanted, for it was Parliament that decided which expenditures local government was responsible for. Spending outside this legislatively authorized area would be *ultra vires* and possibly illegal. This in itself is an important constraint on local autonomy. (Although a notable exception to this rule was to be allowed section 137 of the 1972 Local Government Act. This empowered local authorities to spend the proceeds of a 2p rate on anything 'of benefit to local inhabitants' and this provision was to have important implications for local–central conflict, as we shall see). Nevertheless, local government was responsible for a wide range of state functions, including intervention in areas of central political importance. The provision of public education and public housing are noteworthy in this respect, being both large spenders (accounting for 60 per cent of local government expenditure in 1975, or 18 per cent of total public-sector spending) as well as issues never very far from the active political agenda.

The importance of local autonomy within overall constraints

seems to have been one reason why electoral local government has been progressively stripped of a whole range of responsibilities. Among the most important transfers, poor relief was removed to central ministries in the 1920s and 1930s (and greatly expanded in scope after 1945), electricity and gas were taken over by public corporations in 1947 and 1948, local hospitals were taken over by the National Health Service in 1947, as were other local health services in 1974, while water-supply and sewerage also went to regional water authorities in 1974. Whether central government was reacting to the inability of local governments to provide a uniform services, that is, to the problem of underspenders (as was the case with the post-war nationalizations) or to the problem of overspending by politically conscious councillors (as in the 1920s and 1930s, and apparently also in the 1974 reorganization) it is clear that it was local political and financial autonomy created the problem in the first place. Transfer out of direct electoral politics did not wholly solve the problem, however. There still had to be regional or local units to deal with locally specific uneven development, and these were often able to maintain or even increase expenditures in line with their own internal objectives (see chapter 7).

It is tempting to see this pre-1975 picture as a golden age for the local state. Indeed, in some ways it was, at least when seen from the perspective of the mid-1980s, following progressive cuts in public spending and the imposition of close central control over the spending and policy of individual local authorities. Newton and Karran for instance, see the five years since 1980 as 'a jump towards a highly centralised state' (1985, p. 114). It is, however, important to establish two points that qualify this perspective. First, this golden age of local government financial autonomy coincided with the economic golden age of the post-war boom. In turn this boom coincided with both the development of the welfare state and a final consolidation of what we may call the 'infrastructural state', in which central and local governments absorbed much of the social necessity of providing physical infrastructure like roads and sewerage. Local government, even if not the initiator, was usually closely involved as that arm of the state in touch with local conditions. The decade 1965–75 marks the zenith of local government spending as these developments were generalized in a period of relative economic prosperity (see table 3.1). Secondly, even in this relatively unstressed economic environment, there was always a central concern over local government spending and the self-reinforcing linkage between this and local government political autonomy. For the Treasury especially, this was a whole area of

Table 3.1 Local government spending in the United Kingdom, 1950–85

	Local government expenditure as % of GDP	Local government expenditure as % of total government expenditure
1950	9.9	16.7
1960	9.9	23.3
1965	13.4	30.6
1970	14.9	31.5
1975	17.6	29.5
1976	17.0	28.2
1977	15.1	27.0
1978	13.0	24.0
1979	14.2	25.6
1980	14.7	25.3
1981	14.4	23.7
1982	13.9	22.9
1983	14.7	23.9
1984	14.6	23.8
1985	13.7	22.9

Source: UK National Accounts (Central Statistical Office, London)

state expenditure essentially outside central control. Sometimes the relationship between central and local government broke down completely, and the issues had to be settled in the courts. The two most famous occasions were in 1953, when Birmingham Corporation was successfully taken to court by the Conservative Government for introducing subsidized fares for pensioners, and in 1976 when the Conservative-run Metropolitan Borough of Tameside successfully resisted the Labour Government's direction to continue plans for comprehensive education.

The 1974 reorganization of local government also reflects these tensions. The problems of local government political and financial autonomy – as epitomized by the Clay Cross saga (see pp. 76–8, 150) – was rationalized as being partly a problem of 'councillor calibre'. Create more professional and more technically proficient authorities and then – so the argument went – the problem of politically motivated councillors who insisted on acting outside central government guide-lines would be side-stepped (cf. Dearlove, 1979). So Clay Cross Urban District Council ceased to exist in 1974: the area became just one constituent part of North-East Derbyshire District Council and an even smaller part of Derbyshire County Council. But if this attempted depoliticization of local government was a concious policy, as Dearlove suggests, it backfired, for the 1974 reorganization only helped create a number of powerful, usually Labour-controlled fiefdoms in the metropolitan counties. (It was probably worth losing Clay Cross to get a South Yorkshire or a Merseyside). Furthermore, electoral trends in the 1970s were making the cities increasingly safe for Labour. The result was a powerful combination of electoral legitimacy, local political security, strategic local powers and a greater local need for public spending. The political results of this reorganization were to contribute first to measures to control local government spending and policy-making directly, then to the increasing transfer of powers to non-elected local state institutions, and finally to another round of 'reorganization' – the abolition of the metropolitan counties in 1986.

The end of this 'golden age' for local government was heralded by the oil crisis of 1973 and the onset of economic depression in the Western capitalist world. This crisis was given a particular political dimension in Britain. The economy was already weak, with rapidly falling profit rates and persistent balance of trade problems, although at the same time trade unions remained strong enough to resist reductions to what were already among the lowest wages in industrial Europe. Similarly, the City of London increased its economic and political centrality as domestic industry faltered, and could easily brush off attempts to redirect investment into the home economy. This impasse was heightened by the triumph of the 1973–74 coal-miner's strike, which led, among other things, to widespread power cuts with a three-day working week and also contributed to the subsequent collapse of the Conservative Government in 1974. To cap it all, inflation reached double figures. Widespread fears of 'ungovernability' combined in establishment circles with visions of economic collapse. These fears permeated leading views of the state and its activity, not least the views of local government which appeared relatively inaccessible to central control.

Two influential publications mark this change in attitudes. In 1975 Bacon and Eltis published a series of widely praised newspaper articles, which popularized and formalized the 'parasite' thesis of Britain's economic ills. (The basis of a book published in 1978). This was essentially a 'pop' version of one of the policy conclusions of monetarism, which was then replacing Keynsianism as the leading economic theory in both academic and government circles. According to monetary theory, the volume of the money supply is the crucial economic variable and controlling this volume is almost the only intervention that governments can sensibly make. Too much money means high inflation, and the reduction of inflation rather than, say, levels of employment or production, is seen as the target of economic policy. Consequently reductions in public spending and public-sector borrowing are the major means of combating this evil. The 'parasite' view takes this further. Here the public sector is seen as being parasitic on the private sector, feeding upon and progessively weakening private-sector wealth creation by diverting investment and resources into non-productive activity. This process was already well advanced in Britain, it was claimed, and the only way to re-establish economic growth was to reduce the size of the public sector. At the same time the White Paper *The Attack on Inflation* (HMSO, July 1975 Cmnd 6151) presented to parliament by the Prime Minister rather than any Government department gave an official policy interpretation of monetary theory. The control of inflation was elevated to a principal social and economic target of government policy, and this meant reductions in public-sector borrowing and therefore spending, combined with the containment of real wage levels. The implications of this new orthodoxy for local government were severe. It was those services for which local government was responsible – housing, education, roads and personal social services – that had shown the highest rates of expenditure increase. It was local government expenditure which was most outside central control. Yet it was also local government expenditure which offered the safer political target. Finally, reducing the wage costs of public-sector employees – predominantly in local government – offered the Government the chance of killing two birds with one stone.

Both the monetarist view of Britain's economic ills and its 'parasite' offshoot have since been heavily criticized as being incredibly over-simple, if not downright misleading. The 'parasite' view in particular no longer holds much intellectual credence (see Newton and Karran, 1985, for a summary). But both fitted in well with the political climate of the time; they were seized upon to give some credence to the establishment panic. Finally, the nearest thing in existence to an abstract capitalist, the International Monetary Fund (IMF), allowed these changes in attitude to be implemented in concrete policies. In trying to escape its fiscal crisis consequent to high inflation the Labour Government borrowed from the IMF in 1976. A condition of the loan was a halt to the growth in public spending. Whether willingly or unwillingly (and the Cabinet was split on the issue), the Government could blame the IMF when carrying out the necessary dirty work and reneging on its electoral promises. As Tony Crossland, then Minister for the Environment, told local councils with his now-famous aphorism, in 1976 'The party's over'.

Two elements were used to close down the 'party'. First, PESC became oriented to monetary control rather than to resource planning. The supply of money became much more an economic issue in its own right, and much less a means of doing things. Secondly, and most importantly, restrictions on current spending were introduced in the form of cash limits on the annual cost of particular programmes. Grants were fixed with reference to price levels assumed to operate during the financial year, rather than adjusting them automatically to take account of inflation. This was first seen as a means of breaking the upward spiral of inflation. But of course this also provided a means of actually controlling and reducing current spending, and by underestimating the rate of inflation the real value of grants could be lowered still more. First implemented in a limited way in 1976/7, the effect of cash limits was to cut into local government spending as a proportion of both overall GDP and of public-sector expenditure (see table 3.1).

In this way central government, for the first time, took direct control over local government spending. The cash ceilings on current spending complemented the existing loan sanctions on capital spending. It is important to note, however, that this tightening of overall financial limits on local government autonomy was still some way from the attack on its political autonomy mounted later by the Conservative Governments under Thatcher. There was no direct control over the policies of individual authorities and, if the political will and political support was there, local governments could still go their own way by raising rate revenue. In this sense local governments still had the autonomous ability to fix their own spending and raise their own revenues. This point is sometimes forgotten by critics who see no difference in principle between the Labour and Thatcher Governments. For them, capitalist states must necessarily act in the interests of capital, and when the latter dictate cuts in the welfare state then the government responds appropriately, in this case by reducing local government expenditure. Hence 1976 becomes the key date, when the IMF cuts were imposed, rather than 1979, when the Conservatives took power of central government. As we have seen, there is something in this argument. However, overall controls over local government expenditure do not necessarily mean direct policy control over individual authorities. The Thatcher Governments found themselves compelled to go much further along this road in pursuing their particular interpretation of capitalist necessity. In this way 1979 re-emerges as a crucial political marker.

There remains, however, one joker card in the interpretation of this first round of expenditure controls. In 1976 the Layfield Committee on local government finance (Layfield, 1976), in a wide-ranging and thorough analysis, accepted the responsibility of central government for overall fiscal control but concluded that increased local autonomy and accountability was equally necessary. This could be produced by replacing the bulk of central grant support with a local income tax. Although intellectually astute, this plan hardly satisfied the political needs of the moment, and the political response to it did less than justice to the report. The Conservative opposition simply promised to abolish rates – a particularly visible, unpopular and hence electorally vulnerable tax. The Labour Government took up the central control part of the argument. The Department of the Environment, in its evidence to the Committee, proposed replacing the Rate Support Grant (RSG) with a 'combined grant'. Similarly, the 1977 Green Paper in response to Layfield floated the idea of a 'unitary grant'. A central feature of these new grant systems was an increase in central direction over local expenditure at the individual authority level. The RSG, which allocated non-specific grants to local government, covered about 40 per cent of total local government expenditure by 1970 and was therefore a crucial element in local spending. In attempting to equalize between poorer and richer authorities and to allow needier authorities to provide uniform service provision, the RSG system used locally based estimates of needs and resources, including the level of previous expenditures as a guide to future allocation. So spending plans were locally determined and, even worse for a central government bent on cuts, increased spending would attract more RSG support. The 'combined' or 'unitary' grant systems would replace this by central estimates of local needs and in this way would have drawn central government into the arena of local policy-making.

These proposals were swept away in the 1979 election, only to reappear from Civil Service filing cabinets as the 'Block Grant' central to the Conservatives' first attempts to reduce local government autonomy. The question 'Would the Labour Government have become Thatcherite if it had won the 1979 election?' is impossible to answer. Our own feeling, however, is that the unitary grant would have been a logical end to Labour's version of restoring capitalist efficiency *vis-à-vis* local government, where the Block Grant was only the beginning of the Conservatives' version.

The Conservative general election victory in 1979 owed something to an effective sloganizing of their vision for regenerating British society and its economy. Saatchi and Saatchi, their advertising consultants for both the 1979 and 1983 elections, became a byword for both the power and the triviality of political propaganda. Their apparent success was a lesson not lost on the 'new urban Left' who were soon to take power in many local councils, and whose 'local socialism' was to become such a scourge to the Thatcher Governments. A central part of this Conservative campaign was an attack on state intervention; individuals should be freed from state controls, for instance over council house sales, and the private sector should be allowed to get on with wealth creation free of state interference and crowding out. This 'rolling back the state' would allow both to work properly in their own interests and so create the self-help culture that would regenerate Britain.

This highly ideological message was not always supported by coherent and practical policy proposals. Nevertheless, it certainly overshadowed the relatively drab Labour campaign of 'more of the same' and, as Labour was to find out to its cost in 1983, practical policies seem not to be the most important part of winning elections. As far as local government finance was concerned, almost the only concrete policy highlighted in the campaign was the promise to abolish rates. As subsequent events were to show, this was itself rather impractical both administratively and politically. Indeed the vagueness of the Conservatives' policy platform, and the *ad hoc* nature of some of its subsequent legislation, has led some commentators to question the received wisdom that Thatcherism was all about consciously breaking the mould of the post-war social democratic consensus. Rather, they say, radical New Right ideas were just a means of keeping Conservatives in power and monetarism was little more than a lifeline in the search for a credible economic policy in a time of crisis. At the other extreme, commentators point to the existence of the 'Ridley plan' (leaked to *The Economist*, 27 May 1978) where the strategy for a future Conservative government were laid out, even to the extent of planning the coal-miners' strike, which eventually happened in 1984–85. In this view of events, monetarism is a mere tool to further these political ends. Certainly, while particular policy plans may have been vague and legislation somewhat off the cuff and subject to last-minute decisions (as local government legislation was soon to show) it does seem that the

Table 3.2 Over-and underspending by local government: 1974–84

Year	Over/Underspend* %
1974/5	+5.4
1975/6	+0.7
1976/7	−1.8
1977/8	−1.5
1978/9	−1.0
1979/80	−3.2
1980/1	+0.1
1981/2	+8.7
1982/3	+7.7
1983/4	+3.3

Note: Local government expenditure minus Rate Support Grant target, England and Wales
Source: Boddy (1984).

direction policy should take and what it should be used for was well established. In this sense the Thatcher Governments can be regarded as consciously radical. Of course, establishing these New Right ideas at the centre of the Conservative Party was not a purely intellectual decision. It had lost four out of the last five general elections and, with the lowest proportion of votes ever, Party support was becoming limited to southern England. The change of political direction was a desperate response to the possibility that the Conservatives were no longer the 'natural party of government' and that time had passed it by. And the gamble worked.

It is not so surprising, therefore, that within weeks of taking office in May 1979 Conservative ministers were criticizing local government as wasteful, burdensome, irresponsible and out of control. This was despite the evidence showing that the Labour Government's centralization measures had succeeded in containing and even reversing local expenditure (see tables 3.1 and 3.2). This was because the Conservatives (or at least its Thatcherites, for a number of 'Wets' still remained in positions of power) were not just interested in total local government expenditure as a macroeconomic variable. For some, immersed in the 'parasite' version of monetarism, any local government spending was undesirable, even if at times this would be a necessary evil. Similarly, fired with visions of restructuring society, the accent was less on how *much* was being spent but *on what* it was being spent on and *how*. The Government's first response was to demand cuts in local government expenditure – but this came too late in the year to have any chance of being implemented successfully. Using this failure as its justification the Government's second response was the 1980 Local Government, Planning and Land Act.

THE 1980 LOCAL GOVERNMENT, PLANNING AND LAND ACT

This Act (see figure 3.1) has been well described as a 'legislative farrago [of] 19 Parts and 34 Schedules of which 12 are themselves divided into between 2 and 14 parts of their own. It is really 5 Acts' (quoted in Loughlin, 1981: see also Burgess and Travers, 1980; Loughlin, 1982; for detailed accounts). It took almost a year to go through Parliament and this was after a previous Bill had been withdrawn as unworkable. Yet this length of passage did little to clarify its contents. *The Guardian* noted that even 'Civil servants seem to have been driven to the conclusion that simplicity is a virtue inherently incompatible with the framework of the Local Government, Planning and Land (No. 2) Bill' (27 July 1980). The confusion was not helped by the way the Government introduced new material into the legislation after it has been introduced into Parliament. As one commentator put it:

> The Government took... principles into legislation before any work had been done to test them in detail. As Mr. King [then Environmental Secretary] was promoting his principles in committee, horrified civil servants were discovering that the more detailed work they did, the worse the mire in which they found themselves. (*Financial Times*, 5 August 1980)

This comment summarizes very well the nature of the first Thatcher Government. It may well have been unsure about exactly how to do things – and in taking policies into uncharted waters civil servants were not sure either – but it was quite certain about the direction in which things ought to go. In this way the Act is not a hotchpotch, but a coherent political document. So although legislation for local economic policy, land assembly and planning were also thrown into the Act – and we will consider these later – this administrative confusion does not detract from its political purpose. This can be summarized as 'rolling back the local government state'.

Local Government, Planning and Land Act 1980

1980 CHAPTER 65

An Act to relax controls over local and certain other authorities; to amend the law relating to the publication of information, the undertaking of works and the payment of allowances by local authorities and other bodies; to make further provision with respect to rates and to grants for local authorities and other persons and for controlling the expenditure of local authorities; to amend the law relating to planning; to make provision for a register of public land and the disposal of land on it; to repeal the Community Land Act 1975; to continue the Land Authority for Wales; to make further provision in relation to land compensation, development land, derelict land and public bodies' acquisitions and disposals of land; to amend the law relating to town development and new towns; to provide for the establishment of corporations to regenerate urban areas; to make further provision in relation to gipsies and their caravan sites; to abolish the Clean Air Councils and certain restrictions on the Greater London Council; to empower certain further authorities to confer honorary distinctions; and for connected purposes. [13th November 1980]

B E IT ENACTED by the Queen's most Excellent Majesty, by and with the advice and consent of the Lords Spiritual and Temporal, and Commons, in this present Parliament assembled, and by the authority of the same, as follows:—

Figure 3.1 The Local Government, Planning and Land Act: the official summary

There was, however, at least one fundamental contradiction in the Conservative Government's position: increased (market) freedom from the state required increased state centralization. The Act reflects this contradiction; while most of the Act deals with measures to increase central government control over local authorities the preamble to the Bill described itself as 'A Bill to relax controls over local government'. Mr Heseltine, as minister responsible, could even say 'We will sweep away tiresome and expensive controls over local government. Local councils are directly elected. They are answerable to their electorate....I am determined to clear the way for local action at all levels' (18 July 1979, quoted in Stewart, 1980). This was ironical in the extreme, but the first part of the Act does 'free' local government from central controls over such things as the regulation of caravan sites, the implementation of weights and measures rules, allotment allocation, dog-breeding procedures and so on. After this almost symbolic beginning the Act gets down to its real business – introducing substantial controls over local government, creating new non-elected state institutions to implement the Government's local economic policy, and repealing the Community Land Act.

The corner-stone of the local government part of the Act is the new system for paying central grants to local authorities. This increases central control in two ways: financial penalties are introduced for 'overspenders', who are determined by the centre, and the basis for calculating and distributing grants is centralized. The new Block Grant, replacing the Rate Support Grant (RSG), is distributed by Grant Related Expenditure Assessments (GREAs). The old RSG had taken local spending patterns as an index of need, and this index underlay the distribution of the largest part of the grant. But GREAs were to be determined centrally, according to the Department of the Environment's calculations of local need. The Block Grant is the balance of the GREA figure after the locally raised rate fund contribution is deducted – but again the latter is assumed from a 'grant related poundage' (GRP) also determined centrally. Furthermore, 'overspenders' who exceeded GREA levels would be penalized financially, their grant would be progressively reduced ('grant taper') in line with extra spending and they would have to levy even higher rates to support their expenditure.

In other words, central government would determine what local needs were and would set spending patterns accordingly – local political processes and local decisions to spend more on, say, school meals were to have no place in this process. If local governments were to insist on spending outside these guide-lines, even though they used their own rate income to do so, they would be punished. There was also a further twist to this central abrogation of local financial autonomy. For, although dressed up in a pseudo-scientific rationale, the actual calculation of GREAs and GRPs can only be a political judgement. This was shown soon enough by subsequent measures to alter the distribution of the Block Grant (favouring the Conservative shire authorities) and to change the definition of GREAs and GRPs so as to catch particular 'overspenders' (see below). This concern with 'overspenders' goes far beyond the earlier ideas for a 'unitary grant' developed under the Labour Government and appears moreover to have little macroeconomic rationale. Local government was only responsible for a mere 4 per cent of the Public Sector Borrowing Requirement (PSBR) and in any case rate income is clearly not borrowing. It is a local tax. This underlies the political importance given to nobbling certain authorities and their policies. The successful experiment by South Yorkshire in developing cheap public transport would hardly threaten the exchange rate. But it might threaten the idea than an individualistic, market-ruled society was the only alternative. After the Act was implemented the South Yorkshire public transport budget came to depend overwhemingly on rate income, and the County attracted heavy penalties for making its local, electorally legitimated choice.

This centralization of current spending was supported by further controls over capital expenditure. The latter was already subject to loan sanctions, after the Labour Government's 1976 measures. As borrowing accounted for 65 to 75 per cent of total capital spending, this meant an overall macroeconomic control. However, local authorities could still, if they wished, spend freely capital that was raised in other ways. Loan sanctions should also have been sufficient for a monetarist economic policy, where public borrowing is the key issue. But again the Conservative Government went further in controlling what individual authorities could do. Centrally determined ceilings for total capital expenditure were to be set for each authority, although this was wrapped up in a somewhat spurious argument that because loan sanctions for individual borrowings were removed, local authorities would actually be freer. Interestingly, unlike the Block Grant, this element of central control is not implemented exclusively by the Department of the Environment. Five expenditure allocations were distinguished – housing, transport, education, personal social services and all other services. Under the Act it was the appropriate minister for each who specified the prescribed amount of capital expenditure for each authority for each year. Only the first two categories come under the Department of the Environment, and in this way local authority budgets become more like appendages of central departments of state. Authorities were allowed to spend up to 10 per cent 'tolerance' over the limit, plus any net capital receipts (in practice these came from the sale of council housing and land enforced by other legislation, although this was later rescinded) and plus profits from any trading undertakings. Authorities can also move expenditure between blocks. The penalty is that any overspending (including the 10 per cent tolerance) will be deducted from the following year's allocation, and that sanctions for the further payments would be refused if they exceeded allocation. Ultimately, an authority would be *ultra vires* in ignoring the sanctions. Finally, at the same time as central control over both current and capital spending was increased, cuts were made in the actual level of funding using the PESC apparatus. By 1981/2 central government grants covered only 55 per cent of local government expenditure, compared with 63 per cent in 1975/6, even though total expenditure had declined by 15 per cent in real terms since then.

Ironically enough, the deficiencies of such a centrally planned system become apparent when the Government had to force local governments so 'spend, spend, spend' in order to revive the construction industry as part of the 1983 pre-election boom. According the *The Guardian* 'Mr Heseltine…performed an astonishing feat of monetarist alchemy by producing a £700m boost for public investment in the coming election without adding anything to the Treasury's basic plan for public spending' (8 November 1982). This immediate spending (although this sum was later halved at the Treasury's insistence) was difficult when councils were geared up to saving in the new system, when overspending had been penalized severely and when proper planning of construction projects takes some time. Similarly, spending on capital projects without increasing revenue expenditure meant that much of what was eventually built had no lasting purpose, while the command to spend created more centrally perceived 'overspending' and eventually meant more cuts. The Conservative-controlled Association of County Councils was reduced to calling annual capital expenditure ceilings 'a nonsensical system of controlling a long-term matter by short-term means' (*The Guardian*, 25 April 1983).

This was not the only part of the Act to expose divisions within the Conservative Party. Often, indeed, the Government's supporters gave the most outspoken opposition. For example, Geoffrey Ripon, a former Conservative Minister for the Environment claimed that:

'This bill, and its financial provisions in particular...constitutes a threat to local democracy' (quoted in Cheetham, 1980). A leading Conservative back-bencher, Anthony Beaumont-Dark, pointed out the united opposition to the Bill when he said in the House of Commons:

> It is unique to have a Bill on which all local government associations of whatever complexion are sensibly united against the Government's measures. It is also unique that no one outside the government has spoken up for the Bill....I have been years in local government and have not come to Parliament to turn a partnership into a dictatorship. (*The Guardian*, 9 July 1980)

The Bill only just survived a stormy passage through the House of Lords where all parties were united after the local government organizations had lobbied over 1,000 peers. Conservative opposition had been bought off at the last minute when the Government conceded four amendments to Tory local government leaders. A Labour peer, Lord Mishan, captured the atmosphere well: 'If provisions like this are passed by Parliament, then one had better alter the name of local authorities because I do not know what authority they are left with. They ought to be called local agents for national government' (*The Guardian*, 9 September 1980).

Government supporters who were not loyal Thatcherites had double reason to be disappointed. It was not just that the Act seemed to go against previously accepted Conservative principles in creating a stronger central state, or that Conservative-ruled local authorities would be threatened just as much as Labour ones. The election promise to abolish or at least reform the rating system had been reneged upon. All that the Act did was to allow ministers to say when new rating valuation lists should be brought into operation, rather than this happening automatically every five years as before. A new list means higher taxation as property values in general increase over time. By this means the Government avoided the embarrassment of actually increasing the tax they had promised to reform – even though revaluation had been due since 1978. This dilemma was to remain the tip of a political iceberg throughout the Thatcher Governments – it seemed practically impossible to do without rates yet the necessary rate increases alienated Conservative supporters.

SUPPLEMENTING THE ACT: TARGETS AND HOLD-BACK

In addition to the odium that the Act had brought upon it, first results were not at all encouraging for the Government. The transitional arrangements for 1980/1 concerning grant taper were even challenged successfully in court by Brent Council. According to the court the Secretary of State had acted unreasonably in failing to consider representations on behalf of the affected local authorities. But worse still, the fully operational system did not seem to work as the Government wished. The estimates for 1981/2 expenditures showed that local councils were proposing to spend 5.3 per cent *above* the Government target. The Act controlled and limited capital spending and central grant allocation, true enough. But many local authorities, even when faced with grant incentives to cut services, had nonetheless opted to try to maintain or even increase service levels and to raise the extra revenue through the rates. Things were just as difficult at the other end of the political spectrum. In using GREAs to estimate desired local expenditure levels, 'underspending' was identified just as much as 'overspending'. These underspenders could now increase their spending to this limit without incurring penalties – and with the implicit approval from the Government in doing so. Some traditionally low-spending Conservative counties, for instance, were under local pressure to increase expenditure on education in the face of central cuts. As with the health service, traditional Tory voters were often not at all keen that those parts of the state *they* valued should be rolled back. This residual political autonomy, even though macroeconomic objectives were by now quite secure, was not at all what the Government had in mind. In response, a whole series of further measures and legislation was introduceed to centralize local government finance even further.

In retrospect, the writing on the wall had been in evidence even before the Act was seen to fail. The Government's interest in controlling the policies of individual local state institutions, not just their overall contribution to public expenditure, had been signalled as early as August 1979. When members of the Lambeth Area Health Authority refused to impose expenditure cuts as demanded by the Government, they were replaced by centrally appointed commissioners. This action was later declared illegal on a technicality by the courts, again underlining the statutory vagueness of the Government's position. The 1982 Health Act was to replace Area

Health Authorities with new District Health Authorities – and representation from locally elected councillors (who had provided the opposition in Lambeth and elsewhere) was reduceed (see chapter 7).

Faced with the apparent failure of the 1980 Act to do everything it wanted, the Government was forced to drop the pretence to a rational system of assessing local needs and services. A number of various schemes were devised to patch up holes in the system of central control, and in this way the Government's imperatives were exposed more directly. First, the Government simply demanded cuts. In July 1981 a new expenditure target was set for individual authorities – the pseudo-scientific apparatus of GREA was ignored, councils were simply told to cut 1981/2 expenditure by 5.6 per cent from the 1978/9 level (in real terms). Local authorities spending above this level would be subject to a new system of penalties, which became known as the 'hold-back system'. Secondly, at about this time Government 'hit lists' began to be published in press reports. These were composed of a number of Labour councils, mostly metropolitan authorities, which the Conservative Government particularly wished to penalize and so push back into line. About a dozen councils usually appeared on such lists (for example, in 1981, the GLC, Inner London Education Authority, Camden, Hackney, Haringey, Islington, Lambeth, Lewisham, Southwark, Tower Hamlets, Manchester, South Yorkshire, Tyne and Wear). The exact status of such lists was not clear, although their release to the media clearly constituted a considerable political threat in itself. It is clear from comments by Government representatives at the time that the objection to these particular councils was both financial (they spent more than most on service provision) and political (they were Labour-held authorities which supported policies that central government particularly disliked, policies like cheap public transport which would actually *extend* service provision or demonstrate *alternative* policies). These authorities were caricatured as being unrepresentative, irresponsible and, worst of all, politically motivated.

The new hold-back system only produced further contradictions, however, as the base expenditure year of 1978/9 was selected quite arbitrarily, it was not surprising that some gross anomalies resulted. For some councils, 1978/9 had been a year of financial windfalls for various reasons, for others the reverse had been true, while many Conservative-run councils had already cut spending quite extensively. So the 'volume' targets threatened to produce a substantial number of councils which would have to make extreme cuts, including Conservative councils. Their service levels and work-forces might be reduced to levels very difficult to contain politically. But, at the same time, a few lucky councils would be able to increase spending. The very highest spenders would also, strangely enough, escape penalties. The hold-back system did not taper like the penalties of the 1980 Act. Grant was simply removed for overspenders. But at 5 per cent of GRE, tapering returned, as though hold-back was not operating, although penalties became more severe at 10 per cent over target. So for high-spending authorities unprepared to make cuts, the hold-back system contained an incentive to spend 5–10 per cent over target.

Faced with oppostition and outrage by the Tory shires, Mr Heseltine once again changed the rules of the game. In September 1981 he announced that the GREA assessments would return in combination with the volume targets. Councils that were under or on the GREA level, but did not meet the 5.6 per cent reduction, would be exempt from punishment. Only those authorities transgressing *both* targets would suffer a loss of grant. These turned out (not surprisingly after all this effort) to be mainly Labour-held authorities, mostly in London.

This manoeuvring clearly strengthened charges that the hold-back system was politically biased. Furthermore, there was some doubt if hold-back was legal. It appeared to lack statutory foundation and Government lawyers advised that to levy hold-back penalties might well be contrary to the law. The whole system of central control was further scuppered by the local election results in 1981. Already in 1980 the GLC had fallen to Labour, under a radical New Left administration headed by the charismatic Ken Livingstone. In May 1981, four Metropolitan County Councils were taken by Labour (Greater Manchester, Merseyside, West Midlands, West Yorkshire) so that now all the 'Mets' were under Labour administrations (the others were South Yorkshire and Tyne and Wear). Nine shire counties also moved to Labour control (only Durham was Labour prior to the elections) and in six more the Conservatives lost effective control. Many of these new Labour administrations were also of the New Left variety, eager to show that there was an alternative to Thatcherism. The Government was now faced with councils not only opposed to their policies but – the same old problem again – with an electoral and democratic mandate for this opposition. Shortly afterwards, in July 1981, inner-city riots spread through the country. Sparked off by repressive and insensitive policing, these were widely interpreted as a response to unemployment and service cuts.

Although 277 of the 413 authorities did propose to cut spending for 1982/3, by £196m in total, 135 increased expenditure by a total of £211m. Just three councils, the GLC, West Midlands and Merseyside, accounted for a full £167m of this increase. This was mostly the cost of cheap public transport which they were committed to introducing as a means of showing that there were alternatives. These policies were to be financed through levying supplementary rates and ignoring government penalties. And, apparently, the local electors supported them in this. The government's response was a further round of legislation. This would retrospectively legalize hold-back and at the same time close the loopholes in the 1980 system. This was the Local Government (Finance) Bill introduced in November 1981.

THE LOCAL GOVERNMENT (FINANCE) ACT, 1982

The new Bill would increase central control of local government in four ways. First, and most Draconian of its measures, the Department of the Environment would set a ceiling on the rates that any individual council could levy. This would remove almost entirely the convention that local governments could set their own level of taxation and expenditure. One outlet was provided as a sop to the idea of local autonomy. A council could levy a supplementary rate above this level, but weighted more heavily on domestic ratepayers than usual, if the electorate approved this in a referendum. The Government clearly thought that few electors would vote for increased taxation.

Secondly, as expected, the Bill would legislate retrospectively for 'hold-back'. The Secretary of State would have the power to achieve 'any reduction in the level of local authority expenditure...which he thinks necessary having regard to general economic conditions' (quoted in Loughlin, 1982). But this was not enough, and power was also to be given to the centre to reduce a local authority's grant half-way through the financial year. Appropriately, this became known as 'super hold-back'. Finally, a new body, the Audit Commission would be set up to supervise the auditing of local government expenditure. Its membership and functions were to be determined centrally. Indications of the Government's attitudes towards local authorities were plainly shown in other policy areas at this time. In December 1981, centrally chosen commissioners were appointed to enforce the sale of council houses in Norwich, while the Government encouraged local Conservative councils to take the high-spending Labour metropolitan authorities to court, notably in the actions against the GLC's 'Fares Fair' cheap fares scheme. The need to deal with local government finance once and for all was underlined by the publication, again in December 1981, of the Green Paper *Alternatives to Domestic Rates* (DOE, 1981). The paper was essentially a collection of negatives. Every scheme for replacing rates had, it seemed to the Department of the Environment's civil servants, insurmountable obstacles. But the Government was still committed to abolishing rates. Perhaps the Act would give it the next best thing.

But this next best thing provoked almost universal condemnation and opposition – not least from the Government's own supporters on the back benches and in local government. One Conservative MP even went so far as to tell his Party's Environment Secretary that 'When you go into a dung heap you can expect to come out smelling of muck' (*The Guardian*, 25 November 1981). The Government was forced to abandon the Bill or face a heavy parliamentary defeat. Instead, in January 1982 it introduced the Local Government Finance (No. 2) Bill. This retained the proposals about hold-back and super hold-back but withdrew the rate ceilings. As a replacement, local authority power to levy supplementary rates would be abolished.

Even these changes were not enough to salve opposition from their own supporters. Allying themselves with the formal opposition, objectors forced the Government to accept several amendments at the committee stage. Super hold-back was effectively removed and changes made to the new Audit Commission to make it more independent of central government. The Commission's code of practice would now be subject to quinquennial parliamentary approval, trade unions and local government associations were given statutory rights for consultation, and words which appeared to give auditors an overt right to make political judgements were withdrawn. Nonetheless, the Audit Commission still allowed an extension of central control over local policy. Previously, auditors were appointed individually by the local authority concerned, whereas now the Commission would appoint them. Originally imposed in the late nineteenth century as a simple accounting check on financial mismanagement or corruption, the audit system was becoming more an audit of policy rather than of financial practice. The Bill seemed to extend this with its demand that an auditor should now expressly 'satisfy himself [sic] that the body concerned has made proper arrangements for securing economy, efficiency and effectiveness in its use of resources'. At the same time auditors were also given greater powers to apply to the courts for a

With its usual care Whitehall has put together some new legislation.

The legislat... ...to keep busy, particularly when it comes to imposing central-ed control on local affairs.

In 1979 they put the Local Government ...anning and Land Bill before Parliament.

Parliament didn't care for it. And the Bill ...as withdrawn.

Swiftly Whitehall put together some new ...roposals, imaginatively entitled the Local ...overnment Planning and Land (No.2) Bill. ...became law, transforming the financial frame-...ork within which Local Authorities work.

Within a year Whitehall was back with the ...nitive Local Government Finance Bill.

So many M.P.s doubted the constitutional ...isdom of the referendum clause, the Bill was ...ithdrawn within a month.

Now, for the fourth time in two years, the ...gislators are back. With (wait for it) the Local ...overnment Finance (No.2) Bill.

And even as this Bill is about to become ...ed in law, there is already in existence a Government Green Paper outlining radical changes to the financing of Local Government.

The conclusion is that Whitehall is in too much of a hurry.

We believe this latest Bill should at least have a time limit imposed on it.

So that it can be replaced or abandoned once all parties are agreed on the proper relationship between Central and Local Government. And upon a new rating system.

To quote G.W. Jones and J.D. Stewart (Professors of Government, and Local Govern-ment respectively),

Whitehall's "record is amazing: four bills in two years; two bills withdrawn; three major changes in intention; and a grant system that is not merely complex beyond belief but contra-dictory in purposes."

Is this the right way to legislate?

If you think not, write to your M.P. Ask him to voice the demand for a time limit on the Bill.

KEEP IT local

Figure 3.2   Keep it local: one reaction to the Local Government Finance (No. 2) Bill
Source: The Guardian, 1982.

declaration that items of expenditure were illegal.

Professional auditors themselves were not particularly enamoured with this development. The Association of Certified Accountants, backed by by several large accounting firms, opposed the idea of a central, government-appointed Audit Commission. Their point was that as auditing could never be value free, accountants would become tainted with politics. This has indeed happened, but ironically in an unexpected way. The Commission has concluded, in a series of detailed reports, that it is the new system of local government finance that is uneconomic, inefficient and ineffective – not, in general, local government itself. No doubt partly because of this embarrassment the Commission has expressed a desire to be left to get on with auditing pure and simple. It felt that others should be responsible for beginning legal proceedings and it has shown some distaste at the more political measures of surcharge and disqualification of councillors.

All in all the 1982 Bill took eight months to become an Act of Parliament. It became further bogged down in a bizarre constitutional issue, resulting from the threat it apparently posed to ban retrospectively a supplementary rate levied by Bedfordshire County Council just as the Bill was passing through the House of Commons. Once this difficulty was resolved, more legal entanglements arose as the Government pondered on how to penalize 'overspending' authorities without punishing too many of its own supporters – Conservative councils. Eventually, these difficulties were also circumvented – although this was to be an ever-present difficulty with all succeeding systems of central control that gave any pretence to objectivity.

3.3   Centralizing Finance: Political Aims and Technical Failures

The 1980 and 1982 Acts combined were the framework for a complicated dual system of centralized control, in which volume and GREA targets combined were the basis for both allocation of RSG and penalties for overspenders. The system was to break down under its own technical and political contradictions by 1985. But even by 1983, confusion had become apparent. First, some councils could spend more. On the one hand, low-spending Conservative shires which fell under the GREA limit could actually increase spending, and break targets without penalty. At the other extreme, some councils were now so penalized for 'overspending' that their Block Grant was completely lost. Paradoxically, this allowed such authorities to reclaim their financial autonomy; they now raised most of their income from their own tax base (the rates) to spend up to levels they determined. The GLC and Camden (both with substantial rate income from commerical users in Central London) and the Inner London Education Authority (ILEA – whcih could raise income by precepting other councils and did not levy its own taxes directly) could escape control in this way. Secondly, even without this 'freedom' to do without Block Grant support, other politically determined and well-supported authorities could continue to juggle rate rises against penalties and still, although with difficulty, follow 'high spending' policies maintaining service provision. Some authorities were still able, therefore, to pursue politically challenging policies which were much to the distaste of central government. Cheap public transport and alternative local economic policies by the GLC, the Metropolitan County Councils, Sheffield and others are cases in point. Finally, other local authorities did not possess the combination of financial and political resources necessary to mount alternative policy regimes but could still use their remaining autonomy to make political points. For example, over half the geographical area of Britain is now covered by local-government designated nuclear-free zones.

A first attempt to tighten up control was made in December 1982. Exemption from 'overspending' penalties would be removed from those councils that broke the volume target but fell under the GREA limit, with tougher penalties than before for transgression. A new, tighter system for calculating the spending targets of individual authorities was also introduced. But yet again, this provoked a furious and worried response from Conservative councils as well as the political opposition and the calculations had to be withdrawn and 'reworked'.

The Government continued to juggle with RSG allocation procedures, target levels and penalty systems over the next few years – and the same technical and political snags constantly re-emerged. From the point of view of completely controlling local government finance the fundamental and glaring failure in the system was that the Government's own supporters had not gone along with the idea of introducing the 'Scottish solution' to England and Wales. Since 1980 the Scottish Office had been able to specify spending levels for individual authorities, and to make cuts if these were exceeded. This had been used to devastating effect in 1981 against Lothian Regional Council, which was threatening to do a GLC and perhaps even lead a Scottish local government revolt

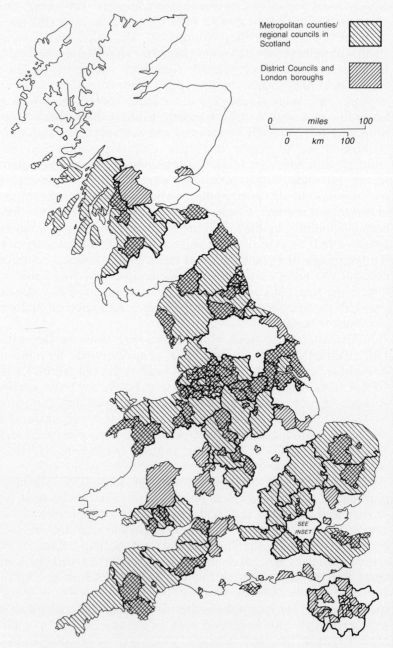

Metropolitan counties/
regional councils in
Scotland

District Councils and
London boroughs

0   miles   100

0   km   100

SEE
INSET

Figure 3.3   Councils hit by hold-back and claw-back, 1983/4
Source: Department of the Environment, proposed
expenditure supplementary reports

against Conservative rule. The Government's own supporters had successfully removed a similar proposal from the 1982 Act. Meanwhile the 'Scottish solution' was extended further in 1982 with new legislation giving the centre powers to set rate levels for individual authorities. The contrast between this system and the much greater room for manœuvre that was possible for councils south of the Border was one stimulus for the 'final solution' of rate-capping and abolition (see chapter 5).

It becomes clearer that the threat posed by local government is mostly a political one if we reconsider the macroeconomic arguments briefly. The loadstone of monetarist economic policy is public borrowing, but by 1982/3 local government borrowing was a mere 4.1 per cent of total PSBR (central government accounted for 79 per cent and the public corporations for 17 per cent). Spending income from rates involves no borrowing at all. Nor is local government expenditure out of control (if academic monetarist theory stresses PSBR, British monetarist practice – corrupted by ideas of 'crowding out' and 'standing on your own two feet' – has become fixed on public spending whether borrowed or not). Between 1974/5 and 1981/2 local government expenditure *fell* by 15 per cent in real terms, while central government spending had increased by 14 per cent (see Boddy, 1984). If anything it is central government spending that is out of control.

Even if we did accept that tight macroeconomic controls were necessary for local authority expenditure and taxation, as well as borrowing, this hardly necessitates the Government's almost compulsive interest in individual council budgets and particular council policies. Why, for example, the detailed adjustments to RSG and targets aimed at trapping particular authorities? One possibility is that ministers have to cling to the notion of local government as a profligate spender and uncontrolled borrower in a self-deluding attempt to preserve monetarist theory as politcial doctrine. Hence, they would have to act on the basis of this illusion; at least this would be offensive behaviour rather than placing the government on the defensive, and this is often the crucial difference between success and failure in electoral politics.

Whether self-deluding or not, the Government's position has steadily fallen away as its own technical and political contradictions have taken effect. The first major report of the Audit Commission (1984) on the Block Grant system confirmed that council spending was in line with overall macroeconomic objectives. Rather, it was the uncertainties created by the centre in creating a complex and constantly changing local government financial system that were at fault. It was this, not local government irresponsibility, that had led to increased rates. Moreover, this inefficient and uneconomic system of central control damaged local accountability. A subsequent report on capital expenditure controls (Audit Commission, 1985) came to much the same conclusion. Furthermore, with capital spending cut by 40 per cent in real terms between 1973 and 1985, even the current unsatisfactory state of local authority housing, schools and roads could not be maintained. The £15bn backlog of repairs was increasing by £1bn per year, and soon renovation would become prohibitively expensive. This was false economy indeed. The Commission's director followed this up with a wide-ranging rejection of the local government finance system, arguing instead for:

1   improved local accountability;
2   local responsibility for how much to spend on capital or as current spending;
3   sufficient built-in flexibility to allow the system to survive changes in central policies; and
4   simplicity even at the expense of capacity.

The sort of inefficiency the Commission referred to was shown up very clearly just as the director's paper was published. An extra cut of 1.5 per cent in RSG was announced in April 1985, far too late for councils to plan for it properly and apparently just in time to deal local Conservatives a heavy blow in the local elections due the next month. But this was not, as *The Guardian* correspondent put it 'a new Kamikaze theory of electioneering' (4 April 1985). Rather, this was the bizarre logic of the RSG system in practice. The GLC had, unexpectedly, spent less than the Department of the Environment (DOE) had estimated. This meant a considerable reduction in penalties and increased grants, in total amounting to 1.5 per cent of total RSG. Hence, 1.5 per cent had to be lawed back. The result was both financial inefficiency and political irritation.

Other authorities supported the Audit Commission line. Even that august and government-appointed figure, the Comptroller and Auditor General, repeated very similar arguments, if in more suitably restrained terms. The Government was to blame for rate increases while the RSG system led to considerable financial inefficiency. This conclusion was based on a year-long study by the National Audit Office. At the same time, a well-publicized study, sponsored by the DoE and carried out by the Cambridge University

Department of Land Economy, removed a further plank in the Government's platform. There was no relationship whatsoever between rate levels or rate increases and local employment levels.

By this time the financial pressures on local governments were intense. RSG had dropped from 61 per cent of expenditure in 1980/1 to only 45 per cent of a reduced total in 1985/6. Rate income, meanwhile, now covered 54 per cent of expenditure where fully 117 councils were subject to government penalties. The Government was not only provoking the opposition but alienating its own most natural supporters from the shires. At almost every parliamentary discussion of council finance, the Government found itself embarrassed by back-bench rebellions. Finally, the Brecon and Radnor by-election defeat in June 1985 seemed to tip the balance. A Cabinet committee concluded that the political costs of keeping targets clearly exceeded the financial benefits to the Treasury, and the Government should act to ensure that the blame for rate increases – that *bête noire* of grass-roots Conservatives – should not stick to them. In July 1985, the Government announced that it would scrap targets and penalties by the end of the 1985/6 financial year. Instead it would revert to a system of GREA levels alone, although with even more severe penalties for transgression. This, it was thought, would hit Labour authorities more, although in the event Conservative urban councils were affected quite badly. 'Recycling' of penalties was introduced at around the same time, with the same sort of political purpose. Previously penalties on overspenders had remained with the Treasury as some sort of bonus: now they were to be shared out amongst underspenders – this was over £500m in 1985/6 alone. The Treasury was losing out to the Government's concern for political survival; indicatively, perhaps, this concession was withdrawn in July 1986, restoring to the Treasury its windfall.

Even so, the pressures remained. The Audit Commission came nearer the political nub of the argument in a report on Cleveland County Council in September 1985. This was the highest-spending non-metropolitan county in many service areas, with the highest rates and also under Labour control. It was frequently cited by Government ministers for extravagance and inefficiency. In spending £17m over target it attracted £22m in penalties. The Audit Commission found that the Council was in no way inefficient. Rather, its high spending and rate levels resulted from local political decisions to provide above-average service levels, and this result was exacerbated by Government policy. The Director of the Commission spoke out again. He was critical of the centralization over the last few years, which had led to 'more waste, more inefficiency and less accountability'....Local government will be replaced by local administration – to the ultimate disbenefit of us all' (*The Guardian*, 26 April 1986). This was followed up by the Comptroller and Auditor General, who complained that central controls over local government finance had in any case failed miserably, and by the Commons Committee on Public Accountss, which said that the RSG system undermined local accountability and increased inefficiency.

At this the new Minister for the Environment (Kenneth Baker) and top officials at this Department appeared to throw in the towel. According to reports he could 'no longer accept the basic intellectual justification for the government attempts since 1979 to control local authority current spending' (*The Guardian*, 7 May 1986). Ministers should be content to impose cash limits on central grants, leave rates to be determined freely and not penalize overspenders, where rates could not add to PSBR or influence the money supply. This conclusion was definitely not accepted by the Treasury (and shortly afterwards Baker was promoted sideways to Minister for Education). However, although a self-indictment of past policy, his statement is perhaps less of a bombshell than at first sight. For by this time the Government had finally managed to destabilize the local government opposition, using rate-capping and abolition (see chapter 5).

This is perhaps why the discovery, made late in 1986, that all RSGs paid since 1980 (up to £70bn of public expenditure) were in fact illegal, seemed more ironical than startling. The Local Government, Planning and Land Act 1980 had been faultily drafted. Typically, it was court cases by aggrieved local authorities (first Birmingham and then the London Borough of Greenwich) that had exposed the flaws. The error discovered by Birmingham could be dealt with by administrative measures. But the Greenwich case was so far-reaching that corrective legislation, the Local Government Finance Bill 1987, had to be rushed through Parliament by the new Environment Minister, Nicholas Ridley. Claiming that 'I am the only person who understands what the law is' (*The Guardian*, 17 December 1986) the Bill appeared to go to new lengths in centralization. It was not only retrospective, but inlcuded catch-all clauses to prevent the legislation being challenged by the courts in the future and overruled any past decision of the courts (such as that in the Greenwich case) 'purporting to have a contrary effect'. At the same time, Ridley pushed through a new Rates Support Grant Bill, which would restore the powers of the Treasury to confiscate the grant withheld from 'overspending' councils, rather than to redistribute it to those keeping within centrally imposed targets. This upset Conservative-run councils yet again, and in compensation the same Bill would legalize the grant redistribution of ex-GLC monies from the inner (Labour-controlled) to the outer (Conservative-controlled) London boroughs, for this too had been found to be illegal.

What Baker's statement on the intellectual bankruptcy of the Government's legislation does, however, is to support our contention that the Conservative Government's macroeconomic policy, like monetarism in general, is more a political tool than anything else. It is designed to hamper those local authorities like Cleveland which are merely responding to local wishes by providing high levels of public services. A central government determined to impose its alternative version of political ideology would clearly want to curb this type of behaviour. Financial centralization on its own was not completely effective in controlling *what* local councils did, even if it severely constrained how much they could spend. To control the content of policy at the local government level more direct and detailed intervention from the centre would be needed. We turn to this in the next chapter.

4
Centralizing the Local Government System II
Policy

4.1 Introduction

As we saw in the last chapter, the Thatcher Government's centralization of local government spending was not just a matter of macroeconomic policy. Rather, the aim of restructuring British society – of changing what people did, how they did it and what they expected – also demanded control over local government policy-making. In this way macroeconomic policy was only a means to an end, and central government became drawn more and more into specifying what individual local councils could do and how they could do it. In this chapter we will look in detail at two policy areas which show this very well – local economic policy and housing provision. In these areas local councils mounted challenges to the Government's accepted free market wisdom, and in each case the Government responded by attempting to remove local autonomy and influence.

Precisely how this removal was to take place was, however, different in each case. Local government involvement in the economy had largely been *ad hoc* with little institutionalization of either local machinery or national legislation. On the other hand, how the economy works and for whom is an area of some political significance and this was the focus of alternative policies from some highly visible left-wing governments as well as from the radical Right in Downing Street. Outflanking local government by creating new, centralized or centrally sponsored local institutions became the Government's strategy in this case.

Housing provision was at the other end of the extreme. This had traditionally been a local government concern, with the centre playing a supporting and enabling role. It was an area where the Thatcher Government wanted to completely change prevailing social and political mores, turning what it saw as a collectivist and labourist culture into that of an individualistic and self-assertive property-owning democracy. Labour-controlled local governments, often well entrenched politically, and where housing was an important local concern, were a major obstacle. Here, the main strategy was to confront these councils head-on, and to use legislation to force them to do what the Government wanted – although as before financial centralization, together with institutional outflanking, remained handy weapons.

Finally, we turn briefly to local policies concerning civil defence. Unlike transport, housing or even local economic policy, the conflict here was not complicated by the spending of substantial sums of money by local governments. This underlines all the more the political and ideological components of the British local government crisis. Ultimately, the threat of local autonomy is a political issue.

4.2   Local Economic Policy: Creating Central Local States

REDEFINING THE FRONTIER BETWEEN THE PUBLIC AND PRIVATE SECTORS

Local economic policy is perhaps where the role of the local state, as both agent of central government and obstacle to it, has become most obvious. The Thatcher Government has introduced a series of financial, legislative and administrative changes with the overall aim of reducing the scope for local authority initiative and intervention in favour of private enterprise. In the words of Michael Heseltine (then Environment Minister), 'The Government is committed to take a radical look at the way in which bureaucratic institutions affect our industrial and economic performance. We see the need to redefine the frontier between the public and the private sector' (Hansard, 13 September 1979). Tom King, Minister for Local Government, extended this line of thought specifically for local economic policy:

> The Urban Development Area, like much of the rest of our inner-urban areas, desperately need the private sector's energy and resources...so do the Enterprise Zones which we have created. In these too we must encourage and enlist the flair, drive, and initiative of the private sector as the *only possible way* of restoring lasting

prosperity to the decaying areas of some of our towns and cities. (Our emphasis, quoted in *Local Government Chronicle*, 12 December 1980)

Note that the definition of two separate and opposed sectors is in itself dubious, over and above the quite illusory ascription of virtue to one and parasitism to the other.

Two of these initiatives, Enterprise Zones (EZs) and Urban Development Corporations (UDCs) were introduced by the 1980 Local Government Act. A number of other administrative measures taken since then consolidate this policy, and new institutions have appeared which represent this new emphasis. Examples are BIC (Business in the Community), FIG (the Financial Institutions Group), ICE (Inner-City Enterprises), the Inner-City Task Forces and Freeports. New Ministers for Merseyside and the West Midlands have also been created to promote these new institutions and the new definition of economic policy in areas hit particularly hard by the recession (and central government's part in creating it).

But electoral local states can still be an obstacle to central government, as well as acting as its agents. Several local authorities, all Labour-held and mostly metropolitan or large urban authorities appearing on various government 'hit lists' of 'overspenders', have attempted to redefine the public/private frontier in quite a different way (see figure 4.1). Rather than bring business into the community, the community is to be brought into business. So Sheffield City Council, for instance, aimed to use economic policy as a means to

> build a confident, local working-class movement which concentrates its strength at its base and which is committed to develope genuine, socialist alternatives to the top-heavy policies of the last Labour Government and the ravages of monetarist policies of the current Conservative Government. (Sheffield City Council 1981)

In similar vein, Geoff Edge, the chair of West Midlands County Council Economic Development Committee, sees their purpose as 'advocates and missionaries of new Socialist ideas' (*The Guardian*, 6 October 1981), while Michael Ward, his counterpart in the GLC, has written that 'Local initiatives can demonstrate that the alternative works: that greater democratic control and the planned use of resources can be used to create jobs. Local initiatives can layout the line of policy that a future Labour government can follow' (Ward, 1981).

It may be that economic restructuring must inevitably be a part of economic policy. But for these councils this should be, to repeat

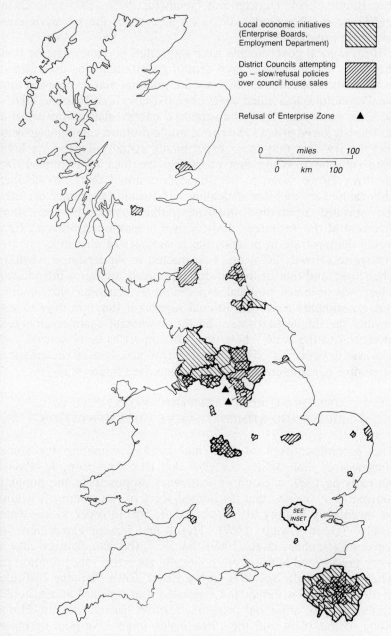

Figure 4.1 Local government challenges: economic initiatives and housing policy, 1980/5

one slogan, 'restructuring in the interests of labour, not of capital' (see Boddy, 1984; Duncan and Goodwin, 1985a, 1985b Goodwin and Duncan 1986, Gough 1985) for analysis of these experiments and their progress).

If these local governments were interested in demonstrating that there *was* an alternative, then central government was determined to show the opposite. In this way the nominal aim of regenerating local economies had much wider objectives. So both EZs and UDCs were set up to show how the supposed energy, flair and drive of a now less-fettered private enterprise would produce economic growth (despite the fact that these experiments actually depend on high state subsidies). When first proposing the idea of EZs in 1978, Geoffrey Howe (soon to be Chancellor) noted that 'two distinct philosophies are on offer' in dealing with Britain's economic decline: the 'socialist alternative' involving public investment and 'state direction of our resources' and his own 'liberation approach'. EZs would demonstrate in practice the advantages of liberating private enterprise (Howe, 1978, pp. 4–5; quoted in Anderson, J., 1983). Their role, and that of the various supporting measures introduced later, was as much political experiment as economic instrument. But experiments need institutional support if they are ever to get beyond the intellectual stage. So the local state again re-emerged as central to the issue – how was this support to be organized and who was to control it? 'Freeing enterprise' necessitated the creation of central government's own local states (see figure 4.2).

THE 'HONG KONG' SOLUTION: INTELLECTUAL ORIGINS AND ADMINISTRATIVE IMPLEMENTATION

The general concept of EZs had been germinating for some considerable time before the 1980 Act (see Anderson, J., 1983). As early as 1969, a group of academics proposed, in the popular journal *New Society*, that 'In limited areas of the country it would be thoroughly healthy to let *laissez-faire* rip, in order to see what results' (Open Group, 1969). This would be 'an experiment in freedom' (Banham et al., 1969). By 1977, this had changed into a more precise and hence more politically attractive interpretation of what would result. Speaking to the Royal Town Planning Institute in 1977, Professor Peter Hall suggested that selected areas should be exposed to 'minimum control', in order 'to recreate the Hong Kong of the 1950s and the 1960s inside inner Liverpool or inner Glasgow' (Hall, 1977; quoted in Anderson, J., 1983) Although this interpretation rested on the shaky ground of analogy, and despite

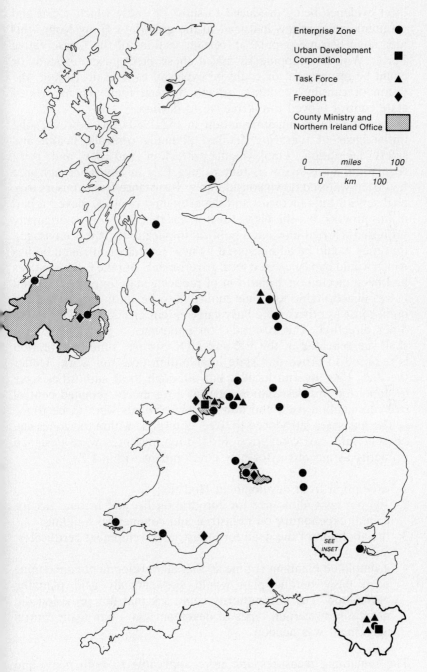

Figure 4.2 Central government local states: economic initiatives, 1980/5

littel evidence being produced to show precisely which social and economic mechanisms had lead to the growth of Hong Kong, this idea soon became popular in certain sections of the Conservative Party. Without stopping to ask if these mechanisms existed, or could be introduced, or could be expected to work in Britain, the vision of causing economic growth through removing aspects of state control proved too attractive to dismiss.

By the time of implementation in the 1980 Act, however, the initial ideas of removing detailed planning controls, health and safety legislation, employment protection and pay and price regulations in as many as four or five EZs in any inner-city area had been watered down considerably. Resistance from conservative civil service bureaucracies and departmental rivalries played a part in this process, but the biggest factor was that the EZs, as originally proposed, carried unwanted political implications. It was envisaged that they would be administered by new centrally controlled bodies which would bypass elected local government. But the Conservatives had been elected on a platform of reducing state intervention, and it was unacceptable for some ministers to be settling up new state bodies just as others were busy carrying out election pledges in the other direction. This contradiction underlines a paradox that we shall see repeated in the EZ and UDC stories; state intervention is required to prove that state intervention does not work. Under the Act, EZs are run locally, but although local authorities have to apply for this designation, central government retained control over designation itself and how the experiments were to be run.

The measures introduced to 'free' enterprise within the zones can be split into two categories. First, four measures were designed primarily as incentives for new development within EZs:

1 exemption from development land tax;
2 100 per cent allowance for corporation tax and income tax for capital expenditure on industrial and commercial building;
3 the abolition of the need for industrial development certificates; and
4 a simplified planning regime so that all development conforming to a basic outline plan would automatically gain planning permission. The EZ authority could ask that this provision did not apply to certain types of developments – but again central agreement was needed.

The remaining measures are more applicable to both neew and existing businesses:

1 reduction in statistical information to be supplied to state authorities;
2 exemption from industrial training levies;
3 accelerating processing of applications for custom-free warehousing; and
4 exemption from paying rates on industrial and commerical properties (the Treasury reimburses the local authorities).

Eleven zones were designated in the first round (between June 1981 and April 1982) and 13 in the second round (between November 1982 and March 1983; see figure 4.2). North-east Derbyshire refused an EZ in the second round and Sheffield City Council had effectively done the same in the first round, by insisting on detailed local planning control. Manchester and some other authorities had determined not to apply.

UDCs share the same underlying principles as EZs, and the same economic and wider political aims. They differ in the important respect of replacing elected local government institutionally. In Urban Development Areas (UDAs), designated centrally where the Secretary of State 'considers it expedient in the national interest', the powers of existing local governments for planning, housing, public health and building controls can be curtailed and given to the UDC. The Secretary of State can 'vest' in a UDC (i.e., appropriate) any publicly owned land in or adjoining the area subject to compensation. In the two UDCs created at the time of the Act, in Merseyside docklands and London docklands, most developable land was owned by local authorities, public utilities and the port authorities, so these land-vesting powers were clearly crucial. In effect, local development is taken out of the electoral orbit of local government and placed in the hands of a non-elected body appointed centrally and responsible to the centre. Although existing local government retains some statutory influence (for instance, it remains the planning body that validates plans for UDAs, even if it no longer draws up plans or judges particular proposals) the implications for central–local relations are substantial.

'FREEING ENTERPRISE': EZs AND UDCs IN PRACTICE

Through their hoped-for economic success, EZs and UDCs have been designed to demonstrate a political lesson concerning the efficiency of the free market. But economically the effects of EZs seem minor and mostly redistributive, and they have mainly shifted existing jobs around as some firms have relocated to take advantage of EZ subsidies (see Roger Tym and Partners, 1981; 1982; Shutt, 1984; Erikson and Syms, 1986). Similarly, the attempt to remove barriers to investment (when these were misleadingly identified as state regulations) has merely led to their redistribution, for instead of paying rates inside the zones firms pay higher rents and property prices (Erikson and Syms, 1986). Developers and landowners have benefited most from the subsidies, which in turn have encouraged large concerns, typically warehousing, at the expense of labour-intensive small businesses.

Paradoxically, what economic success there has been has depended on substantial subsidy from the centre (Shutt, 1984). Aside from the EZ package itself, most zones benefit from other subsidies, such as Development Area status, British Steel Corporation Industry Area funds, and Scottish Development Agency grants. Most had already benefited from considerable state infrastructural support before gaining EZ status, and this continues. Moreover, the more 'successful' EZs are, the more it costs the Treasury in replacing rates. UDCs represent the height of this paradox. They act as state development agencies, employing large sums of money and owning (i.e., nationalizing) large areas of land so that they can make sure the free market works!

Indicatively, the second round of EZ designation concentrated on sites away from the inner cities that were more favourable to capital. Moreover, places such as north Kent and Telford were already showing signs of comparative growth, based partly on heavy state investment in motorway building and local government supported industrial parks. Despite the switch, by 1984 all the EZs put together (some operating for three years, some only for two) could only claim about 3,000 new jobs – and many of these are likely to be redistributed. But the creation of EZs and UDCs is as much political experiment as local economic intervention. So according to Geoffrey Howe in 1978, the EZ policy

> would be designed to go further and more swiftly than the general policy changes that we have been proposing to liberate enterprise throughout the country . . . the idea would be to set up test market areas for laboratories in which to enable fresh policies to prime the pump of prosperity, and to establish their potential for doing so elsewhere. . . . If we find communities queuing up for enterprise zone status we shall have gone a long way towards winning the debate (Howe, 26 June 1978)

Although economic limitations have undermined this goal, the political notion of 'winning the debate' has not been lost. Indeed, technical failure can be presented as grounds for extending EZ principles. Thus, speaking to the Summer School of the Conservative Political Centre in 1982, Geoffrey Howe pointed out that 'Language and tone are often as important as content and policy', before going on to suggest that the 'free for all principles' on which the EZs had been founded might have potential application throughout the country. He continued 'We must go further, state ownership and control should be displaced or supplemented whenever sensibly possible by the discipline and pressure of the market-place' (*The Guardian*, 8 September 1982). But centrally promoted local state institutions have had to be used to carry this out!

This application has been clearest in the Conservative campaign to weaken the land-use and structure-planning system, which is at odds with the free market ideology. According to this, planning should support, rather than regulate, private developers and EZs give a rationale for this. So according to the Minister for the Environment, in issuing a consultative paper, 'The enterprise zone experiment gives us experience of the operation of a greatly simplified form of planning control' (*The Guardian* 2 May 1984). As a result, local authorities have been instructed to fit their planning decisions to the market (Hooper, 1985; Duncan and Goodwin, 1985c), and the 1986 Housing and Planning Act introduced 'special planning zones', (SPZs), in which developers would not need to make planning applications for 10 years. Although it was not incumbent upon local authorities to declare an SPZ, the Minister could direct them to do so. According to the Housing Minister at the time, this would be used against Labour authorities who did not declare SPZs – who wished, in other words, to interpret the notion of planning differently (*The Guardian* 5 February 1986). Finally, following a White Paper revealingly entitled '*Lifting the Burden*' (DOE, 1985), planning permission would normally be granted for any change of use that developers or users may want in existing premises. Given all this, one distinguished architectural correspondent concludes that for the 1947 Town and Country Planning Act 'The holes in the fabric are more prominent than the cloth' (Pawley, *The Guardian*, 10 February 1986).

FREEING ENTERPRISE AND LOCAL-CENTRAL RELATIONS

At first sight EZs and UDCs have had less effect on local–central relations than the Conservatives wished for. In principle, local councils administer their own EZs, and there are only six UDCs.

Nonetheless, both have affected relations between local and central state to a significant extent. First of all, councils lose much of their ability to control industrial and commercial development within their boundaries; one way of achieving electoral influence over economic change is thus removed in EZ authorities. In many, existing public plans for housing and leisure have been shelved in favour of industrial development (Goodwin, 1986b, 1988; Shutt, 1984). Secondly, EZs are in practice administered partly from the centre. The sites are chosen centrally, as are detailed boundaries. Content is also evaluated by the centre – in the first round Sheffield (which refused to bid in the second) was replaced by Wakefield when the city council expressed concern about the effect an EZ hypermarket development would have on existing retailers. Moreover, after designation the centre can modify the plans, but local government cannot. Thirdly, EZs can be used by central government to force ideas onto a recalcitrant authority. Several Labour councils apparently felt compelled to apply for an EZ, or risk being labelled as uncooperative by the centre and inactive by local residents. In this way EZs have been used to divide local opposition to centralization of the local state. Fifteen of the 28 zones are in Labour-controlled authorities, which seem to have accepted the faulty notion that any jobs means economic regeneration and that job redistribution equals job creation.

With the UDCs, where local elected governments are replaced directly by centrally controlled bodies, the implications for local–central relations are even clearer. As Nigel Broackes, the first chairman of the London Docklands Development Corporation (LDDC) put it 'Why face aggravation from councils opposed to the profit motive and home ownership?' (*The Guardian*, 3 July 1981). Broackes clearly saw the LDDC as capital's answer to troublesome electoral politics. He later confirmed that 'We are not a welfare association, but a property based organisation offering good value' (*Docklands News*,).

The LDDC was created in 1981 along with the Merseyside Development Corporation (MDC), and four more, in Tyne and Wear, Teeside, Manchester and the Black Country, were announced in 1986 at the Conservative Party Conference – an indication of the political importance attached to this part of the experiment. Yet another five were announced just after the June 1987 election. The Government clearly takes a special interest in the affairs of these 'property-based organizations', and their boards are appointed by, and responsible to, the Minister for the Environment. The LDDC, at least, has almost daily contact with the Minister's department and at times receives direct instructions from the Minister's office (see Goodwin, 1986b; King, 1987, looks at the MDC). Under this chain of command, existing local political organizations, including local governments as the site of representative democracy as well as local community groups and specific issue groups, are consulted as and when desired by the LDDC. There is no statutory need to listen to any advice, especially when the UDC can take over public land as desired, when it holds its own development powers, and when it is financed generously from the centre. Although modelled initially on New Town Development Corporations, the content of UDC policies is quite different. Rather than development corporations as the physical embodiment of state planning under the terms of a social democratic compromise between capital and labour, UDCs represent government for developers, subject only to central government, which is consciously trying to weaken the position of labour and hence ensure local development in its own image.

JUSTIFYING CENTRALIZATION: THE INEFFICIENCIES OF (LOCAL) DEMOCRACY

At the time of the 1980 Act, Tom King (the Local Government Minister) described the rationale for UDCs as follows:

> The new UDCs . . . will relieve the local authorities of an extremely onerous task. The creation of the UDCs is no reflection on, or criticism of, the efficiency or ability of the local authorities. It is rather recognition of the importance of these areas and the need to bring central government resources to bear in a speedy and *single-minded* approach to solving their area's problems. (*Local Government Chronicle*, 12 December 1980; our emphasis)

'Single-minded' in this case clearly means the removal of elected councils and direct local representation from development issues. The 1980 Act which introduced UDCs was a major means of achieving this and Michael Heseltine, as Minister for the Environment, summarized the situation very well in introducing the legislation:

> Local government must be very clear about the implications of deciding either deliberately to ignore or to fight against measures which a democratically elected government wants to see achieved for the longer term interests of the nation. . . . If individual authorities choose that path it must be open to me to take whatever action I

feel is necessary to secure our essential ends. This is not intended
as a threat. It is simply a reflection of the importance of success.
(18 July 1979); quoted in Stewart, 1980)

Tom King was more colourful – if more distasteful – in condemning
left-wing councillors with alternative policies as 'town hall Pol Pots'
advocating 'municipal Marxism'. (Despite these authorities local
electoral mandates and the Conservative Government's support for
the genocidal Pol Pot regime as the legitimate government of
Kampuchea). Ian Bancroft, head of the Home Civil Service,
appropriately spoke less wildly: 'The process of government
administration can be seen to be inherently inconsistent and even
inherently inefficient, almost by definition.' The problem is one of
'the fundamental inefficiency of any democratic process' (*The
Guardian*, 10 December 1980). This conclusion that democracy is
inefficient is now quite widespread in the establishment of civil
servants, ministers and quango administrators. We have seen some
of its ramifications in our discussion of EZs and UDCs already.
The House of Lords inquiry into setting up the LDDC provides
echoes of this theme (House of Lords Select Committee, 1981).
The Lords recognized that local democratic processes in the London
docklands would be overridden – but nevertheless concluded that
the possibility of quick commercial development justified this loss.
In the words of the Committee:

> The Committee have no doubt that the opposition to the proposed
> transfer of development control from the boroughs to the UDC,
> voiced by the local organisations . . . is perfectly genuine . . . they
> realise that the influence which they can bring to bear on elected
> councillors is greater than any influence which they are likely to be
> able to bring to bear on a UDC: and they fear that if a UDC is
> established, developments of which they disapprove may be carried
> out without regard to their views. But while the committee understand
> – and indeed sympathise with their attitude – they think that the
> approach of some of the witnesses to the problem of the regeneration
> of the docklands was somewhat parochial. (Ibid., para. 8.3)

They concluded:

> The Committee are very conscious that to transfer development
> control over so wide an area from democratically elected councils to
> a body appointed by the Secretary of State is a step which is not
> easily to be justified, especially in an area such as docklands where
> the attachment to local democracy was shown to be so strong; but

for the reasons which they have given, the committee think the government have made out their case. (Ibid., para. 8.8)

Commercial development as an end in itself was given greater weight than the exercise of local democracy. Apparently recognizing the contradictions of imposing development onto people it is presumably meant to serve, the Committee ended by propounding a revised version of democracy: consultation without accountability and certainly without power:

> If a UDC is to be a success it is essential that it establishes and maintains good relations with the local authorities and their officers and avails itself of their advice and expertise. The Code of consultation, provided for under section 140 of the Act, should ensure that this is so. The UDC must also win the confidence of local organisations. It must always let the Docklands Forum know what it is thinking of doing, so that they can express their view on any proposal and it must make it clear that such views, even if not accepted, are always seriously considered. (Ibid., para. 8.)

Yet the two chairmen [sic] of the LDDC have both made plain the true content of such consultations. According to its first, Nigel Broackes, 'Consultations can too easily become an excuse for inaction in the face of lack of agreement...the corporation has no intention of allowing the increasing momentum of development and change to slow down.' His successor, Christopher Benson declared, 'We cannot democratise a Quango. We cannot afford to create barriers by allowing mischievous activists to interface with the pace of progress' (both quoted in Carr and Weir, 1986, p. 7). The barriers of democratic accountability thus have to be removed so that the Government's version of development can be imposed from the centre onto a reluctant community.

FREEPORTS

Along with EZs and UDCs, Freeports have been the flagships of Conservative local economic policy. Like the others, Freeports are a limited experiment in 'free market principles' at the local level. In fact the Freeport concept was an important part of the original debate about the geographical 'liberation' of free enterprise. To a certain extent EZs were a politically acceptable and less extreme version of these initial ideas, which promoted the idea of 'deregulated' zones of 'minimal control'. The right-wing Adam Smith Institute has more recently argued for zones that are completely duty-free, rates-free and regulation-free. In fact, as they say in their report, the idea is 'to suspend for fixed periods the operation, in the Freeports, of most of the Acts which regulate manufacturing in the UK.' (*New Statesman*, 15 April 1983).

Although this report formed the basis of a government working party set up by Geoffrey Howe, then Chancellor of the Exchequer, political pressure again diluted the initial concept. Howe's 1983 budget premissed the introduction of six Freeports with customs exemption but little other deregulation. The measure could placate simultaneously the Treasury, already groaning under the EZ Bill, and push the Adam Smith experiment a little further forward. There were 45 applications for Freeport status, and six were subsequently declared throughout 1984 near airports or docks (Belfast, Prestwick, Birmingham, Cardiff, Liverpool, Southampton). They represent an extension, geographically and institutionally, of the EZ experiment and significantly are managed by public/private consortiums, not by elected local authorities alone.

CONCLUSIONS: A NEW MODEL FOR LOCAL GOVERNMENT

EZs and UDCs have been effective in challenging the accepted ideas about local state forms and powers, and shifting them to the right. It is not just that (despite the heavy central subsidy) these new local state forms are taken to represent the benefits of unfettered private enterprise. More concretely, they have led to demands and campaigns by business organizations for city-wide and even nation-wide abolition of rates or any other form of local taxation. The experiment also raises questions about how local state institutions should operate; in effect it places 'the inefficiencies of democracy' against the 'success of private enterprise'. The real economic failure of EZs and UDCs can be presented as the result of previous and current local government interference in the market, the real state subsidy can be hidden and the real need for people to influence local development can be presented as state oppression of enterprise. A clear message coming out of the EZ and UDC experiments is that local government, because its councillors are elected and thus are to some degree accountable locally, is not to be trusted. If we remember the original plans for each to have its own UDC, and the tenor of current arguments to replace local authority powers by a variety of non-elected state bodies, the UDC experiment becomes very significant. If this model were to be extended it could amount to the biggest change to local government since electoral accountability was finally established at the end of the nineteenth century. By June 1987 there were 6 UDCs in all, with 6 more announced – all 12 were in Labour controlled inner-city authorities.

PRIVATE ENTERPRISE IN THE LOCAL STATE: THE BUSINESS SECTOR AND LOCAL-CENTRAL RELATIONS

It is important to realize that the EZs, UDCs and Freeports are not isolated institutional or legislative developments, specific to particular Acts of Parliament. On a broader scale, the centre's distrust of local democracy as part of existing local government is a constant theme in legislation and administrative practice. The Thatcher Governments have sought to increase the role played by the private sector in local economic policy, inserting these interests into local state institutions, and in so doing, displacing or diluting the role of electoral local government. Existing relationships have thus been redefined and new bodies have been created to take this task further. We will now summarize these developments, drawing extensively on Boyle, 1983 (see also Duncan and Goodwin, 1985c).

The desire to integrate the private sector into policies for urban renewal can be traced back to the 1974 Labour Government. Their 1978 Inner Urban Areas Act, following a 1977 White Paper, *Policy for the Inner Cities* (DOE 1977a) shifted concern over development from the regions to the inner cities. It also stressed that the problems found there were economic and not just social, and hence saw the nature of private-sector investment in inner-city areas as being one of the main *causes* of the problem. However, although the White Paper asked councils to secure private investment it saw local authorities as the 'natural agencies' to direct and control this, and the private sector was not to be represented in the 'Special Partnerships' set up between the Department of the Environment and selected inner-city authorities. In contrast, note the succeeding Conservative Government's portrayal of the private sector as the *saviour* of the inner city, where local authorities are seen as a major cause of decline. Its solution has been to dilute and shrink the boundaries of local government powers while inserting business influence more strongly into the local state.

The Conservatives began by accepting most of Labour's legislation, but insisted that for the Partnership authorities the need was to 'ensure that the balance of the programme is influenced by people employed other than in the private sector' (M. Heseltine, *DOE Press Release*, 309, 1979; quoted in Boyle, 1983). The ministerial guide-lines on the Partnerships issued in July 1981, sharpened the turn away from social policy objectives towards subsidizing capital. Partnership monies would be dependent on local authority consultation with the voice of the private sector...normally through members of local Chambers of Commerce' (DoE, 1981; quoted in Boyle, 1983). Heseltine went so far as to state as evidence to the Environment Committee that 'we could not operate the Partnerships unless the private sector was brought in and consulted about the changes that took place' (Environment Committee 1983a, HC18-11, 0341; quoted in Boyle 1983). These changes were themselves prompted by a secret review of the Partnership arrangements commissioned by the Government in 1980 and carried out overwhelmingly by private-sector teams using criteria acceptable to private capital (see Stewart and Underwood, 1983).

Overall, the resources committed to the 'Urban Programme' (which includes the UDCs) actually increased substantially during a period of public expenditure cuts, from £29.3m in 1977/8 and £165m in 1979/80 to £361m in 1985/6 (cash expenditure). However, this included a shift away from Partnership and Programme local authorities (which had accounted for the bulk of the funds) to the non-elected UDCs and other new policies. Nor was any extra government spending involved. The cash was saved from reductions in RSGs to urban councils, which often lost much more in this way than they gained in the Urban Programme. In 1982 this loss was calculated as around £500m for London alone. And while local governments had some autonomy over how to use RSG, their room for manœuvre within the Urban Programme was reduced and of course removed almost entirely with UDCs.

Initial ideas on how to insert business interests into local government were drawn from the United States and centred on expanding the enterprise agency movement, packaged appropriately as 'corporate social responsibility' (see Duncan and Goodwin, 1985c). But this model was rudely interrupted by the realities of British politics, following a dramatic series of inner-city riots in the summer of 1981 (see figure 4.3). The Government was quickly forced into the position of 'being seen to be doing something'. A hastily arranged bus tour around flame-blackened Liverpool by Michael Heseltine (the Environment Minister) and a number of senior executives and company chairmen, led to the formation of the Financial Institution Group (FIG) in October 1981. This consisted of 26 managers seconded from leading financial institutions, whose role was one of 'increasing private sector involvement in urban questions...and urban problems hitherto regarded as exclusively for the public sector' (Environment Committee, 1983b; quoted in Boyle, 1983).

Although FIG was disbanded in September 1982, and no final report was ever prepared, it did lead to the creation of ICE (Inner-City Enterprises) and UDGs (Urban Development Grants). ICE was launched in January 1983 as a property service company funded by the big financial institutions, whose role was to identify and promote investment opportunities in the inner city which might otherwise be missed by city financiers. Its initial share capital was £1.5m, and it aimed to fund itself through interest charges and fees. Indicatively, office development in the South East was seen as its major opportunity; Liverpool and other declining industrial cities remained peripheral to its activities. UDGs were closely modelled on a similar scheme in the United States (UDAGs), and were designed to enable small amounts of public money to support larger private investment – the subsidy turning marginal projects into profit. A first batch of grants was announced in February 1983, with £10m given to 41 private-sector schemes worth £50m.

Meanwhile, the enterprise agency scheme had come to fruition under the title of BIC (Business in the Community), a limited company 'whose object is to promote the concept of corporate social responsibility and community involvement' (Environment Committee, 1983, 103-x; quoted in Boyle, 1983). By working closely with regional DoE officers BIC has set up local enterprise agencies to bring together local companies, Chambers of Commerce, voluntary groups, trade unions and councils 'to collaborate in projects to assist the local community'. According to the BIC directory, by early 1983 34 of the 100 active enterprise agencies had been established through BIC, but only a few have been particularly successful at generating jobs and few of these are located in inner-city areas.

What is the significance of these initiatives? In direct economic terms, and even in terms of community involvement, little has happened. British firms, both large and small, have shown little interest in corporate responsibility or inner-city investment unless it is made financially safe for them to do so by public subsidy. The early rhetoric of the Liverpool coach tour of leading financiers, with Heseltine at the microphone, compared with the reality of ICE's conclusion that property development in the South East was the best bet, is probably an apt symbol. But rhetoric can have real effects. One is to turn around the portrayal of private capital from being the cause of inner-city decline to being its solution. Another is to alter local–central relations, as councils become passive support agencies for private capital acting in response to central state initiatives.

Furthermore, local economic initiatives are placed in the hands of non-elected bodies which, although using public funds to create urban policy, are dominated by and responsive to private capital. This is the obverse of the new 'municipal socialism' of economic policy in the GLC, Sheffield, West Midlands and other areas. Certainly the Environment Minister was aware at an early stage of the *political* dangers of withdrawing state aid, and the need to replace the vacuum this left with reliable locally-based groups. There was still the same need for local agents of the central government, as we suggest in chapter 2, but the desire was to get away from those heavily influenced by unsympathetic local interests. Speaking to local Chambers of Commerce and Industry on the theme of private urban policy he warned:

> Since the state was withdrawing on a wide front there was a danger that pressure groups would fill the vacuum by default. Already the pressure groups seek to outbid each other with their stories of the hardship brought about by spending cuts. They are blind to the inevitable results of the continuation of the spending policies they cry for. (*The Guardian*, 11 June 1980)

PROTECTING PRIVATE-SECTOR URBAN POLICY: THE COUNTY MINISTRIES AND TASK FORCES

We have seen how the private-sector urban policy of BIC, FIG and ICE depends upon some considerable public subsidy. This is no different from the 'free enterprise' experiments of EZs, UDCs and Freeports. However, in turning their back on the local government system except as a source of funds, the former lacked vital institutional support at the local level. How could this be provided? Certainly not by reintroducing the distrusted local authorities. Indeed as early as 1980, Heseltine, as Environment Minister and Chairman of the Liverpool Partnership, was contemplating new institutional arrangements to replace the council/Whitehall connection. The urban riots of 1981 transformed a relatively minor item into one of some – albeit temporary – significance. The election campaign of 1983 was to have a similar effect.

The first response to this problem – as redefined by the riots – was for Heseltine, as Environment Minister, to assume special responsibility for Merseyside. Merseyside was the site of the worst

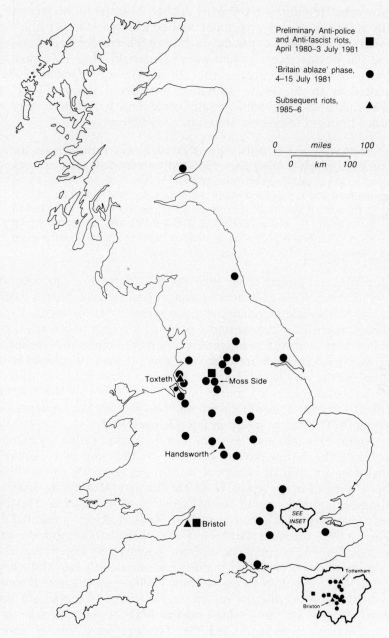

Preliminary Anti-police
and Anti-fascist riots,   ■
April 1980–3 July 1981

'Britain ablaze' phase,   ●
4–15 July 1981

Subsequent riots,   ▲
1985–6

0   miles   100

0   km   100

Toxteth

◄—Moss Side

Handsworth

▲■ Bristol

SEE
INSET

Tottenham

Brixton

Figure 4.3 Inner-city riots, 1981/6
Sources: Race and Class, 1981; Cowell et al, 1982; press reports.

rioting as well as particularly severe and intractable socio-economic problems. Heseltine was promptly dubbed 'Minister for Merseyside'. His role was 'to bring together and concentrate the activities of Central Government departments and to work with local government and the private sector to find ways of strengthening the economy and improving the environment' (Press release, 9 October 1981; quoted in Boyle, 1983). Heseltine interpreted this remit as an opportunity to involve the private sector directly and personally in order to begin to resolve Merseyside's problems.

> I believe it is now self-evident that on a very exciting scale the private sector is being persuaded and 'incentivised' to come back into urban programmes...the private sector is now willing to be involved and is prepared to provide very substantial financial support in pursuit of profits in the urban areas, providing the mechanisms for evolving them are developed, and a lot of what is happening on Merseyside is going towards developing these agencies. (Environment Committee, 1983, 103.-x; quoted in Boyle, 1983)

Heseltine did spend some time on the Merseyside question in 1981–2, even visiting the area frequently (indicatively, he was based at the Merseyside Development Corporation on these visits). Even though the special responsibility role had a strong public relations component (and with hindsight his statement sounds quite hollow), propaganda is much more effective if there is some practice to back it up. At the very least, Heseltine needed a local agency to achieve these objectives, as of course he had little time for the Labour councils in Merseyside or Liverpool. This was the Merseyside Task Force (MTF) finally set up in late October 1983.

Again, this initiative was not merely administrative or purely policy-oriented, but directly political. At the time of Heseltine's first post-riot tour of Liverpool in July, he had been embarrassed by a simultaneous report from the Labour Merseyside County Council outlining a public-sector regeneration programme. Heseltine's unpublished Cabinet report 'It Took a Riot', presented in August 1981, recommended among other things curtailing the powers of metropolitan counties, new central government directorates and ministerial responsibilities for individual inner-city areas, and a new Whitehall committee to ensure that public spending was directly related to subsidizing the private sector. What Heseltine got was responsibility for Merseyside and the MTF – partly because the Department of Industry and the Treasury were uneasy about empire-building on the part of the DOE, as well as the financial implications of these plans. Despite this dilution, however, the

MTF was seen explicitly as a model for a possible new departure in local administration.

The MTF's remit was to co-ordinate a vast range of detailed schemes and policies, and to help pilot new initiatives through bureaucratic labyrinths. It could work over the whole of Merseyside County plus adjoining parts of the conurbation. It was to do this by side-stepping local government and working in collaboration with the private sector 'both in terms of individual companies and groups such as Chambers of Commerce' (Environment Committee, 1983, 18-11; a, 322/23; quoted in Boyle, 1983). To this end the MTF was headed and staffed by civil servants from the Department of Industry and the Manpower Services Commission, backed up by managers seconded from local firms. There were no local authority or trade union representatives.

Over time the work of the MTF altered from the co-ordination of government activity to realizing individual projects. After some considerable tension between the civil servant and private manager sides, a *modus operandi* was established where the former put together packages of public subsidy while the latter took the lead on external contacts. These tensions have debilitated the Task Force and, without any statutory power, the impetus of MTF clearly depends on direct ministerial support. When the 'Merseyside question' goes away, or returns in another form (for example, direct conflict over rates, see chapter 6) so does ministerial support. The MTF has withered and now appears as just one more local state agency (see King, 1987).

Indicatively of this 'flavour of the month' status, the whole idea of County Ministries and Task Forces was briefly rejuvenated in the run-up to the 1983 election. The West Midlands, site of many marginal seats won by the Conservatives in 1979 on the basis of working-class votes, was thought to be a key to electoral success. Since then, the region has shown the highest rate of unemployment growth in Britain. In April 1983, John Butcher was made 'Minister for the West Midlands'. A second Task Force, although this time called an 'innovation team' was set up. Aims were similar to those of the MTF – to co-ordinate and marshall existing resources rather than use more public money. At around the same time, proposals were floated to set up Task Forces in Workington, Teesside, Brixton, South London and Wigan. Little more was heard of either Butcher or the Task Forces after the June 1983 election victory for the Conservatives.

Little, that is, until the next climatic event in the inner cities — more riots in Handsworth (Birmingham) and Tottenham (north

London) in October 1985. Urban Aid, which had been cut earlier in the year, was expanded with 'grant direct' powers to give money direct to private-sector companies. Local councils would be bypassed. Yet again, proposals to set up centrally controlled inner-city renewal agencies were dusted off. The political climate for this had changed somewhat, however, since the early 1980s. The Government had lost the propaganda war in abolishing the GLC and the Metropolitan County Councils, and had been taken aback by peoples' attachment to local democracy. More ambitious plans for government-appointed development corporations to take over from local councils were shelved in favour of the softer (and cheaper) non-statutory Task Force option. By February 1986, ten experimental Task Forces (renamed 'City Action Teams,' perhaps to distance them from the now rather discredited Merseyside Task Force) were set up for inner-city areas in London, Leeds, Middlesborough, Leicester, Manchester, Bristol and Birmingham. Most of these areas had experienced riots over the previous five years and total funding of only £8m was widely greeted as being derisory. Manchester alone, for instance, had lost £21m in housing subsidies and £36m in RSG between 1980/1 and 1984/5. The 'inner-city' issue then remained dormant until the June 1987 election. Eight more City Action Teams were set up immediately before the campaign in Coventry, Doncaster, Hartlepool, London (Tower Hamlets), Nottingham, Preston and Wolverhampton. Nonetheless, in the election itself the Conservative Party was virtually wiped out in almost all the large cities except for London, and it was generally agreed that their campaign had suffered from a complete lack of a 'caring image'. Hence a series of post-election proposals to regenerate inner-cities – although again under funded and notably antipathetic to local government involvement – including five more UDCs.

In terms of either policy development or economic regeneration the County Ministries, Task Forces and City Action Teams have only had very slight impact. Nonetheless, the experiment has a wider significance. This is partly because Task Forces can act as regional extensions for Whitehall departments without their own regional network. More fundamentally, like EZs, UDCs, Freeports and the private-sector urban policy, they provide an alternative model for local–central relations. City Action Teams are completely non-elected, but bring together different government departments (DOE, DOI, MSC) with private capital, and are directly responsible to ministers. Local authorities, pressure groups and the labour movement can be left out of local economic and social policy, and, unlike UDCs, Task Force and City Action Team operations leave the shell of local democracy intact. Public sensibilities about voting need not be affronted, even if what people are voting for is left out in the cold.

4.3   Removing Local Autonomy: the Case of Public Housing

Public housing – its production, management and allocation – was for 50 years up to the mid-1970s the traditional fief of local government. Central government exercised little direct control, instead leaving individual councils to work within a loose structure of legislative guide-lines and subsidy incentives. Housing was also one of the major items of public spending, accounting for 10 per cent of total expenditure by 1974/5. Both the degree of local government autonomy and the significance of its budget distinguished public housing from other welfare services. In many ways it was the very stuff of local politics.

By the mid-1980s all this had changed. On the one hand, expenditure had been cut massively, so that by 1984/5 housing accounted for only 3 per cent of public expenditure. On the other hand, central control reached extreme levels. One commentator was even driven to conclude:

Even for those most in favour of centralized services, the developments, particularly of the last three years, have made proposals for a central government agency almost a redundant task. First, local authority autonomy is so reduced that there must be little remaining purpose in transferring its housing powers to a quango. Secondly, government has developed in parallel with local authority housing a set of housing agencies which are more easily controlled by central government. (Karn, 1985, p. 181)

Three strategies have been used in cutting this local government fief down to size. First, housing finance has been centralized; secondly, alternative non-elected state institutions have been fostered to carry out local housing policy. Finally, local governments have simply been compelled to do what the centre wishes. We have seen elements of all these in our previous discussions of local government finance and local economic policy. But it is with housing that the centralization process has been most Draconian, if only because local autonomy was once to significant. We will look at each of these strategies in turn.

CENTRALIZING HOUSING FINANCE

As early as 1969, Dame Evelyn Sharp – doyenne of the Ministry of Housing and Local Government (note the combined responsibility) – expressed her irritation with local authority autonomy in the housing field. This was because of the 'limitations' of local councils and 'political disagreements' (Sharp, 1969, p. 26). One reason for this increasing irritation was probably the shift in housing policy during the 1960s. Rather than concentrating just on the direct provision of public housing, where it was more or less accepted that local governments were responsible for local policy, central policy became wider and more comprehensive, including for instance, improvement grants to the private sector and the provision of local authority mortgages for owner-occupiers. This also increased housing expenditure. For both these reasons central subsidy for local policy was no longer accepted as a fact of life. But whatever the reason, two events were to forcefully demonstrate just how significant, and how dangerous, local authority autonomy could be.

The first was the controversial 1972 Housing Finance Act, passed by the Conservative Government in an effort to cut subsidies for public rented housing (although, as has nearly always been the case, the massive subsidies to owner-occupiers were left untouched). The means of doing this was to prescribe rent levels centrally. This immediately transgressed the time-honoured convention that local councils should set their own rents. Moreover, some Labour councils set low rents and subsidized them further out of the rates (a form of local redistribution). This would now be less possible while other, Conservative councils would be able to make a profit on their housing accounts. This would breach the previously maintained non-profit principle of public housing. The Act provoked considerable opposition outside Parliament, and several Labour councils refused to implement it. But the Act had provided for centrally appointed Housing Commissioners to deal with just this eventuality. During a bitter campaign a commissioner was sent in to administer public housing at Clay Cross where the elected councillors were taken to court, disqualified and surcharged (Skinner and Langdon, 1974). The unfortunate councillors were made political martyrs, and this did much to unify the opposition in the run-up to the 1974 election lost by the Conservatives. The Act was subsequently repealed by the incoming Labour Government but the precedent of replacing recalcitrant councillors – whatever they might say about local electoral mandates – was set.

The radical manifesto on which the 1974 Labour Government was elected did not last very long in the face of economic crisis and the International Monetary Fund. The fund asked for cuts in public spending and, as we have seen, limitations on local government capital expenditure was one result (see section 3.2). Housing stuck out like a sore thumb in this situation – it was a very large item of expenditure over which central government had less than effective control. But, luckily, a ready-made central instrument was at hand. Housing Investment Programmes (HIPs) had been introduced for improvement expenditure as part of the 1974 Housing Act, which had expanded this part of the housing programme. The forward planning of local housing policies and programmes was combined with the central allocation of investment capital. In 1976 the HIP system was extended to all capital expenditure for housing.

The expressed objectives of the HIP system were contradictory from the beginning, being seen at the same time as a means of controlling public expenditure and 'increasing local discretion by putting greater responsibility for deciding the right mix of investment on the local authorities' (DOE, 1977b, p. 77). The argument for the latter was that rather than receiving separate allocations for each programme (new build, improvement, etc.), councils would receive a total allocation covering their investment needs, and they could then decide precisely how it should be spent. But this increased freedom has proved largely illusory. Rather, the HIP system has been used as a vehicle for detailed central control over capital expenditure, and this control has been used to enforce cuts. On taking power in 1979 the Conservative Government not only endorsed the HIP system but used it to turn the screw even tighter.

What happens is that each council submits a programme of desired spending to the Department of the Environment. This is then largely ignored. Instead a national HIP allocation is made which seems based purely on macroeconomic criteria (for example, reducing PSBR). This is then broken down to regional allocations using the general needs index as a distributive indicator. Local allocations come next, and although some attention is at last paid to what councils planned to do – as expressed in their HIP submission – this is still weighted through a 'locally determined element'. How this element is calculated remains a secret, but it seems that a centrally determined index of local needs is combined with 'Brownie points' for following favoured government policies. But all this is only to licence what expenditure can be made. Councils still have to decide whether to borrow or use cash receipts to finance the spending programme the centre has determined for them. Central controls re-emerge at this point, as financial policies and administrative requirements (for instance, those introduced in the 1980 Local Government Finance Act) push councils into selling land and houses. In this way the private sector is favoured over the 'parasitic' public sector, while PSBR can be reduced. For the same reasons, the 1980 Act compelled councils to operate their Direct Labour Organizations (DLOs) under far more restrictive conditions, and the conditions were tightened further in 1982 and 1983. This was in direct response to the influence of construction companies who wanted the field for themselves (see Flynn, 1985). Again, while the Government knew what it wanted to do it did not – as with local government finance – know exactly how to do it. This meant a confused regulative system which made it even worse for DLOs. As Flynn says: 'They knew the *effect* of what they were trying to achieve. They did not know precisely which rules and regulations would achieve those effects. They chose, therefore, to devise legislation which allowed the rules to be changed as the results became apparent' (1985, p. 131.)

The HIP system may have dealt with capital expenditure on housing, but current expenditure was still relatively uncontrolled when the Conservatives took power in 1979. Most of this was accounted for by rent subsidies, by making up deficits on councils' Housing Revenue Accounts. The previous Labour Government had been wary of touching this issue, for it would mean alienating its own supporters as it re-entered the area of the despised 1972 Housing Finance Act. Nonetheless, by 1979 Labour introduced a Bill which would have given greater central control over local rents. This followed the 1977 Housing Review which had been set up to pour oil over the troubled waters of housing politics (DOE, 1977c). In somewhat complacent tones the Review had concluded that the housing problem was more or less solved, legitimizing the widely held view that increased owner-occupation was the best way forward, while the cost of public housing should be reduced (Harloe, 1978; 1980). While the HIP system would be standard for all housing expenditure made through local authorities, and controls on rent subsidies would be introduced, the highly regressive and ever-increasing direct subsidies to owner-occupiers (principally mortgage tax relief) would remain untouched.

The 1979 Bill was lost in Labour's electoral defeat the same year, but Conservatives eagerly seized upon and expanded the proposals in thier own 1980 Housing Act. Notorious for its statutory requirements for local authorities to sell council houses (see below), the Act was almost as severe as far as finance is concerned. Where the 'right to buy' provisions compelled councils to sell their houses to tenants, the financial provisions removed producer subsidies as of right and took away local control over rent levels. Although varied in scale, financial incentives for councils to build dwellings had been an accepted part of the housing system. Prior to the Act, councils automatically received two-thirds of the debt-charge element in their Housing Revenue Account (HRA). Now authorities deemed by the centre to be 'in surplus' receive no general housing subsidy of any sort, even for building. Instead the centre makes up the difference between the income needed by the council to break even on the HRA and the income the Government considers it should have raised through rents, sales and rates. A further level of cuts is introduced by making deliberately optimistic assumptions on future rates of inflation on which these calculations are based. For 1984/5 only 46 of the 367 housing authorities (13 per cent) were considered to be in deficit and therefore eligible for central 'deficit financing'.

In this way central government also determines the minimum rent levels councils should be charging, and each year the DOE calculates how much local authorities should pay to their HRAs. This effectively means that rent levels rise, and each year expected increases have been in excess of the inflation rate. Transgressors who try to keep lower rents or build new housing will not only have to make up income from rates (or rents in the latter case), but will fall foul of the 1980 Local Government Finance Act and, more recently, the rate-capping penalties of the 1984 Rates Act (see chapter 5). The Block Grant system (see section 3.2) was designed so that authorities have every incentive to raise rents. This applies just as much to those few councils notionally in deficit as to those in surplus. For housing the GREA measure used is that of notional, centrally calculated, rate-fund contributions to the notional, centrally determined, HRA. If the real levels desired locally are different then councils would be penalized accordingly. Over and above this level of penalty, the grant is allocated according to the so-called 'E7 formula' which punishes further councils not following government policies. For instance, high-spending authorities with lower than average rents will receive less grant (see McCulloch, 1982).

As with local government finance in general, the practicalities of implementing this system exposed the political aims of the Government. For the E7 formula produced many authorities with negative GREAs, meaning reductions in the housing Block Grant.

But this included many Conservative councils, so from 1982/3 all negative values were simply treated as zero.

The overall distributive effect of all this is highly regressive. Low-spending, affluent councils gain larger grants than their needs imply and high-spending authorities with bad housing (mostly urban, Labour councils) receive a smaller share. Rent levels in the former are more easily kept low than in the latter, although many Conservative authorities (89 in 1984/5) have chosen to make substantial profits instead. Sometimes large surpluses on rents from low-income households are used to subsidize the rates fund. This effectively means a transfer to higher-income owner-occupying households, which also receive mortgage tax relief and other subsidies. East Cambridgeshire is one notorious example (see Fielding, 1984). The principles of council housing – to subsidize non-profit housing for poorer families – have been turned upside down. Measures of 'success' are that rents have increased on average by 82 per cent in *real* terms between 1979 and 1987 while council house building has collapsed to its lowest level *ever*, excluding the war years, at around 25,000 new starts per annum.

CREATING ALTERNATIVE AGENCIES

By the end of the nineteenth century a large number of housing trusts, charities and societies had been established with the aim of providing good-quality rented housing for the working class. This was to be an answer to the late-Victorian housing problem, which private-sector renting was conspicuously incapable of solving, without involving the state and so without completely dropping cherished notions of *laissez-faire*. It was the failure of these 'voluntary' housing institutions to make any significant impact that finally drove home the point that financial and institutional support from the state was necessary if lower-income households were ever to gain decent housing (see Merrett, 1979, chapter 1, for a summary). Hence the development of council housing and later, owner-occupation, in making up for the failures of the free market.

Nevertheless, these trusts, charities and societies continued to exist. Mostly dormant as far as house-building was concerned, they continued to manage their small stocks of dwellings and even attracted some financial support from central government in the form of loans and grants. They were, it seemed, almost completely pushed off the housing stage. But during the 1960s council housing began to be criticized for inflexibility in its allocation procedures – it could not deal adequately, it was claimed, with the needs of various minority household types. 'Housing associations' (the voluntary institutions renamed) were rediscovered as an ideal means of supplementing local government activity. Funding was increased and in 1964 this was rationalized by setting up the Housing Corporation. This government-directed quango took over responsibility for allocating state money to the housing associations and for supervising their activities. Funding was increased again under the 1974 Housing Act, including a particularly generous capital grant system, and the powers of the Corporation over the associations extended. By this time housing associations accounted for 8 per cent of annual new build in the public sector.

Since then, support for the associations, channelled via the Housing Corporation, has grown as support for council housing has fallen. By 1982/3 local authority net expenditure on housing had shrunk to only £755m, but Housing Corporation net expenditure had reached £680m. As well as taking on a substantial amount of improvement work in buying out private landlords, the housing associations (or at least the 50 or so with any significant activity) were responsible for building a quarter of the social sector stock. There are however, disadvantages in this 'third arm' in purely housing terms. The associations have no responsibility to meet local housing needs comprehensively, and they often lose both economies of scale and co-ordination. Nor are they politically accountable – at least not locally – but this is of course no disadvantage from the Government's point of view.

There seems little doubt that the expansion of housing associations owes a great deal to the opportunity for bypassing local government. Furthermore, the Housing Corporation is set up by and responsible to central government, while the associations are now in hock to the Corporation. Thus, for instance, there was little protest during the 1970s when housing association rents could be set higher more easily than in the public sector; similarly there has been little choice but to switch towards housing for sale in the 1980s. It was only when the government imposed the right to buy on housing association stock in 1986 and thereby challenged their historical rationale, that protest made itself felt. Housing charities escaped this provision after successful amendment in the House of Lords. This is perhaps an ideal local state system from the centre's point of view – local implenting units supposedly responsive to local variations but lacking local poltical autonomy or electoral legitimacy. This contrast is disguised by a heavy dose of spatial ideology. Despite their metamorphosis to local quangos, housing associations are constantly referred to as 'community based'. But despite their electoral mandate, local authorities are never referred to as 'community based' in official literature.

CENTRAL COMPULSION – COUNCIL HOUSE SALES

The 1980 Housing Act has been most visible, not to say notorious, in its 'right to buy' provisions, making it mandatory for local authorities to sell their houses if tenants wished to buy. This high profile was partly a result of the political and ideological role that the 'Right to Buy' played for the Conservatives. According to Michael Heseltine, Environment Minister at the time, the Act would ensure 'the wide spread of wealthy through society, encourage a personal desire to improve and modernise one's home, enable parents to accrue wealth for their children and stimulate attitudes of independence and self-reliance' (quoted in Ginsberg, 1981, p. 27). Not only this, but the Conservatives expected to gain working-class votes in traditional Labour strongholds.

Whatever else the 'Right to Buy' might have achieved, it has certainly led to a dramatic change in local–central relations. According to *Roof* (Shelter's housing periodical), the Act contained

> the most far-reaching changes in the council housing system since its effective origins at the end of the First World War. The changes go to the heart of the basic principle on which council housing was established – that central government provided the financial support but left local government to run its own housing stock...there is little doubt that we are witnessing a revolution in the central–local relationship in the housing field. (Schifferes, 1980)

The mandatory sales component of the Act establishes a 'Right to Buy' and 'Right to a mortgage' for all public tenants of more than three years' standing. Previously, although sales were quite common in some councils and had sometimes been encouraged by central governments, councils had had the freedom to decide whether to sell or not. Under the Act every council is now obliged to sell on request, and must also arrange a mortgage and price discounts of between 33 per cent and 50 per cent depending on length of tenancy. (These discounts have since been increased to keep the level of sales up.) Statutory procedures for sales and mortgage allocation are also established. Resistance to this complete turn-round in local–central relations was clearly anticipated, so that if it appears that tenants have difficulty in exercising their 'right to buy' the Minister has powers to force councils to sell, including sending in commissioners to take over sales at the cost of the authority. Section 23(3) of the Act gives the Secretary of State powers to 'do all such things as appears to him necessary or expedient to enable secure tenants...to exercise the right to buy'. As with 1980 and 1982 Local Government Acts, legislation in this way gives the centre general as opposed to specific powers of over local authority action.

Again, like the 1980 and 1982 Acts, this centralization of state power provoked opposition from some of the Government's own supporters, who otherwise might be expected to be avid supporters of sales. Opposition was directed particularly at those sections of the Act giving the centre powers to compel. One back-bench Conservative MP, comparing Hugh Stanley (then Housing Minister) to Ghengis Khan, complained 'I did not join the Conservative Party to be centralist and autocratic, and I am in good company' (1980; quoted in Forest and Murie, 1985a, p. 23). Among this company was the Conservative-ruled Association of County Councils, but here more material concerns combined with these higher principles. Cheap public housing had always been a godsend to farmers and landowners, who could then pay lower wages all the more easily. Council house sales threatened this and it was farmers and landowners who dominated many County Councils. It was in fact behind-the-scenes work by the Country Landowner's Association and the National Farmers' Union that succeeded in gaining one significant amendment to the Act. In designated 'rural areas' councils could impose pre-emption or locality clauses on subsequent sales. This, is was hoped, would halt the drift of ex-council houses into the second-home market.

Nationally, Labour Party opposition was muted after its defeat in the 1979 election, where the general popularity of council house sales (in certain key areas at least) had helped them lose the election. The same was not true of many Labour councils. Not only was their housing stock the jewel in their municipal crown, and very often a key part of local political cultures of labourism, but they also had secure majorities and electoral mandates apparently legitimizing their stand. Nearly 100 Labour councils openly opposed the Act even before it was implemented, and many of these councils took part in the attempt to form a national campaign against sales culminating in a conference sponsored by the London Borough of Lambeth. Sheffield City Council, for example, backed by NALGO, had affirmed opposition to sales as early as July 1979. The chair of the Housing Committee stated that: 'We have been elected on our policy of not selling Council houses. We believe that it ought to be up to a local authority to make this decision'. (*The Guardian*, 10 July 1979). This line was apparently reinforced by an increased local majority in May 1980, where the manifesto clearly stated opposition to sales. However, as with resistance to the Conservative Housing Finance Act 1972, (see Skinner and Langdon, 1976), it proved impossible to organize a national campaign. No agreed strategy could be reached, and the national Labour Party – while supportive in principle – did not provide any practical means of resistance. By October 1980, when the right to buy was introduced, it came down to which councils if any would refuse to implement the risk the sanctions the centre could now impose.

This was easier said than done. Immediately after the Act became law, the chair of Rochdale's housing committee announced that 'We won't sell our houses, even if it means going to gaol' (*The Guardian*, 7 October 1980). In fact, as elsewhere, such outright opposition dissolved into delaying tactics when it became apparent that personal surcharge and enforced sale through commissioners, not gaol, would be the penalty. In Sheffield the District Labour Party recommended co-operation by a two-to-one majority in October 1980 and the Labour group, with some dissent, fell into line the next day. Without solid local labour movement and union support, and without a national resistance campaign, there was thought to be no political future in another Clay Cross (that is, individual martyrdom). Rather, implementation should be delayed, obstructed and subject to counter-information explaining why sales were bad for Sheffield people (see Alcock and Lee, 1981).

However, the Act implied central monitoring of council perform-ance and this was exactly what the DOE was doing. By April 1981, Sheffield and 39 other councils found themselves on the Housing Minister's 'hit list' of councils not considered to be implementing the Housing Act fast enough and against which legal action would have to be taken under section 3 of the Act (see figure 4.1). In May, this list was reduced to eight councils (Sheffield , Stoke-on-Trent, Wolverhampton, Barking, Dagenham, Camden, Greenwich and Newham) and the centre imposed a deadline for sufficient obedience by 13 May 1981. Beyond this date, legal action would begin. Sheffield, like the others, found itself reluctantly moving fast enough to escape such action and by the end of May 1981 had sold its first council house (although it still managed to score one point in arranging this sale to a buyer with £5,500 ready cash). By November, only Norwich City Council refused to comply with the centrally approved timetable and so moved into the Clay Cross situation (see Forest and Murie, 1985a, for details).

**Department of the Environment
City Hall
NORWICH NR2 1NH**
Telephone: Norwich (0603) 612522

Figure 4.4   Department of the Environment, Norwich, letterhead
Source: Crown copyright. Reproduced with the permission of the Controller of
Her Majesty's Stationery Office.

The issue was again highlighted as one of local democracy and accountability. The leader of Norwich Council explained that it 'had a right and a duty' not to comply with the Act because it alone had 'the knowledge of the situation in Norwich' (*The Guardian*, 4 November 1981). In December, Mr Heseltine ordered his agents into Norwich to take over the sale of council houses, headed by the DOE's regional controller for East Anglia. The City Council was granted an injunction at the last moment to challenge the legality of this move. The council lost its case but was given leave to appeal.

The courts expressed considerable misgivings about the powers of the Act and its effects on local–central relations. In the House of Lords, Lord Denning, Master of the Rolls, said that he had never before seen a piece of legislation which gave such power to a minister, stating 'It's a very very strong power. It looks like a very big stick to me' (*The Guardian*, 23 January 1982). He reiterated these feelings in the judgement, calling Mr Heseltine's intervention 'a very drastic action' under 'a most unusual power' which 'goes as far as anything I have soon hitherto' (*The Guardian*, 10 February 1982). He also pointed to the drastic nature of this legislation with regard to central–local relations, saying that 'This default power enables central government to interfere with a high hand over local authorities. Local government is such an important part of the constitution that to my mind the courts should see that the power of the government is not over-used' (ibid.). Despite these misgivings, the court upheld the centre's legal right to enforce sales and so confirmed the changes in local–central relations introduced through the 1980 Act. The final insult to local autonomy came when the DOE set up offices in Norwich City Hall to oversee the sales, even printing stationery with the letterhead shown in figure 4.4. This is perhaps a fitting comment on the turn-around in local–central relations pushed through by the Act.

Despite all this, a small space for local manœuvre remained. Sales could be delayed on the margin of legal action, and made subject to counter-information to reduce the number of right-to-buy requests. Sheffield, Greenwich and Camden, among others, have used these tactics. Such action has to be paid for in terms of a gap between the centrally expected and actual revenue from sales. Even Norwich retained some margin for manœuvre, and this is why it chose in the end to co-operate rather than go the whole way down the road of refusal (see Forest and Murie, 1985a). Logically, wherever managerial autonomy must remain to deal with local variations, then political autonomy also remains – although pared down to the very minimum as in this case. This is probably why there is considerable council variation in sales levels, which cannot be accounted for solely by variations in the nature and cost of the stock or by the income and characteristics of tenants (see Forest and Murie, 1984).

Further legislation was introduced in 1983 to remove some of these variations. Furthermore, sales were beginning to slow down as effective demand was satisfied and the recession began to bite. Sales discounts were increased and their qualification period was decreased, while the 1980 powers were to be extended to dwellings owned by housing associations (including leasehold properties), and council dwellings meant for the physically disabled and pensioners (there are over one million special dwellings for pensioners alone). These categories had been excluded from the 1980 Act because it was here that the iniquities of putting the market before the need were most obvious and hence opposition to the Act had been more successful. The House of Lords had been particularly important in getting this exclusion, because this body is both necessary to legislation yet partly insulated from the parliamentary majority. Furthermore, a 'social democratic' consensus could be built up of opposition peers, independents and old-style 'Wet' Conservatives. Such opposition cannot be consistent, however, and the House of Lords has only minor powers to hold up and possibly amend legislation. This time the Lords' amendments could only exclude the sales of dwellings owned by charitable housing associations (even so, tenants were to receive cash hand-outs in compensation) and give councils more extensive rights of repurchase for pensioner and disabled dwellings. In the same spirit, the Government had already granted cash aid to buyers of defectively built council dwellings, while denying such help to tenants or the authorities themselves.

Despite the scant room for manœuvre left to the opposition, the

1980 Act must be counted an overall success in political terms. Rents have been increased, on average, by 82 per cent in real terms, although some councils with a secure electoral base and the political will are still able to set rents at lower levels using rate income to make up. The 1984 Rates Act may well put an end to this. Over 550,000 council houses had been sold by the end of 1984, and every single council had been bludgeoned into sales policy. Compare this with below 100,000 sales in the last sales boom under the 1970–4 Conservative Government. Labour councils were actively carrying out Conservative policy. True, sales have declined rapidly from their 1983 peak, despite the Government's attempts to jack up the rate by increasing financial incentives or finding new stock to sell (hospital residences for health service staff was the latest ploy by 1985). But this is because most people able and willing to buy have bought, and also much of the best stock has been sold. From a housing point of view, the picture is not at all so rosy. Most accounts see long-term economic losses to both national and local government, and a strong reinforcement of already severe iniquities in housing distribution (see Forest and Murie, 1984, 1985b).

Local government has gained one new housing function, however. This is the administration of the Housing Benefit scheme introduced in April 1983, to replace a number of social welfare payments for housing. But this transfer from central to local government emphasizes strongly the difference between local policy formulation and local administration. Councils can only *manage* the scheme, payments are standardized according to centrally determined rules and any non-standard benefits are referred to the Department of Health and Social Security (DHSS) for authorization. In fact the transfer was effected to reduce the number of central civil servants and so fulfill electoral dogma, while jettisoning a politically contentious area onto local government. At the same time the level of benefit eligibility and individual autonomy over the benefit were all reduced. The transfer has also been chaotic. Local government has effectively been prevented from taking on extra staff because of the centralization of its finance while at least 10 DHSS circulars have been necessary to try to explain how the new scheme works. This in itself has caused considerable hardship, over and above the effects of the cuts in benefit levels (Kemp, 1984). In some areas housing benefit allocation has all but broken down.

4.4   The Continuing Threat of Local Autonomy: the Case of Civil Defence

THE ISSUES: POLITICAL CHALLENGE FROM THE LOCALITY

Unlike public transport or housing provision, civil defence has not used large sums of money. (At least not so far as local government is concerned. It can be argued that to be in any way convincing, with mass provision of public shelters as in Sweden or Switzerland for instance, civil defence would be very expensive indeed.) The central–local conflict over civil defence is thereby all the more interesting as it underlines the crucial ideological and political elements of such discordant approaches. This is not to say that thermonuclear war would be an immaterial event – quite the contrary. But local government has little or no direct control over military policy. It can, however, make a political and ideological challenge to one of the most cherished but at the same time least convincing elements of central government policy. What is more, local government is open to electoral influence and in this way reflects and represents widespread public opposition to government policy. Hence the fuss.

ATTEMPTING TO ENFORCE LOCAL OBEDIENCE, 1974–84

On April Fools' Day 1974, the Civil Defence (Planning) Regulations came into force, giving County Councils (including the GLC and metropolitan counties) the duty to make civil defence plans in view of the possibility of an unlimited nuclear war. These new regulations used the 1948 Civil Defence Act, which was passed at the beginning of the first cold war. The original regulations had involved intense opposition from some councils at the time of the first rise of the Campaign for Nuclear Disarmament (CND) in the 1950s and 1960s. This led to commissioners being sent in St Pancras and Coventry councils in the 1950s to take over and implement civil defence policy. Subsequently, both the issue and the policies lost steam with the apparent stability of *détente* in the later 1960s and 1970s. More recently, this situation has been rudely interrupted by a new cold war, an escalation in the arms race and the rise of widespread popular opposition on a national and European scale.

The 1974 regulations required counties (supported by other

councils in some tasks) to appoint Emergency Planning Teams and make civil defence plans, and envisaged council provision of control centres, staff training, volunteer recruitment and so on. The Conservative Government considered these to be necessary legal duties but, influenced by the intense and widespread popular opposition to government nuclear policy, over 150 councils including 27 Counties had declared themselves 'nuclear-free zones' by 1983 (see figure 4.5). There was a growing realization that most civil defence tasks were not mandatory in any case. The nuclear-free zone authorities determined to have nothing to do with government policy, which they considered quite unworkable except for deluding the population about what would really happen in a nuclear war. Many councils mounted counter-campaigns, exposing the futility of existing measures as well as supporting and widening public opposition to government policy.

This conflict came to a head when the Government was forced to cancel a major civil defence exercise, 'Hard Rock' in July 1982. This was because 20 counties refused to take part, and another 7 agreed to only limited co-operation. This left a mere 33 councils, predominantly shire counties in England, participating. The Government itself compounded the problem, because its political considerations made any realistic exercise impossible. Not only were all nuclear installations, all United States bases and all large cities, deemed to be outside the Soviet 'target' list (a hardly convincing scenario) but the Governmentt insisted that all Conservative marginal constituencies should also be missed. At this point, even the Government's own planners threw in the towel. The Government's response, outlined at the same time as Hard Rock was 'postponed' indefinitely, was to change the law in order to force councils to engage in civil defence as required by the centre.

The new regulations were announced in April 1983. Councils were not only obliged to make plans but to maintain war-time HQs, to see that staff took part in planning to organize and train volunteers and so on. A direct legal duty to participate in civil defence exercises was imposed. The usual catch-all in recent local government legislation, the duty of individual councils to follow specific instructions made by the minister, was also added. Councils were only given copies of the draft regulations after protest, having received only a summary in the first instance. This was a break from the normal consultation procedure – the 1974 regulations were debated for almost a year and amendments were made at the suggestion of local authorities. The passage through Parliament was planned to be just as quick, the new rules coming into force in

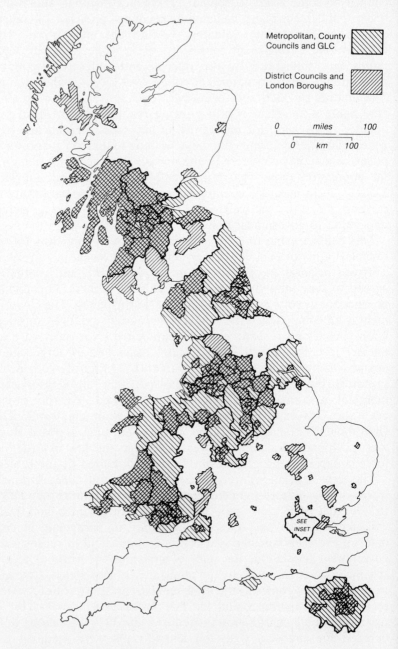

Legend:

Metropolitan, County Councils and GLC

District Councils and London Boroughs

0   miles   100
0   km   100

SEE INSET

Figure 4.5 Local government challenges: nuclear-free zones, 1982
Source: Campaign for Nuclear Disarmament

July. They were, however, held up by the general election, and finally came into force in December 1983.

When asked if these powers did not impose absolute duties on councils regardless of expense, the Home Office Minister responsible for civil defence replied: 'The main thing is that local authorities shall not be able to flout the will of Parliament' (*The Guardian*, 18 February 1983). The article continued: 'Imposing duties on local authorities was very different from employment law, Mr Mayhew said. You could not legislate for good industrial relations, but you could properly require local authorities to be *agents* for Parliamentary policy' (our emphasis). Nevertheless, local governement opposition has continued. Many unions, including NALGO, the National Union of Public Employees (NUPE) and the Fire Brigade Union, declared their opposition to the regulations and their support for any members refusing to take part on grounds of conscience. Legal advice to the GLC held that nothing need – or should – be done until the Home Office provided precise details of what local authorities were supposed to be planning for. These details have not been forthcoming, as a Home Office circular promised several times has failed to appear up to the time of writing. Ironically, Tory councils wanting to co-operate are unable to do so properly. Even the long-expected questionnaire demanding information on progress to date has failed to materialize. The Government has, however, recently announced plans to withhold grants from any authority which persists with opposition to the 1983 regulations (see *The Guardian*, 23 July 1986).

It is doubtful if even this measure will work because the Home Office is in a catch-22 situation. To get co-operation and efficient planning it must issue detailed and realistic instructions. To do so, however, would reveal the futility of civil defence measures and expose official Home Office figures on death, destruction and social collapse as considerable underestimates. This would only increase support for an already powerful peace movement. The attempt to use civil defence to delude a worried population would be counter-productive. Similarly, if Government, as widely alleged, is using civil defence as part of a 'counter-force' strategy (i.e., the readiness to fight and supposedly survive nuclear war), this strategy could only appear credible with large-scale expenditure on mass shelters. But again this would give support to more realistic views of what nuclear war means (for example, recent reports of the nuclear winter) and so undermine the Government's policy further.

Meanwhile, the nuclear-free zone councils have formed a nuclear-free zones national steering committee, meeting regularly to co-

ordinate opposition to current government policy. Many are
continuing to mount counter-campaigns and actively support anti-
nuclear groups and events. For instance, the GLC declared 1983
to be Peace Year and sponsored festivals, concerts, meetings and
discussions centred on the theme of disarmament. Leeds City
Council has produced and published a booklet detailing the effects
of a nuclear bomb on the City, which has already sold out twice.
Even more influential was the GLC's *Greater London Area War
Risk Study* (GLAWARS) published in 1986. Written by a team of
international experts, it is one of the most detailed and comprehensive studies ever made of the likely effects of nuclear war on a
large modern city. It is also a powerful indictment of the British
Government's civil defence policy. Published just before abolition,
the GLC had no option but to pass it on to one of its succeeding
quangos, the London Fire and Civil Defence Authority. The
Government had been forced to lie low and – yet again – wait for
abolition and rate-capping. These measures remove some of the
more active anti-nuclear councils and sap both the will and the
ability of the remainder. Like transport, civil defence was given to
non-elected regional quangos in the metropolitan counties and in
London.

4.5   Conclusions

In technical terms, the Conservative Government's attempt to
centralize local policy during the period 1979–84 has been largely
successful. Local government autonomy has been removed or
severely controlled in a number of key policy areas considered in
this chapter, either through specific legislation (for example, the
1980 Housing Act) or by removing policy competence to non-
elected bodies (for example, London public transport – see chapter
7). This success has been less complete with local economic policy,
but only in the case of civil defence is the outcome still much in
doubt.

   This last example, however, underlines the limitations of 'technical' success. It is possible, eventually, to compel policy change at
local state level. But success may be much more limited in terms
of removing political and ideological opposition. So, as we shall
see, the Fares Fair fiasco was in fact a political own-goal for the
Government. Similarly, local government economic policies have
had some success in demonstrating that a practical alternative to
'Thatcherism' is possible. Both these conflicts, and the others we

have described, have brought the question of local government autonomy firmly onto the political stage. Furthermore, this is an issue where the Government has been convincingly placed on the defensive. It is not just what local state institutions do that is important. It is how they do it and who does it (see chapter 1.) Centralizing local policy was not quite the success it may seem in purely policy terms. Hence the attraction of the 'final solution' of rate-capping, which finally received parliamentary approval in mid-1984, and abolition. It is this solution to which we turn in the next chapter.

5

Destroying Local Government Autonomy

Rate-capping and Abolition

5.1   The Logic of Central Control

By the summer of 1982 the Government was becoming increasingly and uncomfortably aware that the greatly increased controls over local government were still not giving them what they wanted. First of all, there was an apparently insoluble macroeconomic problem. Despite all the promises of monetarism and the new realism, indications of economic recovery were hard to find. Worse still, unemployment showed a frightening increase to well over three million even on the Government's conservative figures. As a consequence, public spending was pushed up. Expenditure on unemployment benefit alone increased by over £2.5bn between 1979 and 1982/3 – more than 50 per cent in real terms. Despite cuts elsewhere – notably on public housing – total public expenditure had still increased by 6 per cent in real terms. Not only was the rhetoric of monetarism difficult to maintain in the face of such facts, but failure seemed to be the Government's own fault.

What was the solution? Paradoxically, further controls and cuts in local government spending seemed to offer a way out. This was despite the fact that local government expenditure was stagnant as a proportion of Gross Domestic Product (GDP) (between 13 per cent and 14 per cent between 1979/80 and 1982/3), while it was central government spending that had increased (from 32 to 35 per cent). While it was politically difficult for the Conservatives to cut unemployment benefit or defence spending, local government welfare services were much easier to define as superfluous 'fat'. This would also take the limelight off central government. This plan seemed all the more reasonable when it was rumoured that, despite the 1980 Local Government Planning and Land Act and the 1982 Local Government Finance Act, local authority spending for 1982/3 would be 7.7 per cent above the control target.

This strategy combined rather nicely with the second problem posed by local government. It was still able to mount effective challenges to central policy and to the Thatcherite message that 'There is no alternative.' While ministers were supposed to be implementing radical reform of British society, they found themselves caught up instead in skirmishes provoked by local governments over local economic policy, public transport or police accountability. Sometimes the Government found itself on the defensive, as with the GLC's 'Fares Fair' policy, where public support coalesced round the Council's charismatic leader Ken Livingstone. This political problem strengthened the resolve to curb public spending and centralize local government finance even further. For those councils in the vanguard of opposition were usually the very councils that had little to lose in the way of penalties. They had already been penalized up to the hilt and made their own political decisions to spend from their rates. This was the major reason for the projected 7.7 per cent 'overspend' (although the Government had to an extent engineered this through its pre-election boom, with relaxations in both loan sanctions and rate support). In the face of these continued political challenges the Government began to tackle the 'representational' role of local council (i.e., removing their ability to represent local electorates effectively) as well as their 'interpretive' role (i.e., removing their influence on policy content).

Two quotations from Cabinet Ministers show very well the Government's thinking about local councils at the time. They also show how, in the euphoria of electoral popularity generated by success in the bizarre Falklands conflict in the spring of 1982, the Government was confident that it could do almost anything and get away with it. Leon Brittan, Chief Secretary of State to the Treasury, started with the financial problem:

> Local government spending plays such an important part in our economy that a failure to overcome the problem of overspending is bound to lead ultimately to developments which the friends of local government will find extremely unwelcome. It is bound to cause central government to intervene ever more obstrusively and seek even greater power over local authority finances. The political strength of local government may for a period check the growth of such an assumption of power. But any such check will only be short-lived if overspending continues, whichever government is in power. (17 July 1982)

Norman Tebbit, Employment Minister, started from the ideological perspective. The GLC he claimed, was 'creating poverty, killing industry, breaking the law and helping criminals'. London was

> in the hands of Marxists bent on revolution. The Labour Party is
> the party of division. In its present form it represents a threat to the
> democratic values and institutions on which our Parliamentary system
> is based. The GLC is typical of this new, modern, divisive version
> of socialism. It must be defeated. So we shall abolish the GLC. (*The
> Guardian*, 15 and 18 March 1983)

The context for this policy direction had been established in a
Cabinet committee, code-named MISC 79, set up in the summer
of 1982. Its brief was to consider how to change the rating system
in line with the 1979 election commitment. They soon concluded
that no alternative to rates was possible – except perhaps a local
income tax and that of course would just make their problems with
local government much worse. It would be better to nationalize
local government services like education, with direct central control
over what rates could be set (rate-capping) and abolition of the
GLC and the Metropolitan County Councils – the flagships of the
opposition.

This relative failure of central control was forcefully illustrated
by comparison with Scotland. In England and Wales the 1982 Local
Government Act had been watered down during its passage through
parliament, but in Scotland separate legislation allowed central
control of both expenditure and rates. This proved both politically
and financially successful. In 1981 and 1982 Lothian Regional
Council (centred on Edinburgh) in particular had been threatening
to do a Scottish version of the GLC, but found it lacked the
financial and legal power to do so. Eventually its political will was
fragmented. The way the Government was thinking was signalled
shortly afterwards, when the 1983 Water Act for England and
Wales abolished local authority representation on the Regional
Water Authorities (see chapter 7). The pressures of the 1983 general
election campaign were to transform these various messages and
attitudes into concrete policy commitments, and subsequent electoral
success was to give the Government the power to carry them out.
But first we should look at the 'Scottish solution' which provided
the object-model for the imposition of rate-capping in England and
Wales.

5.2   The Scottish Solution

It may be overly facile to explain the existence of Scotland and England as separate but united countries simply in terms of uneven development, although convincing arguments can be made (for example, Foster, 1980). Among other things, each country has had its own legislation and its own distinctive local government system – although both are part of the British state ruled from Whitehall and the Prime Minister's Office. This uneven national development has forced corresponding responses in the form of the state. In particular the Scottish Office (SO), located in Edinburgh and with its own civil service departments, cabinet minister and junior ministers, was set up in the late nineteenth century to deal directly with the problems of governing Scotland. These have always been a heady mixture of nationalism fuelled by economic disadvantage and political radicalism. At first concentrated on the peripheralization of the Highlands in the nineteenth century, this problem for central government was made potentially far worse by the increasing marginalization of the central industrial belt in the twentieth century, where 80 per cent of Scotland's population lives. The Government created specifically Scottish economic development quangos in response, first the Highlands and Islands Development Board (HIDB) in 1965 and most important – in the face of an electorally worrying surge of nationalism – the Scottish Development Agency (SDA) in 1975. Both bodies dispense substantial funds for economic development schemes.

The position of Scottish local government has always, then, been significantly different from that in England and Wales. The evidence is that central control was already stronger in Scotland even before the Thatcher Governments. It was the Scottish Office and its Minister which allocated financial support and approval, while powerful central state economic agencies could range freely around the local level. The central state was already entrenched more deeply in local affairs than south of the border. Furthermore, the procedures for distributing Rate Support Grant (RSG) were more centralized than in England, while since 1973 control had been exercised over capital expenditure itself, rather than over borrowing (see Page, 1982). The flip side of this was, however, the possibility of greater financial support from the centre. The attempts to salve economic problems demanded public expenditure, while the Secretary of State for Scotland might try to built up his own empire. Certainly both local authority expenditure per capita and total public spending per capita were higher in Scotland than in England.

The 1979 Conservative Government built upon this existing situation of greater central control and quickly created what became known as the 'Scottish solution' to the local government problem – direct central control over both expenditure and local rate-taxation. The first stage came in 1980 when George Younger, Secretary of State for Scotland, resisted plans to introduce the Block Grant system to Scotland. This was the major part of the 1980 Local Government Planning and Land Act, widely seen as 'the death of local democracy'. The old RSG system was retained in Scotland. But this was not out of any respect for local government autonomy on Younger's part. Instead he went further and introduced even more Draconian legislation for Scotland – the local Government (Miscellaneous Provisions) (Scotland) Act 1981 and the Local Government and Planning (Scotland) Act (1982). As Jones and Stewart (1983) point out, these are statutes of major constitutional significance and they were accepted by Parliament 'virtually unknowingly' (p. 43). It has also become clear that the success of this legislation (from the Government's point of view) was the model for rate-capping in England and Wales.

Why was the final solution to the local government problem first tried out in Scotland? There are two main reasons, both of which return us to uneven development. First, Scotland, with its separated legislative procedures, has traditionally been used by the British Government for policy and administrative experiment. Secondly, however, there are specific features about local government in Scotland that – until this legislation – posed a potentially severe problem for a right-wing government bent on centralization.

The reason for Scotland's role as a guinea-pig is its relative remoteness from the English London-based establishment and media. Even Parliamentary interest in Scottish affairs is low. If the experiment goes right it can be extended to the rest of Britain. If it goes wrong almost no one who is seen to matter will know. Two recent examples of such experiment are the Criminal Justice (Scotland) Act 1980 and the relaxation of licensing laws for public houses. The former strengthened police powers of arrest and detention and, like the 1981 and 1982 Scottish Local Government Acts, was a direct precursor of more authoritarian legislation for England and Wales (the Police and Criminal Evidence Act 1984).

Secondly, there were powerful political reasons for tougher centralization in the context of Scotland and Scottish local government. First, local government reorganization in 1974 had taken a different form in Scotland. The country was split into nine Regional

Counties (with three separate Island Authorities). These had much wider powers than their counterparts in England and Wales (the County and Metropolitan County Councils) with responsibility for water and police, as well as education, structure planning, social welfare and fire services. Beneath this level 53 District Councils (DCs) concentrated on housing, local planning, libraries, refuse, environmental health and leisure services. The three Island Authorities combined both tiers.

Not only did these Regional Councils (RCs) and Island Authorities have greater powers than elsewhere, but they could also draw on a stronger political base than usual across the Border. Several of the most important RCs were centred on large, dominant cities while the largest, Strathclyde, centring on Clydeside, contained half of Scotland's population as well as a built-in Labour majority. The three Island Authorities (Western Isles, Orkney, Shetland) were also distinctive local areas with possibly high levels of mobilization against the centre. But the crucial factor was the pervasive feeling of Scottishness which, in political terms, was largely expressed through the Labour Party (see Smith and Brown, 1983). This was especially so in the dominant central belt stretching from Clydeside to Edinburgh and Dundee, with 80 per cent of Scotland's population in five RCs (although widespread flirtation with the Scottish National Party between 1970 and 1974 has left a more permanent SNP political Scottishness in parts of the North East, the Highlands and Galloway). Opposition to the centre and to the Conservatives is strongly buttressed by nationalism. This was emphasized in 1979 and 1983 when Scotland voted more solidly for Labour just as, in England, the swing was to the Conservatives, who then became Scotland's rulers. The 1987 election was to reinforce this difference still further (even if Wales and parts of Northern England were to move to Scottish side of the fence). Local government, with its more extensive powers in Scotland, was left to represent this potentially explosive mixture of nationalism, political opposition and local feeling. Its representational role was all the more meaningful because many Scottish areas were among the most deprived in the United Kingdom and needed state expenditure on public services more than most. A Scottish/Labour revolt against Conservative rule, spearheaded by local government, was perhaps on the cards and this was something the Government wanted to stop. Its legislation, the 'Scottish solution' succeeded all too well.

The first element of this solution was the Local Government (Miscellaneous Provisions) (Scotland) Act 1981. The anonymity of this title betrays its back-door, experimental status. However, it is anything but anonymous in its powers. These are summarized pungently by Jones and Stewart:

> The Act gives the Secretary of State for Scotland virtually direct control over the level of expenditure of each local authority. He can report to Parliament that there should be imposed on any local authority a reduction in rate support grant if he is satisfied that the estimated expenditure of the authority is 'excessive and unreasonable'. No criteria are laid down as to how the Secretary of State will determine that the expenditure planned by the local elected representatives is excessive and unreasonable. No principles or guidelines are stated about how the Secretary of State should calculate the reduction of grant. The discretion of the Secretary of State is allowed free rein against the judgement of the local authority on its own level of expenditure and of local taxation – a judgement for which it is accountable to its own electorate. (1983, p. 41)

A prohibition on council borrowing without central permission was also imposed, and in the absence of supplementary rate powers in Scotland this means a centrally set expenditure ceiling. Grant reduction could even be ordered retrospectively after the beginning of the financial year.

The effects of the Act were equally stark. In June 1981, action was taken against Lothian RC and six DCs (Cumnock and Doon Valley, Dumbarton, Dundee, East Lothian, Renfrew, Stirling). The composition of this list was clearly politically motivated – Conservative-run authorities which could equally well be included were notable by their absence, whereas Lothian RC, Dundee DC and Stirling DC had been picked out as needing correction before the supposedly objective selection procedure took place (Midwinter et al., 1982; see also Crompton, 1982; Elliot and McCrone, 1982). Indeed, Lothian was threatened by an immense £53m reduction in RSG, 15 per cent of its total budget. The region had several areas with intractable socio-economic problems as well as some of the best service provision in Scotland, especially in non-statutory areas like nursery provision (see *New Society*, 27 August 1981; Nupe/ Titterton, 1983). After prolonged negotiations and bitter local protest this penalty was reduced to £30m. Despite the will to fight back, the Council found it had little left to fight with. The consequence was severe cuts in service levels and, eventually, in Council employment. At the same time some of the other threatened councils made 'voluntary' reductions while Dundee and Stirling DCs had £1m and £700,000 withdrawn respectively. The efficiency of the Scottish solution was plain for all to see.

This contempt for local electoral politics was demonstrated by Younger's response to proposals for rates referenda. This idea was introduced in October 1981 as a possible supplement to the 1981 Act. It became clear, however, that referenda might well sanction rate rises to finance local service expenditure and could, in effect, become referenda on the Government's policy on local government as a whole. Younger maintained that even if a council won a referendum he reserved the right to ignore the result, and the proposal was quickly withdrawn in November 1981. The next year further action was taken against Lothian RC and Stirling DC. This time Lothian made its own 'voluntary' reductions after the authority had changed hands, partly because the constant pressure and inability to act in line with political commitments had split the Labour Party in the area. Stirling eventually lost £1.2m in RSG.

Jones and Stewart claim that, with the 1981 Act, 'The very basis upon which local governement acts, the very reason for its existence, has been destroyed' (1983, p. 42). This basis was the ability of local government to determine its own levels of expenditure as long as this was financed from its own local taxes and subject to local electoral mandate. For the Government, however, the destruction had apparently not gone quite far enough. The 1981 Lothian settlement had not resulted in substantially lower rates; the Regional Council had still been able to juggle its accounts financially and avoid some redundancies and local councils could still use their elected status to good effect in bargaining with the Scottish Office. The 1982 Local Government and Planning (Scotland) Act filled this gap. Clause 1 of the Act gives the Scottish Office powers to impose a reduced rate poundage on councils supposedly guilty of 'excessive and unreasonable expenditure'. Again, criteria are vague and the discretionary powers available to the centre are extremely wide.

In May 1983 'selective action' was announced to fix the rates of five councils on the largely unsubstantiated basis of their 'excessive and unreasonable' budget expenditure in comparison with centrally determined guide-lines. None had experienced recent rate rises above the Scottish average – indeed one planned no rate increase at all. Detailed arguments presented by the councils, showing why their planned expenditure should be made, and representations of their local electoral mandate, were largely brushed aside. Finally, penalties were lowered somewhat and Lothian RC received a 6p reduction in the rate poundage, Glasgow DC 3p and Stirling and Kirkcaldy DCs 2p. This was equivalent of a total spending cut of £18.8m. The procedure for imposing these cuts (needing an individual report for each council) was apparently too slow for

Younger who was given quicker and extended powers in the 1984 Rating and Valuation Scotland (Amendment) Act. At the same time the RSG was cut and, using the 1981 Act, 'claw-back' withdrew RSG from councils proposing to spend more than centrally determined plans allowed. In 1982/3, '£27m of a total Scottish 'overspend' of £200m was claimed back, and in 1983/4 £45m of an alleged excess of £121m. Again the composition of a 'hit list' was selective and the calculation of both centrally planned targets and claw-back levels seemed arbitrary. The largest penalties affected either Labour strongholds like Strathclyde RC, and Glasgow and Kirkcaldy DCs, or less secure but more 'local socialist' councils such as Lothian RC and Stirling DC.

By 1983 it was apparent to the Government that its Scottish solution had worked well. Local government expenditure and taxation was brought under central control. All that was left was local bargaining on the terrain already determined by the centre. Political opposition had been demoralized and weakened (most notably in Lothian). The threat of a Scottish/Labour revolt against Conservative rule, based on local government, had been removed.

5.3   Exporting the Scottish Solution: Rate-capping

PRESSURES ON THE CENTRE

In Scotland, central controls over expenditure and rating had achieved both financial cuts and political security. In England and Wales, however, the centralization of local government was relatively less successful; local government could more easily present political alternatives and could, it seemed, still spend to support these alternatives. A version of the Scottish solution seemed one way out for the Government, and this became a major item for discussion in MISC 79, the Cabinet committee charged with doing something about the rates problem.

Three other factors reinforced this conclusion. First, the Treasury, which has usually been monetarist in the sense of opposing public spending, regarded local government spending with considerable distaste. This was all the more heartfelt as the Treasury had only indirect control over what amounted to as much as a fifth of all public expenditure. Secondly, the existing and controversial penalty system had come up against internal limitations. Some councils were so penalized that they lost all their grants, although this apparently had little effect on their capacity for independent action.

For the same reason penalties had to be made more severe every year to have an effect – but then every year more authorities were entering the more autonomous grantless category. All the system was apparently creating was political controversy, not least among Conservative supporters. Why not deal with the whole messy business in one fell swoop? Finally, the Government had made an election pledge in 1979 to abolish the rates system of local authority taxation. The trouble was, experts, civil servants and ministers were united in seeing no practical alternative. But by the next election, in 1983, some action was clearly necessary. So if you couldn't abolish rates, at least you could control them. Enter the Scottish solution once more.

All the evidence suggests that it was the Treasury, and its Chief Secretary Leon Brittan, who started the campaign for rate-capping in 1981/2. The Government should specify permanent upper limits on rate rises and this would at last give the Treasury complete control over local government spending. Brittan raised the issue on at least four occasions in Cabinet – but not a single minister supported him. Quite possibly they were aware of the political dangers rate-capping would bring, and they were perhaps more willing to give the considerable controls over local government already established a chance to work. The 1983 election changed all this. Apparently rate-capping was adopted for the election manifesto at the last minute at the insistence of Mrs Thatcher, (*Financial Times*, 14 January 1984). If the Scottish solution was the logical extension of earlier centralization, it needed the stress of an election to provide the political impetus. This stress must have been intensified for the Government by the dangers of *local* challenges to Thatcherism. Certainly the simultaneous proposals for the abolition of the GLC and Metropolitan County Councils, which reached the manifesto in a similar way, bore all the marks of an ill-conceived outburst.

The policy leap, from centralized Block Grant with penalties to rate-capping, is shown up very well by the statements of Government representatives. In trying to defend the Block Grant system as early as March 1980, Tom King the Local Government minister said: 'To hear some people you would think that we were introducing individial cash limits. You would think we were fixing a maximum percentage for rate increases. We are not doing any of those things that would be really damaging to local autonomy' (quoted in the *Financial Times*, 14 January 1984) He expanded on this in Parliament:

When the public funds have been distributed, it is then a matter for individual local authorities and their councillors as to what their expenditure decisions are. It is their choice between services, and *their choice to the rate levels that they decide to impose*. That is the freedom and discretion that exists in local government. It is this partnership: public, ministerial and parliamentary responsibility for the public funds, the national taxpayers' funds, paid to local government: *the local councillors' responsibility for the final rating decisions and the expenditure of their own local authority*. That is the basis on which the local government and central government partnership exists. We each have our responsibility to our own electorates in that respect. (8 July 1980; quoted in Stewart, 1984; our emphasis)

But by the run-up to the election, King was saying the exact opposite:

We shall ask them to present preliminary budgets and we shall indicate what we think is an appropriate level of expenditure and rates. Parliament would then have to approve what would be the valid rate for each of these high spending councils. Any other rate would not be valid and could not be collected....If there were problems and it was clear that the need to contain expenditure and the need to recognise the position of the ratepayer was not being sufficiently recognised across authorities then it would not be possible to extend the (selective) scheme more widely. One would then go on to a policy of general levels of rate increase limitation and then operate by a policy of exception by which people would apply for derogation from that overall level. (*The Guardian*, 27 May 1983)

The only difference from 'the Scottish system' would be that central demands would not be made retroactively; rather 'We shall call for budgets in advance of the rate-capping period.' Under the pressure of trying to defend rate-capping in the House of Lords, Lord Bellman later let the political cat completely out of the bag:

A number of local Labour councils are now in the hands of extremists. Their influence and numbers are growing and there is no will or ability among the national leadership to curb them. What if the present irresponsible behaviour of the few spreads to 60, 80 or 100 authorities? (*The Guardian*, 10 April 1984)

In addition, if these councils refused to pass budgets making necessary spending cuts, the Government threatened to send in its commissioners to take over. For the other side, the message was clear. According to *The Guardian*, 'The move is regarded by many left-wing Labour council leaders as the ultimate weapon in the hands of central government to combat attempts by local authorities to uphold promises to their own electors in defiance of Whitehall and Westminster' (2 July 1983). So in both political camps the proposed legislation was recognized for what it was – a means of curbing the representational role of local government.

THE PROPOSALS AND THEIR (LACK OF) RATIONALE

Unlike the complex and confusing system of central control established between 1980 and 1983, the rate-capping proposals were relatively straightforward. That is perhaps in the nature of an 'ultimate weapon'. Indeed, the 'clearest English seen in a Bill for many years' was almost the only feature of legislation to receive any praise from ouside government circles.

Government influence over councils would become direct control with two separate but complementary powers. The first was a selective power to set a legal top limit on the rate levels of local authorities judged by the centre to be 'excessive' spenders. Councils so designated could ask for this level to be raised but, if the level was raised (and it need not be, it could be lowered even more), central government had the power to intervene further by determining exactly how cuts were to be made. Next a rate limit would be set for each of the authorities. This would allow them to raise just enough money from rates so that, with normal government grants, they could spend the stipulated expenditure and no more. The Government would also take account of council's financial reserves so that these could not be used to circumnavigate the cuts. If a council did not agree to its approved rate level this would be enforced by an order for which approval of both Houses of Parliament would be necessary. This would be a single umbrella order covering all defiant authorities in any year, and the Secretary of State would be able to fix a maximum rate in the interim. Councils spending less than GREA or less than £10m p.a. would be excluded. In 1983 this would have excluded 275 of the 296 shire district councils but inflation since then has brought most over the £10m limit.

This selective power is a means of crippling certain local authorities that are particularly offensive in Government eyes – official statements made this clear enough with estimates that between 12 and 20 Labour councils would be involved. But the cuts which could be made by so few councils – many of which were soon to be abolished in any case – could hardly eliminate more than a part of the cited local authority excess. The second part of the Rates Bill provided for general reserve powers by which *all* councils' spending and rates would be controlled, although an appropriate order would be needed from both Houses of Parliament. A second order would then enforce rate limits for all councils that would not accept the limits set by the Department of the Environment. Finally, the tail end of the Bill addressed itself to the residual problem of rates as a method of taxation. Councils would have a duty to consult with local business ratepayers before fixing budgets. (The government had argued unconvincingly that business 'had no votes' while paying taxes.) Similarly, all ratepayers would have the right to pay by installments.

Despite a storm of protests and condemnation from all sides, the Rates Bill was passed with only a small amendment in April 1984. The first batch of victims was identified in August 1984 and the new legislation came into power in 1985/6. In effect this legislation removed the direct link between local taxation and the local electorate, giving the Government the power of a majority vote on on any local council. If the general reserve powers were to be brought into use (and observers thought this would have to happen if any significant cuts were to be made to local government expenditure as a whole) then local government would be reduced to no more than a local administration of central instructions (see SAUS, 1983; Stewart, 1984).

The White Paper simply entitled 'Rates' (DOE 1983a, see also DOE 1986 for Government views), which introduced the legislation, tried to provide a technical rationale in terms of economic policy and accountability. As any number of commentators soon showed, this rationale did not hold even according to the Government's terms (see SAUS, 1983; Midwinter and Mair, 1987). Local government spending and certainly its borrowing, was not out of control. Any increase in rates could be attributed largely to central cuts and penalties. Rates were and are clearly no part of public-sector borrowing, nor is there any simple connection between total taxation (of which rates are a small part) and economic performance. Indeed, later evidence suggested that rate-capping would actually increase public borrowing (see below). Economic theory and experience suggests that rates have no adverse effects on incentive, nor are they a particularly heavy burden on business. Finally, rates are not a crucial element in the inflationary cycle. Above all, selective rate-capping would reduce aggregate taxation by less than 0.5 per cent, and would be imperceptible in relation to the macroeconomic variables discussed. The White Paper's rationale in terms of accountability was equally weak. The arguments that only a minority pay rates directly (which is spurious if households rather than individuals are the units used) turns the principle of 'no taxation without representation' into 'no representation without taxation'. Universal suffrage is revised in favour of property and income qualifications. It is equally spurious to argue against rates on the grounds that non-domestic ratepayers have no vote, while it is surely illogical to point to shortcomings in accountability and then recommend a reduction in accountability.

Not surprisingly, these 'official' arguments for rate-capping were little used by Government spokespeople charged with defending the Bill. There was little point in doing so. They relied instead on two, somewhat off the point, persuasions. First, they claimed that rate-capping would only be used against a small number of extremist Labour councils. The majority, especially their own supporters, need not worry. Secondly, Britain was a unitary state not a federal one – so it was quite in order for the Government to take total control over local government if it wanted to.

Upon serious examination neither argument is convincing. Given the huge discrepancy between the very large cut in local government expenditure planned by the centre (around £2-2.5bn by 1986/7 according to the 1984 White Paper, Cmnd 9143), and the relatively small cut in overall terms made possible by rate-capping the 18 authorities finally selected (at most £198m in 1985/6), it seems that the general powers would have to be used if this argument were to be taken seriously. Certainly many Conservative councils took this view, pointing out that if the general powers were not needed and were not going to be used (as the Government argued) then why was the Government so adamant about keeping them in the legislation? Their scepticism was reinforced by experience with the Block Grant policy system. Despite similar promises, as many as 153 councils were penalized in 1983/4, including many Conservative ones, compared with only eight 'extremist' Labour councils when penalties were introduced in 1980/1 (compare figures 3.3 and 6.4; see also Travers, 1986). Similarly, while it is true that Britain is a unitary state, this does not mean that there should be only one possible politics or policy applied uniformly everywhere under central direction. The Environment Secretary had claimed that 'There can be no room in our unitary state for unilateral declarations of independence by individual authorities, relying on claims of a local mandate' (14 September 1983; quoted in Stewart, 1984.) But as Stewart points out, local governments have not claimed independence, only the right to pursue local policies within national laws. It is equally true that Parliament is the supreme legislative body but this hardly helps to establish whether legislation is good or bad.

REACTIONS AND RESPONSES TO THE RATE-CAPPING
LEGISLATION

As with the 1980 and 1982 Acts, there were few outside immediate government circles who supported rate-capping – although this time the response was even more unfavourable. All the local government associations and nearly all local governments, whether Conservative controlled or not, strongly opposed rate-capping. This was despite the Government's attempt to destabilize opposition with the two exemptions for selective rate-capping for councils spending less than the GREA or less than £10m p.a. This would respectively exclude most of the shire counties, represented in the Conservative-controlled Association of County Councils (ACC), and most shire districts, represented in the Conservative Association of District Councils (ADC). Even if they had been willing to ignore the threat to local government autonomy in accepting these uncertain short-term bribes, both Associations were worried that selective rate-capping would soon be followed by the general powers that could include every council. The ADC voted 49 to 3 to use 'all lawful means' to oppose rate-capping where:

> the government proposals would result in an unacceptable centralis-ation of power, in practice in the hands of executive rather than Parliament, and the further weakening of local democratic control. The price to be paid is too high for a problem which is over stated. (*The Guardian*, 29 September 1983).

The ADC also voted overwhelmingly in favour of calling on the Government to reconsider its 'totally unacceptable' proposals, which were a 'constitutional change which would be a fundamental breach of local democracy and accountability, and be wholly unworkable in practice' (ibid., 15 September 1983). The ADC chair had already commented 'I don't feel bought off at all', adding that the Government's proposals 'represent state intervention on a scale unprecedented in this country. They smack of Big Brother, on the threshold of 1984' (ibid., 3 August 1983).

The Labour-controlled Association of Metropolitan Authorities (AMA) saw the Scottish solution as 'an abuse of ministerial position and a breach of constitutional rights'. Its extension to England and Wales would mean that: 'When the government has absolute control over the spending and rating decisions of each local authority, then local accountability, local democracy and local government would effectively cease' (ibid., 22 September 1983); Labour Research Department, 1983).

Although the minority Tory group in the AMA supported less vigorous condemnation, arguing that some Labour councils had indeed overspent 'unjustifiably', they too concluded that the 'excess of a few authorities might not be sufficient reason to justify dismantling the relationship between central and local government' (according to *The Guardian*, 22 September 1983).

Indeed, one of the few AMA supporters of rate-capping showed the illogicality – but also the deeply political aim – of the Government's case: 'I would rather be governed by an elected Conservative government with a mandate to cut local government spending than be governed by Moscow' (Mrs F. James, ibid.). Local government opposition was so strong and united that, just before the vote in the House of Commons, Conservative Central Office took the unusual and faintly ludicrous step of issuing the names and telephone numbers of all 21 councillors, across the whole country, who had signed a message of support for the Bill.

Nor could the Government find much support elsewhere. Academic commentators and local government specialists were totally opposed to rate-capping (see SAUS, 1983; Stewart and Jones, 1983; for examples), as were most of the press. The proposals were regarded as being unwarranted and would effectively remove local authority autonomy. The *Financial Times*, for instance, called it 'this sad little document.... It deserves to be thrown out' (18 August 1983). Social policy interest groups, in health , housing, social services and education were also totally opposed to the Bill (see *The Guardian*, 2 February, 28 July, 2 August 1984; *New Statesman*, 4 May 1984; Bramley, 1984). They saw rate-capping as a back-door means of enforcing welfare spending cuts that could not otherwise be so easily – or so indirectly – carried out.

Even the Government's 'natural' supporters in business, who traditionally oppose welfare spending and local government rates, were split on the issue. Although the Confederation of British Industry (CBI) welcomed rate-capping, further down the line the troops were not so sure. Construction companies saw further threats to their already reduced order-books, while the City of London was worried that rate-capping might threaten councils' credit-worthiness in the money markets. In any case, City institutions argued, the scheme would be ineffective in reducing public expenditure. At the local level, Chambers of Commerce were split on the issue. Their National Council could give only qualified support while particular regional areas and individual Chambers were opposed, especially to the general part of the Bill. Not only did many have good – and profitable – relations with local councils but they were wary of being associated with the ending of local democracy.

Opposition continued in Parliament, again crossing political boundaries. Labour's Shadow Environment Minister, calling the Bill 'the Abolition of Local Democracy Bill', described it as 'one of the most sinister measures to control individual freedom proposed by any British government this century. Its central purpose was to eliminate the right of local communities to elect councils to provide services people wanted' (*The Guardian*, 18 January 1984). He was joined in this condemnation by a number of leading Conservatives. Edward Heath, former prime minister, claimed 'I came into this House in 1950, having fought an election on Mr Churchill's theme that we were to set the people free. It was not that we should set the people free to do what we tell them'. He was joined by, among others, Geoffrey Ripon and David Howell, both former ministers (the latter in a Thatcher cabinet). Ripon called the proposals 'one of the most deplorable Bills I have known brought before the House all the time that I have been a member. . . . It's nature is undemocratic and contrary to the spirit of our unwritten constitution' (ibid.). Howell denounced the Bill as an extension of central government power, arguing for the ballot-box and the rule of law as opposed to edicts like those used in tsarist Russia (ibid., 5 January 1984).

The Government attempted to defuse a Tory rebellion by promising lesser Block Grant restraints on shire counties. But the counties' parliamentary representatives did not take the bait, partly because some shires suffered considerably in Block Grant allocations announced in January. In fact the opposite happened, with a back-bench rebellion of shire MPs against the allocation. In the event, discussion of the rate-capping Bill was restricted by appropriate timetabling ('a classic example of elected dictatorship' according to Ripon, *The Guardian*, 23 December 1983) and the second reading in the House of Commons was passed with a three-line whip on 17 January 1984, despite a massive revolt, in the circumstances, of 40 Conservative MPs voting against or abstaining. This revolt was enough for the Government to concede the 'Pym pledge' to prevent any repetition (Pym, a sacked cabinet minister and senior

Conservative politician, carried considerable weight with back benchers). The Pym pledge stated that for shire counties spending above target, but below GREA, targets would be raised by 4.5 per cent for 1984/5. In the event this was of very temporary significance. By the 1985/6 allocation shires were already complaining bitterly of increased cuts. Finally, debate in committee was cut off by a guillotine on 1 March 1984. Despite Conservative back-bench protest that it was 'a scandal' that vital clauses of the bill were not to be considered, the Conservative Leader of the House of Commons explained that the Government 'had no alternative but to introduce a guillotine...to meet the objective of having the legislation in place for the 1985/6 rates' (ibid., 1 March 1984). One Conservative protestor, saying that 'Nothing epitomizes more the politics of the elected dictatorship under which we now work' than the Bill and its guillotine, concluded that 'The whole thing now rests on the House of Lords in its whole anachronistic glory to preserve the traditions and liberties of England' (ibid.). Here a similar story repeated itself. Senior Conservatives as well as opposition and independent Peers spoke out against the Bill, and indeed a minor amendment slightly limiting the general powers was approved (following another House of Commons Tory back-bench revolt during the Bill's report stage). But strong whipping, unprecedented Government lobbying and the flooding of the House of Lords for a key debate, with specially imported backwoods aristocrats who normally never appear in Westminster, was enough to carry the day. Nevertheless, at one stage the Government's majority was cut to ten and the last-ditch import of backwoodsmen was to have some important consequences. This desperate operation can only, apparently, be carried out successfully once every three or four years. Using up this lobby fodder on rate-capping was later to lead to an important parliamentary defeat for the Government's abolition campaign. The sole amendment would exempt from *general* rate-capping those councils that had met their spending targets for three previous years. This was enough to gain some crucial Conservative support from the shires and their backwoods contacts.

A final condemnation of rate-capping arrived with the Audit Commission's report on 30 August 1984 (Audit Commission 1984). By this time, the general impression was that the Environment Minister, Patrick Jenkin, had made a fool of himself with the whole episode. This was because rate-capping clearly had little logical rationale and was opposed by almost everyone outside Cabinet circles, yet the Government, personified by Jenkin, persisted in pushing through the measure. While winning the legislative battle, there was considerable danger of the Government losing the political war. To cap it all the Audit Commission report 'blew Jenkin out of the water' (*New Statesman*, 27 July 1984). It is probably for this reason that final publication of the Commission's report was delayed until rate-capping was safely through Parliament, although leaks began to emerge in July 1984.

The report makes two main points. First, quite contrary to the Government's claims, current spending by local authorities was roughly in line with the targets set centrally. Secondly, the Rate Support Grant system, with its shifting targets and penalties was unfair, ineffective and inimical to proper advance planning by local authorities. At one stage local authorities were even spending £1bn *below* DOE guide-lines while, at the same time, overspending according to the Treasury. Indeed, because of this centrally imposed inefficiency, rates were £1.5b higher than necessary over 1981–3, as councils had had to increase their revenues as a cushion against the uncertainties caused by the centre. The Audit Commission recommended the speedy abolition of spending targets and penalties for individual councils, thereby also dismissing two crucial arguments for rate-capping. This was all the more damning because the Audit Commission, although independent, had been created by the Government in 1982 (see chapter 3). All Jenkin could say, rather weakly, was that while most of the report's recommendations seemed reasonable he believed that they were based on a number of wrong-headed arguments. Shortly afterwards the Service Advisory Board (the local government pay negotiating body) released a report showing that staffing increases in English and Welsh local government – heavily criticized by Jenkin – was entirely the result of central government decisions to devolve work from Whitehall to town halls.

Conservative Party leaders and managers were shaken both by the revolts against rate-capping in Parliament and the depth of antipathy for the measure among their supporters ouside it. Rather than amend the legislation (as in 1982), the response (to quote from a leaked Government paper, written by the Prime Minister's Press Secretary) was to 'treat, as a matter of urgency, dissident elements among the Government's own supporters to ensure that they are neutralized if not positively harnessed to the Government's cause' (*The Guardian*, 20 January 1984). This action was to proceed on two fronts. First, in Parliament, the military discipline exerted by the Whip's Office should be restored. The problem was that deference had apparently broken down in the modern Tory Party and this breakdown had been encouraged by influential figures, often former Chief Whips themselves, like Heath and Pym (who led the revolt). One suggested solution was to reintroduce the convention that Chief Whips should be removed from Parliament after their period of office.

Secondly, opposition outside Parliament should also be neutralized. The Government should take 'remedial action with troublesome journals whether national, provincial or specialist', mount a publicity campaign using favourable outlets (for example, appearance in the chat show run by the Prime Minister's acolyte, Jimmy Young), and create a civil service-run 'information unit' to put the record straight. The whole campaign would be overseen by a civil service interdepartmental official committee and an interdepartmental team of ministers (ibid., 20 January 1984). Various parts of this operation were put into practice early in 1984.

The final irony of rate-capping is that it does not work even in terms of financial cuts. Selective rate-capping of the 18 councils chosen in 1984 could do little more than cut local government expenditure by £198m in 1985/6, compared with plans for a £2-2.5bn cut by 1986/7 and a centrally defined 'overspend' of £900m for 1984/5. Furthermore, most of the savings from this list were from the GLC, ILEA and the six Metropolitan County Councils, all of which were abolished on 1 April 1986, so in future years significant savings would be even harder to achieve. In addition, rate-capping has its own reverse rachet effect. The rate-capped authorities will no longer attract the same level of penalty for spending in excess of DOE targets. These penalties were in effect a financial bonus to the Treasury as councils raised rates instead of using Treasury grants. This bonus will now disappear if an authority is rate-capped. In addition, non-rate-capped councils will continue to 'overspend' and the Treasury will be asked to fund this – unless these councils are to be left to raise rates considerably and so recreate the situation that rate-capping was supposed to remove! Estimates are that the Rates Act will actually *cost* nearly £1.5bn extra in central funding. To pay a lot of money for marginal savings is not what the Treasury had in mind when it sold rate-capping to the Prime Minister. If rate-capping is to achieve Treasury aims of significant local government cuts then the general powers scheme will have to be applied. As yet, there is no sign of this happening. The political costs would be far too high.

On the other hand, the Cabinet may primarily see rate-capping in political terms. To destroy the capacity of Labour councils to present alternative policy may be worth some expense. Compare this with the Chancellor's notorious statement that the cost of the

1984/5 coal industry dispute was worth it if the National Union of Mineworkers was broken (which it was). This interpretation is certainly supported by the story of abolition, to which we now turn. For with abolition there seems little chance of making any financial cuts; quite the contrary. The operation can only have purely political aims but even these have turned out to be partly counter-productive.

5.4   Abolition and the Fear of Local Alternatives

THE THREAT OF LOCAL AUTONOMY

We have seen that the centralization of local government is not merely an issue of macroeconomic or financial policy. The desire to control public spending does not necessitate the detailed and blanket control of local authorities sought by the Conservative Government – still less if it is public *borrowing* that is crucial (as monetarist doctrine would have it). Indeed, some of the Government's actions are counter-productive or at least peripheral to this aim. Rather, we claim, it is the political objective of removing local government autonomy that is at issue. This has both a short-term and a long-term objective. In the short term, the centre can make cuts in public service provision and enforce its own policy aims in every local area. In the long term, alternative political and policy positions can be weakened – there will be no government framework to give them any institutional voice or credence. The Government's fear of locally expressed alternatives reached its extreme with the legislation to abolish the GLC and Metropolitan County Councils.

Central government fear of local alternatives was not something suddenly discovered by the 1979 and 1983 Conservative Cabinets. It has a history as long as elected local government itself – although as we shall see the Thatcher Governments have been especially sensitive. As early as 1894, only five years after the London County Council (LCC) was created (and just 14 years after a wide male suffrage was allowed in local government) the Conservative leader, Lord Salisbury, attacked the LCC as 'the place where collectivistic and socialistic experiments are tried...where a new revolutionary spirit finds its instruments and collects its arms' (quoted in *Time Out*, 13 October 1983). In 1895 Salisbury's party won the general election and – with the Progressives (a coalition of Liberals and Fabians) still in control of the LCC – a bitter rivalry developed between what contemporary writers called 'the two parliaments'.

Salisbury attacked the LCC at every opportunity, backed by a predominantly Tory press; like Ken Livingstone 90 years later the LCC leader was driven to complain about the one-sided sensationalism of 'a corybantic press' (ibid.).

There are even closer historical parallels than this. In 1978 a commission of inquiry into local government recommended that the GLC's power be increased on a wide scale, through 'devolution of power from Whitehall to County Hall'. The commission was set up by the Tory GLC and chaired by Lord Marshall – who was soon afterwards appointed Vice-Chair of the Conservative Party. With other leading Conservative MPs, Patrick Jenkin sent his own views to the commission arguing that 'I therefore believe we have got progressively to return to the concept that the GLC is a strategic authority' (ibid.). By 1983, Marshall was responsible for running an election campaign round a manifesto including the abolition of the GLC, his report ignored; Patrick Jenkin was responsible for legislation to abolish the GLC, his ideas of the necessity of direct elections in local government now unmentionable. In 1895 a royal commission on the LCC had also recommended strengthening local government throughout London.

But after the Progressives won control of the LCC for a further term, Salisbury would have none of it. Arguing, like the Thatcher Government, that his reform would reduce rates (it actually increased them), Salisbury diluted the power of the LCC by setting up local borough councils beneath it. This would disorganize the opposition, and the Moderates (Tories) could at least win some boroughs. The only difference was Salisbury did not dare go so far as complete abolition.

Ironically, one of the inner London councils created by Salisbury – Poplar – became the focal point for the next central scare produced by local alternatives. Dubbed 'Poplarism', this became a municipal socialist movement, which during the 1920s was taken up by hundreds of local councils and boards of guardians who administered the Poor Law in local areas (see Branson, 1979). The Conservative Cabinet saw this as a revolutionary movement in the making, and toyed with the idea of removing the local government franchise from all those receiving poor-relief – a significant minority or even a majority in many areas (see Deacon and Briggs, 1974). Sixty years later, the Thatcher Government also argued that local council elections were somehow undemocratic because those who benefited most from council services sometimes paid no rates, while business owners only had one vote each! The 1920s Conservative Cabinet drew back from this course. Just as effective, and less obviously anti-democratic, was the response of removing key policy areas like poor-relief from the orbit of local government. Instead of dealing with locally elected councillors and Poor Law guardians with the 'wrong ideas' – and some power to put these ideas into practice – poor-relief would be run by a central department directly responsible to the Cabinet. Exactly the same response lies behind the Thatcher Government's success in removing the control of London Transport from the GLC (see chapter 7).

Poplarism was effectively controlled through the restructuring of local–central relations at a time when the balance of power shifted away from the Labour Government (see Duncan and Goodwin, 1982b). But early in the 1930s Labour took permanent control of the LCC. Again, the mildly redistributive policies achieved a political effect far out of proportion to their intrinsic importance. Labour's leader, Herbert Morrison, was attacked as a profligate and dangerous socialist spender who put an intolerable burden on the rates. Again, the rallying cry of Conservative horror was the abolition of the LCC in order to remove the threat of an influential and democratically elected body with a built-in Labour majority. But the problem was that outright abolition always smacked too much of anti-democratic leanings. This would confirm that the British state was indeed a capitalist state, or at least an establishment one, rather than one depending on representative democracy. Conservative national governments seemed caught in a cleft stick.

But during the 1950s the Conservative Party hit upon a better idea – enlarge the LCC by including the Conservative-voting outer suburbs. This is what happened in 1963, when the GLC replaced the LCC after yet another royal commission. Why this was seen as a solution is clear enough. Roland Freeman – then a director of the Tory London Municipal Society and playing a significant role in drawing up the Conservative Government's proposals to the royal commission – puts this very well: 'All our discussions turned on the fact that we couldn't win the LCC as it was then constituted. We wanted the maximum powers for the boroughs, and a metropolitan authority covering as wide an area as possible – so we would have permanent control' (*Time Out*, 13 October 1983). This is very nearly what happened. The GLC's role remained ill-defined and poorly resourced in relation to the boroughs (see Young and Kramer, 1978), while the built-in LCC Labour majority was removed. But unfortunately for the Conservatives some outer London areas had successfully resisted inclusion in the new authority. They had to settle for control of the GLC only half the time. This had turned out to be not enough for the Thatcher Government (see also Young, 1984a; 1984b; for a review of the political status of the GLC and its opponents).

In May 1981, Labour took control of the GLC and four Metropolitan County Councils (Greater Manchester, Merseyside, West Midlands, West Yorkshire). Existing control of the other two Metropolitan County Councils (South Yorkshire and Tyne and Wear) were strengthened further. Not only this, but these councils were elected on the basis of manifestos promising increased public service provision and even extension of public influence into new areas, like the local economy. Both their electoral success and the leftward shift of their policies owed much to a reaction against the radical Right of the Thatcher Government. Very soon they were in the forefront of opposition to central government. West Midlands took the lead in alternative economic policy, South Yorkshire in transport and Merseyside in police accountability. These initiatives were widely applauded and began to spread to other Labour councils. The GLC, headed by the charismatic Ken Livingstone was prominent all in these areas and also challenged the Government in the wider terms of attitudes towards the family, sexuality and authority. Among other things, the GLC gave institutional and financial backing to gay groups, women's organizations, black groups and set up people's planning initiatives and committees to monitor police behaviour. The GLC even took issue with the Government on matters like the British presence in Northern Ireland and nuclear military policy. Sometimes these opposition policies received considerable popular support – cheap public transport is the notable example. At the very least they gave an opportunity for pressure groups to mobilize and a platform for their ideas, on policing for instance – already a highly contentious issue in the aftermath of the 1981 urban riots. Perhaps most of all ministers found themselves being constantly put on the defensive by sniping from a number of directions, which diverted their efforts from what was supposed to be a radical reform of British society.

As with rate-capping it was the Cabinet committee MISC 79 and the tensions leading up to the 1983 general election which produced an answer to this problem. The committee had concluded that no alternative to the rating system was viable. Nor should a ceiling be put on business rates (as the Trade and Industry Minister wanted), or education expenditure transferred from the rates to central government (as the Education Minister suggested). In the first instance, the committee had even rejected the Treasury's demands for rate-capping in England and Wales as well as Scotland. This left two problems to be resolved before the next election: how to fulfil promises to do somethings about the rates, and how to solve the continuing problem of local government that legislation had so far failed to do. A temporary answer was to make London Transport directly accountable to the Department of Transport and to weaken the political cohesion of the Inner London Education Authority (ILEA) by replacing GLC members with borough nominees. In the long term, however, the problem would be solved by abolishing the GLC and the Metropolitan County Councils. Like rate-capping, these recommendations were put into effect under the pressure of an election. It was only then that the whole-hearted personal backing of Mrs Thatcher was achieved, after she had personally taken control of MISC 79. Abolition of the GLC and Metropolitan County Councils were incorporated into the Conservative manifesto for the June 1983 elections.

The Conservatives won the 1983 election with an increased majority of seats in the House of Commons (although only 44 per cent of voters, or 35 per cent of the total electorate voted Conservative). But on its return to Westminster the Government found itself with a timetabling problem. The snap election, called to capitalize on favourable electoral signals, had left important legislation unfinished. Even the Finance Bill, incorporating the April budget, had been abandoned and parts of the budget were not yet implemented. Most of this existing legislation had prior claim on parliamentary time, while the task of producing practical legislation from the abolition proposals looked like being a very complicated process – as both civil servants and knowledgeable ministers like Heseltine and King at the DOE had forewarned. Nobody quite knew how to replace the GLC and the Metropolitan County Councils, or what precise mechanisms should be put in their place for the day-to-day running of fire services, refuse disposal, charity support and a hundred-and-one other functions. The decision was taken first to deprive the GLC of London Transport, and to give rate-capping parliamentary priority. Abolition would be introduced later.

In turn this timetabling difficulty created a political problem. The next GLC and the Metropolitan County Council elections were due in May 1985. But it was clear that legislation could not be produced in time to allow the complete installation of alternatives before the spring of 1986. If the elections went ahead the opposition would be handed a major weapon – voting would effectively become referenda on abolition and what would happen, as seemed very likely, if the Conservatives lost? The Government would plainly be seen to be shutting down political opposition in the face of the democratically expressed wishes of the electorate.

A series of leaked minutes between Patrick Jenkin, Secretary for the Environment, and Mrs Thatcher records how the Government tried to resolve this problem. Summarizing the deliberations of MISC 95 (the successor to MISC 79 now dealing exclusively with abolition) Jenkin wrote on 20 September 1983:

> Elections to the GLC and MCCs are due in May 1985. The Group (MISC 95) are agreed that they cannot be allowed to go ahead: other objections apart, abolition would be a major issue in the elections, so that there would be a major public debate going on after the House of Commons had voted for a second reading of the abolition Bill. (*The Guardian*, 26 March 1984)

The minute goes on to describe two alternatives – 'deferral' or 'substitution'. The first involved deferring the elections for a year (i.e., effectively cancelling them) and allowing the elected councillors and hence the GLC and Metropolitan County Councils to continue for another year until abolition on 1 April 1986. Substitution meant that the present councillors would step down as normal when the new elections were due in May 1985 – but no elections would take place. Instead councillors nominated by London boroughs and the metropolitan districts would take over their role and run the authorities as a stop-gap measure for a year until abolition and the introduction of alternative structures.

Both options were problematical:

> Both our own supporters and the wider public would find it incomprehensible that we should, in effect, extend the terms of office of the GLC and the MCCs. Moreover, to do so would provide these bodies with scope for obstruction at a time when this would be most damaging to our policies. (Ibid.)

But the political implications of substitution were also a problem, for the political control of nominating authorities differed from those being abolished:

> Some members argued that there were constitutional and political objections to substitution: in particular, that we should be accused of creating a new procedure in order to engineer a change in political control in the GLC area and possibly...some of the MCC areas. (Ibid.)

MISC 95 was divided, but, while recognizing that 'in political terms this is probably one of the most sensitive decisions we have to take', both the group as a whole and Jenkin came down in favour of substitution. Although Mrs Thatcher initially disagreed, this is what went into the White Paper *Streamlining the Cities*, published in October 1983, and hence into the legislation process (DOE 1983b). As MISC 95 had predicted, the Government was widely perceived to be gerrymandering and this provoked one of the worst legislative defeats of the Thatcher Government.

MISC 95 was also divided on how closely central government should control the joint boards of borough and district nominees that would take over some of the abolished councils' functions in 1986. Certainly, control of expenditure and policy was necessary. As the leaked minutes show, ministers originally favoured direct ministerial control of budgets and staff numbers for two or three years. However, the group drew back because central ministries

> would require substantial increases in the staffing of the departments concerned; even so departments would be likely to be swamped by the resulting workload. They would moreover, open up the possibility of the extensive challenge in the courts by way of applications for review of ministerial decisions. (Ibid.)

The group clearly reckoned that the local state is at least useful for a scapegoat role – it is better for the people, and the law, to blame the council (even if it is merely an agent of the centre) rather than the Government itself. In the end the group recommended relying on rate-capping along rather than further controls. But the Treasury held out for direct central control and got Mrs Thatcher's support for this view. Provision for central approval over manpower, rate precepts and budgets, for at least the first three years, was written into the White Paper.

THE PROPOSALS AND THEIR (LACK OF) RATIONALE

The major provisions of the White Paper published in October 1983 were:

1 Abolition of the GLC and MCCs on 1 April 1986.
2 Substitution of the existing councils by borough/district nominees on 1 April 1986. These nominees would run the GLC and MCCs for their final year.
3 After 1 April 1986, the GLC and MCCs would be replaced by:
   3.1 At least three statutory, but non-elected, joint boards in each ex-county made up of councillor nominees from

boroughs and districts. These would run strategic, county-wide services in the absence of all seven counties (for police, fire, public transport, also ILEA in London and possibly waste disposal).

3.2 Transfer to existing regional or national quangos (for example, the Thames Water Authority would take over the Thames Flood Barrier, trustees of museums and galleries would take over arts sponsorship).

3.3 Transfer to boroughs and districts (for example, highways, waste disposal, planning, coroners, libraries). For some of these functions a single district or borough would act for all the others in the ex-county (for example, for traffic lights, rent officers, libraries). This would mean at least eight central bodies for each ex-county run by a single borough. For other functions (for example, planning, arts, voluntary service support) voluntary joint arrangements would suffice, possibly leading to six more bodies for each ex-county.

3.4 The creation of new bodies to deal with county-wide functions which could not be broken up in any of these ways (for example, a London Planning Commission, statutory boards to manage debts and pension funds).

3.5 Transfer to central government (highways, reserve powers and the power to set up new boards and bodies). The transfer of London Transport to central government, already accomplished by separate legislation, could be included here.

4 Central government would control the joint boards as regards staff numbers, budgets and rate precepts for at least three years.

Even in such a brief summary, these proposals seem complex enough (see Flynn et al., 1985). In practice they were soon to become extremely messy. In particular 'new' functions were continually discovered over the next year or so and categories 3.2, 3.3 and 3.4 seemed capable of considerable expansion.

Having formulated some sort of structure for abolition, two major tasks remained: first, producing a 'technical' rationale for such seemingly extreme action and gaining some support for it, and secondly, obtaining parliamentary approval. The first task failed almost completely, the second suffered major delays and even some temporary reverses.

Before dealing with the technical rationale for abolition – and its almost universal rejection – it is worth reminding ourselves of its political rationale. According to George Tremlett, GLC Conservative councilllor and former deputy leader of the Party's GLC group: 'She [Thatcher] believes Red Ken can be abolished by wiping out the GLC. She believes the Labour Party can be crippled by destroying the Metropolitan counties, their principal power base outside Parliament' (*City Limits*, 13 January 1984). Any number of similar, if less blunt, statements have been made by the Government's own supporters. But what better source is there than the Cabinet itself? William Waldegrave, Environment Minister responsible for the parliamentary progress of the GLC abolition, admitted that Labour boroughs might take up the torch of the abolished GLC and would have greater powers 'for causing trouble in their own areas'. But, he added 'That is the cost of this measure. It seems to us a lesser peril than allowing the metropolitan counties to continue as they are.' For the 'root evil' was electoral legitimacy: 'If you have a thing that is elected, that gives it a legitimacy, and it is bound to try and widen its role' (*Evening Standard*, 22 March 1984).

It was not then, that the GLC and Metropolitan County Councils were in some way inefficient or inadequate, although this was the justification for abolition that the White Paper conspicuously failed to establish (see below). In that case they could be replaced by some other more efficient electoral body. This was the solution favoured by GLC and other local government Conservatives. The latter were dismayed by their own party's policy, claiming that it would lead to an administrative shambles, reduce democracy and give Labour a sizeable electoral advantage. The task was, to quote the title of one of their pamphlets. *How Do we Get Out of this Mess Without Appearing Disloyal* (*The Guardian*, 9 October 1984). They proposed a number of schemes for various London-wide electoral authorities. But the Government would have none of it. Kenneth Baker, Local Government Minister, saw such proposals as a 'mini-GLC' and was 'completely unconvinced by the arguments for such a body' (ibid.). Mr Jenkin was 'not persuaded. . . . I simply have to say firmly but gently that they do not wash' (*Time Out*, 13 October 1983).

The reason for this obstinacy is summed up in the leaked minutes from Jenkin to Thatcher, commenting on the deliberations of MISC 95. The group had decided that 'Any political pressure for a statutory provision for a body representing London should be resisted, such a body could well become a focus for the sort of pressures we already have from the GLC' (*The Guardian*, 26 March 1984).

THE FAILURE OF THE TECHNICAL RATIONALE

The White Paper for abolishing the GLC and Metropolitan County Councils *Streamlining the Cities*, was published on 7 October 1983 (DOE 1983b). As one wag pointed out it was a living example of the premiss that the most important thing about a White Paper was its cover, for the title alone could solve the problems that the contents completely failed to reach. For while there were no forecasts or estimates of the savings in costs, staffing or rates, abolition was supposed to save public money. The White Paper claimed that abolition would simplify local government, but over 100 new state bodies would replace the seven that were to disappear. Similarly, while it claimed that the abolished councils lacked the strategic role for which they had been created, it proposed setting up numerous county-wide strategic bodies. Finally, if there were problems of accountability in metropolitan local government it would hardly help to abolish elections and replace elected authorities with various sorts of quangos.

But the White Paper also pointed to other, less technical reasons for abolition. The GLC and Metropolitan County Councils were 'preventing further progress' in the Government's objectives of reducing inflation and improving 'efficiency' in the public sector. These councils were guilty of 'overspending' and not only that, their strategic role had led 'them to promote policies which conflict with national policies which are the responsibility of central government' (*The Guardian*, 8 October 1983). While the shire counties (mostly Conservative controlled and accounting for 87 per cent of council spending in their areas) would be allowed to remain, the GLC and Metropolitan County Councils (all Labour controlled and accounting for only 16 per cent and 26 per cent respectively) would go.

The technical rationale for abolition was largely demolished in the debate that followed. Turning first to the purely financial rationale, the White Paper itself could only lamely admit that 'It is not possible to put a figure on the savings arising from abolition, or the transitional costs.' This is hardly surprising, for all the considered estimates concluded that no savings would be made, although Conservative Central Office claimed a reduction of 9,000 jobs (18 per cent) and a saving of £120m per year after transitional costs (mostly redundancy payments) of £20–70m (*Local Government Chronicle*, 25 July 1983). These claims appear totally ill-founded. Few services were to have disappeared with abolition so the vast majority of staff and the bulk of buildings and equipment would have remained. But their administration would be duplicated and fragmented in the various replacement bodies, each with its own premises, staff and procedures. Economies of scale would be lost while administrative costs would increase.

Interestingly, the Conservative Cabinet was aware of such conclusions before publication of the White Paper. The GLC Conservative member for Bromley, Michael Wheeler, had estimated abolition costs for London, based on services already transferred from the GLC. He found that the ambulance service, removed from the GLC in 1974, had 'an increase in real terms (1974–81) of 27 per cent despite the fact that 300,000 less patients were carried and less miles were run. Staff increased in the period by approximately 400' (quoted in *Time Out*, 13 October 1983). Sewage services were also taken from the GLC in 1974, and handed over to the Thames Water Authority – here Wheeler discovered an 'increase in real terms of 21.5%'. Wheeler concluded that the Government had 'failed to appreciate the dramatic effect the abolition of the GLC will have on rates'. They would go up. This prediction was confirmed by events. In May 1986, the first levies made by the residuary bodies and joint boards exceeded the Government's targets more than any other type of local authority. The DOE had seen 3.5 per cent as the 'correct' increase for 1986/7 over the previous year. In the event, the metropolitan police authorities were 14.6 per cent over, the metropolitan fire and civil defence authorities were over by 15.4 per cent, and the metropolitan transport authorities by 6.8 per cent. Similar London residuary bodies had increases of between 8 and 11 per cent.

Asked about Wheeler's costings and the conspicuous absence of his own, Patrick Jenkin brushed this aside with 'I am sure I have the full support of Mr Wheeler and his colleagues.' It was not just that the White Paper was completely inadequate, if quite unique, in not providing any costings for such important legislation, but that existing evidence was ignored. Alternative estimates soon filled the gap and the Government's case fell by default. West Yorkshire Metropolitan County Council estimated that its abolition alone would cost £8.1m p.a., plus a transitional cost of between £20m and £29m at 1982/3 prices (*The Guardian*, 14 July 1983). This was soon confirmed by an authoritative study by the management consultants Coopers and Lybrand (1984), commissioned by the Metropolitan County Councils. Even with the best of assumptions for the Government's case, abolition of the Metropolitan County Councils would yield only paltry savings of £4m p.a. at most with a loss (or 'saving'!) of 500 jobs. This small margin was well within the margin for accounting error, and would be overshadowed by transitional costs of between £50m and £90m. In all probability abolition would cost up to £60m p.a., unless the Government ordered substantial increases in bus fares, cuts in police and fire services and reduced standards in waste disposal, road building, etc. (Coopers and Lybrand, 1984). But of course, such 'savings' would have nothing to do with abolition as such. Jobs would *increase* by 1,400 and transitional costs would be between £150m and £240m. As for the GLC, the leader of the Tory Group, Alan Greengross, costed abolition at £204m p.a.

The White Paper had provided figures for Metropolitan County Council and GLC 'overspending', however. Even if the Government refused to cost its own proposals, it could at least point to the guilt of others. According to the White Paper the Metropolitan County Councils had increased cash expenditure, from 1978/9 to 1983/4, by 11 per cent, compared with 8 per cent by other authorities. The volume of Metropolitan County Council expenditure had increased by 13 per cent rather than 1.5 per cent while rate precepts had gone up by 29 per cent since 1981/2, compared with 20 per cent. Similar figures applied to the GLC. This of course completely rejects the view that local electorates should be able to vote for higher local service provision if they wish. For instance, the Metropolitan County Councils spent 15 per cent of their budgets by 1983/4 on keeping down public transport fares, and this had been a highly visible issue in the 1981 council elections. Even so, much of the apparent 'overspend' was approved by central ministries. The Metropolitan County Councils and GLC spent above DOE targets for police, but police budgets had been approved by the Home Office. They spent more on highways, but no more than allocated by the Department of Transport through the Transport Supplementary Grant. Higher fire service expenditure was merely in compliance with national fire standards. But even accepting the White Paper's narrow assumption on what overspending was, Coopers and Lybrand found the Government's case 'overstated and hence misleading' (1983, p. 3). This was because the Metropolitan County Councils

1 provided a mix of services which had been subject to a higher-cost inflation than the mix provided by other authorities;
2 experienced higher needs for their services;
3 expenditure was affected more adversely by factors largely outside their control;
4 had been affected relatively adversely by the Government's

policies on Block grants and expenditure targets; and
5 had not used balances to keep down rate increases as much as
   other authorities.

Taking all these factors into account, spending in Metropolitan
County Councils was not very different from that of the other
authorities and rates had increased by only 2 per cent more than
elsewhere.

The costs of abolition would also mean increased rates – directly
contradictory to the Government's expressed aims. This would
happen in two ways. First, the increased cost of providing services
(if large-scale cuts were avoided) would be reflected in rate levels.
Many district and borough councils would then transgress targets
and suffer from rate-capping or grant penalty. Secondly, especially
in London, the intricate complexity of existing rate equalization
between authorities would be damaged. GLC Conservatives agreed
and claimed that their own proposals for a 'mini-GLC' would save
£287m p.a. in rates compared with complete abolition (*Evening
Standard*, 2 March 1984).

Although the White Paper so conspicuously failed to cost its
proposals, Coopers and Lybrand found 'that it should be perfectly
feasible to produce soundly based order-of-magnitude estimates for
the financial costs and/or savings or the proposed structure compared
with the present arrangement, as well as for the costs of transition'
(1984, p. 6). The civil service at the DOE apparently agreed, and
had privately estimated much higher costs of abolition than they
could admit to publicly, as well as increased rates.

Faced with all this evidence the Government could only respond
by reversing its previous position. By the end of 1983, having
declined to allow the Audit Commission to make independent cost
estimates (as the Metropolitan County Councils had suggested)
Jenkin was arguing that expenditure issues were not central to the
case for abolition. But even if this startling turn-round from the
official position could be accepted, the rest of the White Paper's
case hardly stood up to examination.

This residual case for abolition consisted of the assertions that
the Metropolitan County Councils and GLC had no strategic role,
that their activities merely produced conflict and duplication and
that the proposed changes would increase administrative efficiency.
Commentators found none of these points convincing and most
thought that abolition would make metropolitan government much
more complex and difficult. The White Paper itself admitted as
much, with regard to the strategic role of county-wide authorities

– hence the proposal to set up county-wide boards to run police, fire, transport and to keep the ILEA. According to the White Paper: 'Since the GLC and MCCs were created, substantial amounts of human and financial resources have been devoted to building up county-wide services in these areas. It is not practical to dismantle these arrangements for every service' (section 2.2). Many other functions would also be run by some form of central or strategic body, either by a new special unit, an existing quango or by District Councils/London Boroughs taking on responsibility on behalf of others. It is here that the complexity and likely inter-authority conflict becomes obvious. To take just one example – structure planning in London – 44 lines of communication between various bodies would become over 500 after abolition; for financial precepting and equalization the situation would be even worse, see figures 5.1 and 5.2. A two-tier system of government would be transformed into a multi-tiered system with at least 13 kinds of authorities and over 50 new bodies. In the same way, commentators were sceptical about the ability of 32 London boroughs or the metropolitan districts – with some very different political, social and demographic characteristics – to create common policy voluntarily as the White Paper envisaged. This could hardly be called 'streamlining'. This fact was recognized by the House of Lords at least, which passed a series of amendments to the Bill in May and June 1985, creating strategic, city-wide authorities for waste disposal, and a number of other services. Indeed, when the joint boards began operations in May 1986, they soon became notorious for their slowness and clumsiness in reaching decisions.

On top of all this, indirect election of nominees to boards and joint committees, or no election at all, would replace electoral accountability. The members of the residuary boards, appointed by the Government, were nearly all retired businessmen or quango managers. On the same day that the Metropolitan County Councils were finally abolished – 1 April 1986 – the Local Government Information Act became law. This allowed greater public access to local government including the opening up of sub-committees. But the residuary bodies at once went secret. Only board members and Environment Ministers could see their minutes. As many commentators pointed out, the whole result would be to return metropolitan government to the chaos of Dickensian London – in its day a byword for inefficiency and lack of accountability.

There was, then, an almost complete failure to provide the abolition proposals with any convincing technical rationale. Sometimes no rationale at all was presented, as with the White Paper's

The disappearing GLC precept

The Government has claimed that abolition of the GLC will lead to a saving in bureaucracy. This diagram illustrates the existing financial relationships compared with the complex set of relationships flowing from the number of joint boards, quangos and joint arrangements consequent upon the abolition of the GLC. Because the Government is committed to replicating the existence of the GLC in financial terms, the number of such relationships would increase from the present 33 to about 500 were its proposals to be carried through.

This is but one example of the many processes of local government in London which would be made more complex by abolition.

NOTES
1 The link from the GLC to the boroughs accomplishes precepting, changes for services, and London Equalisation share adjustment.

The Existing 'Complex' Arrangements

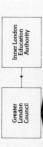

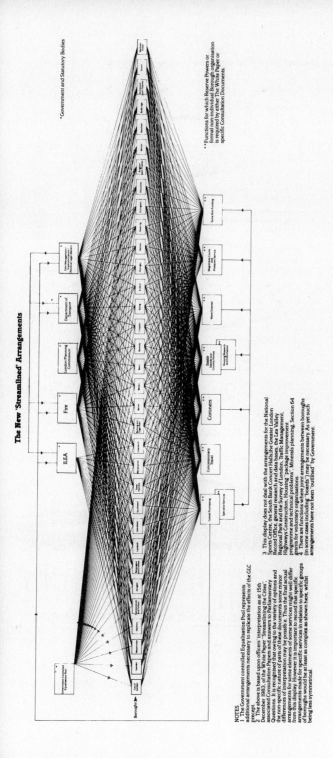

Figure 5.1 'Streamlining' metropolitan government: precepts and financial equalization

Source: GLC, 1984

The Government's proposed 'streamlined' system for structure planning

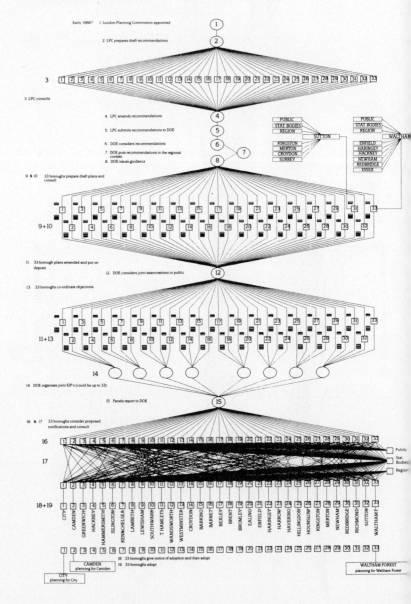

Figure 5.2 'Streamlining' metropolitan government: structure planning
Source: GLC, 1984

complete and astounding lack of costings. Commentators on all sides were left with no option but to see abolition as a purely political move, an attempt to close down opposition and deny alternatives. As we have seen, this is more or less how the Cabinet itself saw abolition. A leader comment in *The Guardian* summed up the White Paper very nicely: 'The White Paper is therefore squarely in the old and dishonourable tradition in which governments claiming to be acting for the highest motives of administrative efficiency and financial prudence have manipulated local government for their own political ends' (8 October 1983).

How were these political ends to be achieved with abolition? First, a base for political opposition and political alternatives would be removed. As one Conservative GLC member put it 'The Prime Minister cannot tolerate London remaining the base of a political group opposed to her. It is simply too powerful a base for opposition' (*The Guardian*, 27 March 1984). This base was not only institutional, allowing resources for policy development and political visibility, but was also given an electoral legitimacy. After the abolition of the GLC, for instance, non-statutory initiatives on police accountability, women, employment and minorities were either truncated or reduced to a more conventional approach, while many local pressure groups – like those, fighting privatization or the LDDC's development plans – were suddenly left bereft of funds. Secondly, replacement institutions would be inimical to the emergence of coherent opposition. It would be far more difficult for a dozen or more co-operating, or more likely conflicting, bodies to present alternative political and policy positions – especially when many no longer had electoral legitimacy. Thirdly, central government would take budgetary control of the key replacement bodies for three years.

LEGISLATING FOR ABOLITION – A POLITICAL OWN-GOAL

First reactions to the proposed legislation can be summarized as condemnation from all parts of the political spectrum and all sorts of organizations. Of the 1,500 responses to the White Paper, only 91 supported abolition, while public opinion polls regularly produced figures showing very high levels of disagreement with the Government. Abolition and rate-capping began the attrition that was to reduce the popularity of the Conservatives from the heights of 1983, following the Falklands War, to a historic low for a governing party by 1986.

Not surprisingly, those councils directly threatened with abolition opposed the Government's plans most fiercely. The GLC and the Metropolitan County Councils mounted a persuasive and effective counter-attack varying from in-depth professional investigation to widespread newspaper and poster publicity. They were widely perceived to have won the argument, both in technical terms and in terms of public opinion. Although this made little difference to the legislative outcome, given the Government's massive parliamentary majority and its 'elective dictatorship' it helped manœuvre the Government into a political own-goal. Instead of fighting on its own grounds of rolling back the state and punishing overspending, the Government was forced to defend taking away the right to vote. For almost the first time since 1979 the ideological offensive reverted to the Left.

The response of Conservatives in local government is indicative of the mess the Government found itself in. Indeed, one GLC Conservative pamphlet, published for the 1984 Conservative Party conference, was titled *How Do we Get Out of this Mess Without Appearing Disloyal*. As early as the run-up to the 1983 election the GLC Tory group signalled its worries about the abolition commitment and endorsed a GLC report opposing the Government's plans. Increased centralization and the creation of non-elected quangos, it argued, were no answer to the problems of the GLC and to London's need for a democratically elected voice. Trying to tread the tightrope between siding with Labour in opposing their own party, and accepting something they saw as fundamentally mistaken and wrong, the group ended up arguing for a new, reformed elected London authority if abolition were to go ahead. Even so, some GLC Conservatives could not contain themselves even before the election, and their ex-chair of council condemned the Government's manifesto abolition plan as 'fraudulent, ignorant and deeply insulting' (*The Guardian*, 25 May 1983).

The same pattern repeated itself after the general election, only with even greater fervour. The Conservative London boroughs had originally applauded the legislation; their hated local enemy would disappear. But in most cases their support became lukewarm when they realized what abolition would probably mean in terms of costs, rates and central control, while the Conservative-dominated Association of County Councils had always been wary of abolition. The GLC Conservatives put forward any number of proposals for a compromise that would preserve some sort of elected London authority. At the very least there should be an open-ended inquiry into the problems of London government. Despite campaigning and support in the Conservative Party and local government, they got nowhere. But their failure is hardly surprising. As we have seen, it was local electoral legitimacy itself which the Government feared. To that extent the technical justification for abolition was a smoke-screen.

As the debate abolition moved more and more in the victims' favour, the GLC Conservatives became more desperate. Their political opponents were winning the debate and, what is more, they were driven to support them. They ended up appearing on joint platforms with Ken Livingstone, or supporting GLC condemnations of the Government's plans. Some broke ranks completely. Most notable was George Tremlett, former deputy GLC leader. Disagreement with the Government's plans on constitutional and practical grounds was coupled with a strong attack on Mrs Thatcher and her style of leadership (see, for example, *City Limits*, January 1984). By the time of four GLC by-elections held over abolition he was advising electors to vote Labour. This was because:

> The government is making a major error to constitutional judgement in taking away the right of people of London to have their own elected city-wide government. The reason it is being taken away is that the Prime Minister has an obsession with the way the Labour Party is run in London, and with Mr Livingstone in particular. (*The Guardian*, 5 September 1984).

One of the few London Tories who supported the Government's plans whole-heartedly, Lady Porter, leader of Westminster Council, stated the other side of the arguement: 'We are in the days of true marxism. There is no use worrying about being dictatorial. Nobody loves you anyway. Get on with the job and do it properly' (ibid., 12 March 1984).

Normally responses to government consultation documents are placed in the House of Commons library. Not so with responses to the abolition proposals. Only a list of respondents were published – but a list that neglected to say whether they opposed abolition or not, and which even 'forgot' to list some of the organizations that replied: it is almost superfluous to go through their responses, which read like a litany of criticisms of the Government's plans (see Duncan and Goodwin, 1985c). For industry, only the CBI and the Institute of Directors (where the latter in particular is strictly monetarist) came out in support. Further down the line, industrialists with everyday pragmatic concerns did not share their views. The construction and transport industries ('appalling', 'a retrograde step', 'disastrous', 'indecision, delay and increased bureaucracy') were most worried. This concern was matched by the Trades Union Congress (TUC) and those unions or professional bodies most involved like NALGO, the Fire Brigades Union, the County Surveyors Society and London magistrates. At the other end of the spectrum, churches and religious organizations were equally opposed. The 1984 Methodist Conference voted overwhelmingly to ask the Government to reconsider its plans, given the 'increasing opposition at all levels of society', and saw alcoholics and homeless people as just two particularly vulnerable groups who would suffer as a result of abolition.

The London Churches Group (all denominations) saw the abolition plans as 'disastrous, hasty and undemocratic'. The poorest groups and poorest areas of London would be the worst hit (*Evening Standard*, 4 June 1984). Somewhere in the middle were professional organizations and interest groups less directly concerned about abolition like the Transport Board, the Civic Trust, the Royal Town Planning Institute ('a reliance on the supernatural'), the Countryside Commission, the Royal Institute of British Architects ('a return to the sort of arrangements deemed inadequate to cope with the urban problems of the railway age') the Automobile Association, the Ramblers Association, the London Wildlife Trust, the National Council of Voluntary Organizations and so on. Whenever possible, the Government tried to buy off such opposition by promising replacement fundings for a transitional period, for the arts, sports or charities, for instance. But the longer the debate went on, and the more advanced plans became, the more organizations saw the disadvantages and costs of abolition. Even the *Evening Standard*, a paper that set out to hound both Ken Livingstone and the GLC, ended up opposing abolition if no replacement elected London-wide authority was to take its place:

> That job to speak for London, to be answerable to Londoners, to provide the indissoluble minimum of capital-wide services – is clearly best done by a single authority. There is no way round that logic. And a Tory government should surely be the last to allow dogma to overrule practical facts. *Evening Standard*, (leader comment, 20 January 1984)

The results of public opinion polls showed how widespread lack of support for the Government's plans were. A series of polls in the Metropolitan County Council and GLC areas regularly gave results of only 15–20 per cent for abolition and 60–70 per cent against.

The Euro-elections in June 1984 showed a significantly higher-than-average anti-Tory swing in London (8 per cent instead of 5.1 per cent since June 1983) while Labour gained three new seats in London and six more in Metropolitan County Council areas out of 15 gains across the country. Turn-out was low however, as it was in September in four GLC 'by-elections' caused by Labour resignations specifically over abolition. But here too, the Labour share of the vote increased significantly. By this time a voting poll showed a massive swing to Labour in London of 16.1 per cent since the 1983 general election, enough to hand Labour 33 Conservative seats in London alone. For the GLC elections, the swing to Labour would be even higher. This almost universal condemnation was to combine with the Government's own internal problem to produce a startling set-back in its legislative programme. In turn, this set-back meant that the own-goal would get much worse.

As we described earlier (pp.192–4) the government chose 'substitution' as a solution to the impending GLC and Metropolitan County Council elections of May 1985. This demanded separate legislation to cancel the elections and to enable nominees to replace elected councillors. The aim was that this should be much shorter and simpler than the abolition legislation itself, and so should not take up too much parliamentary time. This was the Local Government (Interim Provisions) Bill which entered Parliament on 30 March 1984. Because its function was to pave the way for aboliton it became known as the 'Paving Bill'. The main abolition legislation itself would follow in the Autumn of 1984 and in 1985.

But the Bill could not remain simple as planned. The councils to be abolished, together with many other Labour councils involved in the new arrangements, as well as several unions, had threatened non-co-operation and various sorts of sabotage. The Bill tried to preclude this resistance by outlawing such tactics. In doing so, however, it became a much longer and more complicated document than originally intended, running to 15 pages. This made it a much easier target for the most effective focus of parliamentary oppositon – the House of Lords.

The Bill followed shortly after the rate-capping legislation and stimulated a similar response. Labour's Shadow Environment Secretary denounced the measure as 'a constitutional outrage and a democratic nightmare which will lead to a fundamental diminution of democracy, local freedom and accountability' (*The Guardian*, 31 March 1984). Outside Parliament the Labour GLC Leader, Ken Livingstone, complained, 'For the first time in the peacetime history of this country we are faced with the frightening prospect of a British election being cancelled' (ibid.). Speaking later on radio he said that the Government's actions reminded him of the slogan often seen scrawled about London – 'If voting changed anything they would abolish it' – 'The Government have done exactly that', he said (*Evening Standard*, 12 April 1984).

Similar denunciations soon followed from senior Conservatives. Leading a motion opposing the second reading, Edward Heath (Prime Minister, 1970–4) said the Bill was bad because it was unnecessary, a negation of democracy which proposed changing the political make-up of local authorities by diktat and, in addition, 'It puts the Conservative party open to the charge of the greatest gerrymandering of the last 150 years of British history' (*The Guardian*, 12 April 1984). Another rebel and former minister, Ian Gilmour, said elsewhere that 'The abolition of properly elected bodies whose politics and policies are opposed to one's own is perhaps a trifle crude, especially if they are to be succeeded by quantities of quangos' (ibid., 2 April 1984).

In all 19 Conservative MPs, including four former ministers, voted with Labour against the Bill. The Government's paper majority of 140 was cut to 93, and feeling against the Bill was so widespread that the Government's House of Commons managers thought it best to allow the detailed committee stage to be taken on the floor of the Commons. This led in turn to further delays, denunciation and rebellions focused on a series of critical amendments. These were co-ordinated by two former ministers in the Thatcher Government, Pym and Gilmour, with the backing of Heath. Geoffrey Ripon (former Conservative Secretary for the Environment in the Heath Government) called it 'squalid and shameful that a Conservative government should come forward with a proposal to substitute a directly elected socialist authority...by an independent nominated quasi-quango of another political party' (ibid., 10 May 1984). Heath called the proposals for nomination 'completely immoral, unpolitical and impractical' and Gilmour saw them as 'seeking to give some spurious respectability to an obvious gerrymander'. These Conservative rebellions failed to halt the legislation, although this is hardly surprising given the Government's large majority and strong parliamentary discipline which had been improved after the rate-capping revolts. But they had the important effect of signalling support for dissenters in the House of Lords.

At this stage the Government made things worse for itself

by apparently accepting part of the opposition's point of view. The ILEA had long been viewed with considerable distaste by the Conservative Party. It had a permanent Labour majority and spent a lot on education, using a rate precept on inner-London authorities which could not be challenged. But, unlike other rate precepting 'regional' quangos such as the water authorities, it was not under government control. ILEA councillors were predominantly nominated by inner-London boroughs. Mrs Thatcher herself, education Minister in the Heath Government during the early 1970s, had some unhappy memories of the obstacle presented by ILEA.

One traditional Conservative answer to the ILEA problem was to press for direct elections – this would allow greater public accountability and hence, they thought, less spending on education. This was the view Patrick Jenkin, among others, had taken. This become something of an embarrassment when he found himself responsible for removing electoral accountability wholesale. The other Conservative response was abolition of ILEA and this was incorporated into the original abolition proposals. Unfortunately, however, it soon became clear that a strategic education body was still needed for inner London. So while the ILEA itself would go, it would have to be replaced by something else. This would be an inner London education board, run by councillors seconded from the boroughs but without direct rate precept powers. There would, at last, no longer be specialist ILEA councillors and they would no longer have financial autonomy.

So far, so good for the Government's plans. But when civil servants looked at the issue more closely, they found another almost insuperable problem. The abolition proposals threatened to throw into chaos the complex rate equalization procedures in the Metropolitan County Councils and especially the GLC. Civil servants were already desperately working out alternative mechanisms once the councils had gone – none of which looked very good – and now they were faced with the prospect of abolishing ILEA, which itself undertook a large slice of education finance equalization. Unless education expenditure was to be reallocated to central government (something already ruled out) it looked as if the ILEA would have to stay if equalization was not to break down completely.

The story so far of self-imposed administrative mess is perhaps par for the course as far as abolition is concerned, but then Keith Joseph, Education Minister, threw in his own bombshell. ILEA supporters were already conducting an anti-abolition campaign through posters, leaflets, meetings, letters and demonstrations, while the ILEA Conservative group, among others, pressed for electoral accountability. In November 1983, all the political parties represented in the ILEA voted in favour of keeping a unified London educational service that was elected directly, and moved to back the anti-abolition campaign. Public consultation drew over 2,000 protests but only three expressions of support. Apparently accepting these arguments, Joseph announced in April 1984 that the ILEA would stay (although with central power over the budget and staffing levels for three years) and that its councillors would be elected directly. ILEA would be the only London local authority institution remaining with direct elections, because, Joseph claimed, of the 'nature, scale and importance' of London's education service' (*The Guardian*, 6 April 1984). But if the case was a good one for the ILEA, wasn't it the same for the GLC?

The day of reckoning came on the 28 June. The Government had previously kept its legislation on course by unprecedented whipping and importing large numbers of 'backwoods' members of the House of Lords for the event. According to one source, government managers were going up to previously unknown Lords and saying things like 'I was your fag at Eton' (*The Guardian*, 12 June 1984). But the 28 June held more alluring attractions for these men despite their temporary and bizarre importance to the Government. This was the first day of the Lords Test (cricket), the first day of the Henley Regatta (rowing) and well into Wimbledon (tennis) – all important events in the aristocrat's calendar – and few remained in the House of Lords. An amendment delaying the implementation of the Paving Bill until the abolition legislation proper received royal assent was passed by an anti-government majority of 48. This was widely seen as the most damaging parliamentary defeat for the Government of the 16 in the House of Lords during its five years of office (see *Financial Times*, 10 July 1984 for an analysis of voting in the Upper House). The size of the majority was such that the Government had little option but to accept defeat. Although it could continue with the abolition programme and measures to control the activities of affected councils in the interim, it decided not to use the Parliament Act to enforce the decision of the House of Commons on the Lords. According to *The Guardian* this 'would be seen as an intolerable intensification of the controversy over the abolition of the right to vote in London and the metropolitan areas' (29 June 1984). One own-goal was enough.

What was the Government to do now? As the Paving Bill had been delayed until the passing of the abolition Bills, the May 1985 elections would go ahead. This had to be avoided at all costs. It was also necessary to keep strictly on schedule whatever replacement Paving Bill emerged, if the major legislation was to take effect by April 1986. The Government had tried to find a compromise acceptable to Tory rebels in both the Houses of Lords and Commons before the Lords' report stage on 18 July, and before the Commons' parliamentary session ended in August. The Lords' revolt had inflamed opposition in both chambers, so that a half-way house position (postponing transfer to nominee boards by a few months) which had been propounded but cold-shouldered by the Government prior to the defeat, was no longer possible. The one card up the Government's sleeve was the start of the grouse-shooting season on 12 August. Apparently, rather than stay in London debating and so miss this all-important date, many Tory and independent peers can be persuaded to accept a lot of legislation quickly.

Despite a public stance of 'business as usual', the Cabinet clearly found all this an agonizing situation. A special ministerial meeting on the 4 July, chaired by the Prime Minister, opted for the original 'deferral' solution as the way to continue, together with safeguarding clauses to prevent obstruction, 'sabotage' and a final spending spree by the doomed councils. In formal terms this meant Government amendments to the Paving Bill to prolong the lives of the councils for an extra year, when the original Bill had done exactly the opposite. Mr Jenkin undertook this humiliating duty in the House of Commons on 5 July 1984 – Mrs Thatcher pointedly leaving the chamber just as he was about to speak.

The proposals to limit the actions of the reincarnated Metropolitan County Councils and GLC during their final year were introduced a few days later, in time for the report stage in the House of Lords. Clauses would require the councils to get ministerial approval before signing new contracts for engineering and building works over £250,000 and for all other schemes over £1m. Any service expenditure over £1m (new or not) would need ministerial approval while 'asset stripping' (for example, sales of land to sympathetic Labour councils) was outlawed. The Government also took the sanction of disqualification from office, and also from future office for an unspecified time, of any councillor in breach of the legislation. The Government had already interfered in the normal course of the annual GLC Money Bill (allowing capital expenditure) to transfer £41m to that part of the budget over which the DOE had detailed control, while an earlier measure prevented the councils hiring new staff on contracts extending beyond abolition date. These measure would also bring effective government control over the rate income raised under the notorious section 137 of the 1972 Local Government Act – money which councils could spend on anything 'deemed to be of benefit' to their citizens. Unfortunately for the Government the GLC and Metropolitan County Councils had outflanked these measures to some extent. They had already signed a number of large contracts including those for the anti-government counter-publicity campaigns – the very contracts which the Government had wanted most to stop. The councils also took some comfort from the prospect of the centre being overburdened by the minutiae of council business. As the deputy Labour leader of the GLC put it, 'Mr Jenkin will be choosing the colour of our school linoleum' (*The Guardian*, 13 July 1984). Others were worried about the impracticability of this form of local government – the British Road Federation expected the snow to melt before snow clearance schemes would get central approval (*Construction News*, 19 July 1984).

Despite the severity of these 'safeguard' clauses, the amended legislation succeeded in the House of Lords. More Tory peers turned out on the day and the opposition received less support from bishops and independents. The Bill finally passed through the House of Commons on the last day of July 1984. Even so, Mr Jenkin delayed publishing the final version of the much-criticized replacement measures – the system of joint boards, compulsory and voluntary local authority co-operation etc. – until after the final vote was taken. The doomed councils had won an extra year in which to oppose government policy, over rate-capping for instance, an opposition they undertook all the more vigorously when they were to be abolished in any case.

As the Tory *Evening Standard* commented, Mrs Thatcher – in insisting on abolition in the 1983 election manifesto – had 'failed to realise the weight of the political albatross that would settle around her administration's neck' (leader comment, 1 August 1984). Mr Jenkin seemed to agree. Trying to explain his conduct to the Tory back-benches after reintroducing the amended Paving Bill, he was reported as saying 'It would be best to get an unpopular plan on to the statute book as soon as possible, so that there was the maximum time gap between its enactment and the next general election' (*The Guardian*, 6 July 1984).

Abolition, seen by many in the Cabinet as the Government's trump card, was in fact raising some difficult political problems. For the Conservatives, as for central governments over the past hundred years, the local government problem would not go away.

6

The Local Government Problem Won't Go Away

6.1 Say No to No Say

We have described in the last chapter how the Thatcher Government attempted to deal once and for all with the problem of local government autonomy: rate-capping would enable the centre to control local government finance directly; and abolition would remove entirely the major centres of opposition. By these means the scope for local government political autonomy would, it was hoped, be reduced to insignificance. As we have seen, however, (chapters 3–5) the local government crisis was not just a matter of the centre acting on its own volition in order to increase its powers. Quite the contrary; very often the centre was forced to respond or was put off course because of local action. Indeed, this is the origin of the whole 'crisis' and hence the Conservative Government's desire in the first place to restructure local–central relations. The same applies to the 'final solution'. The rate-capping and abolition legislation was not only a response to local government action, but the course of the legislation, its final outcome and its political effects were also moulded by the reactions of local government. For local government, especially the local 'opposition' in radical left-wing councils, was also active in opposing and resisting the Government's legislation. We review this counter-offensive in this section. Local government autonomy may be almost dead but, as yet, it hasn't lied down.

This counter-offensive included a publicity campaign against rate-capping and abolition which marked a new departure in local–central relations in Britain. The traditional methods of political lobbying and campaigning were intensified, accompanied by information tailored to both specialized and general audiences and a widespread political advertising campaign. As we have seen, the Government's case was a poor one, both logically and politically; it was not at all difficult for the opposition to win the technical debates about rate-capping and abolition. But it is not unusual in politics to win the technical battle but to lose the war in terms of practical politics and public awareness. The counter-publicity campaign was crucial in bringing the issues of local–central relations to a wider public and to help fix widespread support for the anti-government side. In this way the campaign was a major political defeat for the Government and was perhaps the beginning of the end for the New Right offensive.

In opposing particular legislation the focus of the counter-offensive was of course the parliamentary process itself. Even if the wider war of political awareness and political consciousness was important, this is where the short-term battle would be won or lost. Here the more traditional modes of opposition were well tried, the lobbying of parliamentary target groups combined with parliamentary opposition in debates and committees. The existing local government lobbies – the local authority associations – were already well connected in parliament. We have already seen how all were totally opposed to rate-capping while the Labour Association for Metropolitan Authorities in particular (with tacit support from the Conservative Association for County Councils) worked against abolition. Some influence could be exerted in this way, especially where the formal parliamentary opposition kept up the temperature of the debate and assiduously opposed legislation line-by-line at the committee stage. It was in this way that something similar to rate-capping had been deleted from the 1982 Local Government Finance Act (see chapter 3).

The trouble with this line of attack was the advantage of controlling the parliamentary process that was open to any majority government, coupled with the strong voting discipline exerted by party managers. This advantage was massively reinforced by the large Conservative majority in Parliament. It is doubtful that such dramatic legislation would have succeeded with more normal parliamentary majorities of 10–40, given the opposition of the local government associations and the existence of a group of prestigious Tory rebels. The Government's majority had only been 60 when the rate-capping part of the 1982 Local Government Finance Act was deleted. But now the majority was 140. As far as the House of Commons went, opposition might succeed in raising the temperature of debate, but it could not have much legislative effect.

One response was to widen and intensify the parliamentary lobby. Using contacts in the labour movement and Labour Party, the local government crisis was presented as one of the major political issues of the day which should command prime attention from the opposition. (An impression the Government did nothing to dispel). This was something of a turn-round for Labour where a centralized national party had traditionally relegated local government to the level of spear-carrier. Among other things, the Labour Party National Executive Committee (NEC) upgraded its Local Government Affairs Committee to the same front-line status as the Home Policy and International Policy Committee. David Blunkett, leader of Sheffield's ruling Labour group, an exponent of 'local socialism' (see Blunkett and Green, 1983) and recently elected as the only council member on the NEC, became its chair. The same message, the political importance of local government, was also taken to professional and academic groups, who in general were already convinced of the argument but, for the most part, had not got involved in political lobbying. The lobbying target was also widened. The House of Lords was now seen as the place where the Government's legislation was most at risk. Not only were the local authority associations well connected there, but Conservative Party discipline was much lower and key groups, like the bishops and the 'Butskellite' (centre–Left) Conservative peers were known to be extremely wary of Thatcher's new radical Right and its legislation. So academics sympathetic to the local government position, for instance, were encouraged to lobby target groups in the House of Lords. The wider campaign was promoted nationally by the Association of Metropolitan Authorities (AMA), the GLC and Sheffield City Council and other Labour authorities on the Government's 'hit list' after a conference in Sheffield in June 1983. They helped set up a Local Government Campaign Unit in September 1983, with Sheffield's David Blunkett in the chair, to co-ordinate activities. This was eventually sponsored by over 60 councils. The disaster of the Paving Bill is partly a tribute to their success.

Given the unfavourable parliamentary situation, this lobbying campaign also relied on the outcome of the technical debate. This is where the Government's case was weakest, and we reviewed in the last chapter how their case was shot to pieces for both rate-capping and abolition. What is important to note here is that this debate and its outcome fed into the lobby campaign, and that it became part of the 'received wisdom' of the campaign's targets. For instance, in the absence of any credible official figures, the Coopers and Lybrand reports (1983, 1984) sponsored by the Metropolitan County Councils became a definitive source for quantitative estimates on abolition and so helped influence the debate. The impact of these reports and other studies like them was widened through the use of a whole series of information packages, pamphlets and leaflets tailored to differing levels of interest and knowledge. Political advertising and political image-making/visibility in turn pushed the whole issue of local–central relations into the limelight.

In one sense then, the new departure of political advertising was a direct response to the large Conservative majority in Parliament. Ironically, large-scale political advertising using the services and techniques of commercial advertising agencies was first used in selling the Tories in the 1979 general election campaign. The AMA had followed this breakthrough, in a small way, in a series of press advertisements opposing the 1980 and 1982 local government legislation, and so had NALGO in opposing the Government's privatization plans. The aim was to take the offensive and so define the area of debate, which would also keep the government unsettled and, in turn, on the defensive. Denied access to television and radio (advertisements judged to be political are banned) the campaign primarily used posters and newspaper advertisements, backed up by cinema advertising and videos and leaflets aimed at particular target groups. The campaign, based on achieving widespread public familiarity through a simple and powerful message, was almost entirely used for attacking the abolition legislation – the Government's most vulnerable spot. The complexities of rate-capping were more difficult to convey through simple images.

The GLC was pre-eminent in the political advertising campaign (see Hipkin, 1984). Images and slogans produced by a leading advertising agency were tested by opinion polls and by panels of Londoners of all shades of political opinion. They soon found that the most crucial issue in the minds of Londoners (and it was judged important to involve Conservative voters) was not defending a left-wing council or its policies, but protecting democratic rights. The Government's proposals to cancel elections provided the perfect leverage. Hence the simple black-and-white statement in March 1984, displayed from nearly 500 poster sites across London, 'From now on you have no say in who runs London.' Unlike the previous GLC adverts (the anti-abolition poster campaign began in May 1983) the logo 'Keep the GLC working for London' did not appear, although the signifier 'Say no to no say' remained on all adverts and posters (see figure 6.1).

These early posters and newspaper advertisements quickly lodged the issue in people's minds. By June 1984, polls revealed that 90

"IF YOU WANT ME OUT YOU SHOULD HAVE THE RIGHT TO VOTE ME OUT."

Everyone's entitled to their view. The British constitution says you express it through the ballot box.

That's the law.

Unfortunately the Government doesn't like the law as it stands in relation to the GLC.

Today the first bill relating to the abolition of the GLC gets its second reading in the House.

It's devised to wipe out next year's GLC elections. Whether you're Labour, Tory, Liberal or SDP, you'll have no say.

Not since the last World War has your statutory right to vote been withdrawn in this way.

And it's a cynical dismissal of public opinion.

In a recent MORI poll 61% of Londoners of all political persuasions said no.

Only 22%, by the way, said yes.

In every straw poll, overwhelming public opinion has said no to abolition.

On 26th March Tom King the Conservative Secretary for Employment outlined in the House the elementary rights of people to register their vote without interference.

That was in relation to the Trade Union movement.

This Government steadfastly refuses to apply the same principles to the rights of 7 million Londoners.

You may hold the view of course,

that they were voted into power democratically and have the right to do as they wish.

But, nowhere in the Tory manifesto was there a mention of abolishing your right to vote in local elections.

Ask yourself why the Government is intent on doing away with the GLC in the first place.

There has not been a single proposition motivated by the desire to improve London.

What you might have heard have been outbursts.

"Red Ken spending our money on weirdos again."

(For the record less than half of one

per cent of GLC expenditure is allocated to all minorities.)

Don't let bigoted arguments of this kind blind you to the real issue.

This country's centuries old democratic tradition is at stake.

Local Government is one of the checks and balances which safeguard us against the abuse of central Government power.

And it would be an abuse of power for any Government to abolish a democratic institution such as a local authority, simply because it did not like the incumbent administration.

SAY NO TO NO SAY.

Figure 6.1 The publicity campaign: Ken Livingstone says 'Say no to no say'
Source: The Guardian, 11 April 1984.

per cent of Londoners were aware of the issues being raised and 69 per cent were opposed to abolition. Given the weakness of the Government's case, the degree of opposition is perhaps not surprising – but its breadth certainly was. Based on its early success, the campaign turned to what would happen if Whitehall took over the running of London. At 490 poster sites, snails with bowler hats were seen crawling in from Whitehall to run London, whilst at 10 supersites 'politics met art' as Hipkin (1984) puts it. For two days at the end of May 1984 these sites bore the simple message 'Imagine what London would be like run from Whitehall'. Then overnight these posters were wrapped in a maze of red tape.

In addition to reaching targetted groups (e.g. cyclists, businessmen, academics) by leaflets, information packages, pamphlets and videos, GLC visibility was also raised by cultural festivals, on the South Bank of the Thames and elsewhere, that were already linked to political messages like opposition to racism or support for the peace movement. All this effort clearly spread and consolidated the anti-government case. By August 1984 even 44 per cent of Tory MPs thought abolition a vote-loser for the Conservatives. The GLC alone had spent £10.6m on counter-publicity by July 1984 (three times the budget for the Labour Party's 1983 election campaign), and although other threatened councils were less intense, similar campaigns were run elsewhere. Some authorities had already mounted counter-publicity about rate-capping and found considerable public support. One survey in Sheffield found that 55 per cent disapproved of the legislation, even including 33 per cent of those who opposed the City Council's policy.

Not surprisingly, the Government tried to paint these counter-publicity campaigns as 'council propaganda' and Mr Jenkin attempted to tighten up the legislation under which they were funded. Targetting Mrs Thatcher personally was apparently felt particularly keenly (see figure 6.2). This involved him yet again in a cat-and-mouse game with the 'offending' authorities, especially the GLC, each side using the intricacies of local government legislation and auditor's reports in their manœuvres. The result was that, although the GLC would have to tread more carefully, it was able to proceed more or less as before. Ironically, while the Government criticized council propaganda, it allocated at least £500,000 for its own advertising campaign to promote abolition. And much more was to be spent later on privatizing British Telecom and British Gas.

The message of the counter-publicity campaign was supported by protest action. In January 1984 a march against the abolition of the

THREE OUT OF FOUR LONDONERS WANT A SINGLE ELECTED AUTHORITY FOR LONDON.

One month ago the Harris Opinion Poll showed clearly how Londoners felt their city should be run.

Three quarters believe London as a whole needs a democratically elected authority.*

On the other hand, the Government seems to think that in some cases the 32 individual boroughs can take the place of a single body.

Most Londoners know that a city as large and as complex as London needs one authority to co-ordinate many of its services.

In other cases they seem to think that Joint Committees and Government controlled Quangos will know what's best for the people.

That cannot be right when they're not directly elected by Londoners.

The fact is, no matter what anybody thinks of the way the GLC runs London, Londoners still want a single elected authority to perform the same function.

The Government still has time to listen to what the people are saying. We think they should.

*SOURCE: HARRIS OPINION POLL APRIL 1985 FOR THAMES NEWS (THAMES TV).

Figure 6.2 The publicity campaign: targetting Mrs Thatcher
Source: The Guardian, 17 May 1985.

GLC and ILEA attracted about 26,000 marchers and closed most inner-London schools. Parents' organizations and community groups were joined by teachers, GLC staff and other members of local government unions. This was repeated in a nation-wide 'Democracy Day' of protest in March, covering opposition to rate-capping as well as abolition. This was organized by the Local Government Campaign Union and the TUC. About 50,000 people marched in London, accompanied by mayors and council chairs in full regalia, while demonstrations also took place in the metropolitan counties. These were particularly successful in those areas where councils had strong links with active labour movements, as in Merseyside, where 24-hour strikes of transport workers, dockers and some private-sector workers accompanied marches (*The Guardian*, 30 March 1984). Throughout, the GLC constantly took the opportunity to remind the public what was happening, for example by presenting the DOE with a 100-feet-long telex message requesting authorization, under the new Paving Bill legislation, for items like tea-bag purchases for school canteens. The GLC administration even put its majority on the line, when four councillors resigned in the summer of 1984 – including Ken Livingstone and the deputy leader – to fight by-elections over abolition. This generated some useful publicity, although Conservatives boycotted the elections and turn-out was low in the face of torrential rain and out-of-date electoral registers. Nevertheless, all four Labour candidates won by a considerably increased percentage of votes.

6.2 Non-compliance

The success of the counter-abolition campaign helped to ensure the mangling that the Paving Bill received in the House of Lords. But despite this the Bill did pass into legislation roughly on time and with its essential features intact – the Metropolitan County Council and GLC elections were abolished and Acts followed to abolish the councils themselves. Similarly, the rate-capping Bill had become law more or less unchanged. If the counter-attack was to continue, it would have to be a matter of obstructing legislation and, possibly, breaking the law. Even if the Bills abolishing the Metropolitan County Councils and GLC *had* failed (and some votes in the House of Lords were very close) this would not have made that much difference. For rate-capping gives the centre powers to take an effective majority on councils as far as their spending is concerned. Resistance to rate-capping became the arena for the immediate

WHAT HAS THE GMC DONE TO DESERVE ABOLITION?

BUILT THE BEST EQUIPPED, MOST EFFECTIVE POLICE AND FIRE SERVICES.

CREATED NEARLY 9,000 REAL SEW JOBS AND PROVIDED WIDESPREAD ASSISTANCE TO INDUSTRY/BUSINESS.

ESTABLISHED ONE OF THE FINEST, CHEAPEST, MOST COMPREHENSIVE PUBLIC TRANSPORT SYSTEMS IN BRITAIN.

DEVELOPED A SUPERB TRADING STANDARDS ORGANISATION HANDLING 50,000 COMPLAINTS ANNUALLY.

ATTRACTED £50 MILLION WORTH OF EEC AID TO HELP CREATE SUPER-REGIONAL FACILITIES.

TURNED NEARLY 3,000 ACRES OF URBAN WASTELAND INTO ATTRACTIVE COUNTRYSIDE.

GIVEN MORE THAN £5 MILLION A YEAR TO SUPPORT OUR ARTS, HERITAGE AND SPORT.

TRANSFORMED OUR CITY CENTRES WITH MAJOR ENVIRONMENTAL IMPROVEMENTS.

PIONEERED DEVELOPMENT OF REVOLUTIONARY WASTE PROCESSING – TURNING REFUSE INTO OIL.

This Easter Monday, the Greater Manchester Council will be abolished.

During its two year trial by Parliament, the GMC – along with the other doomed metropolitan county councils – stood accused of running the county's affairs in a cavalier and extravagant manner.

It was, said Government Ministers, "wasteful and unnecessary." It duplicated the work of other councils (the districts). It caused tension and conflict. And, worst of all, claimed the Government, it spent far too much of the ratepayers' money.

Of course, the truth is rather different, as the majority of people acknowledged during the Abolition Bill's progress through Parliament. And as even more people are now rapidly discovering, to their cost.

Abolition's prime and much-repeated aim, you might recall, was "to save ratepayers' money." Indeed, former Environment Secretary Patrick Jenkin told the House of Commons: "If we don't achieve substantial savings (£100 million a year was the figure he quoted) when this exercise is completed, we shall have failed."

GMC always warned that far from saving money, abolition would cost Greater Manchester ratepayers dearly. And today,

even before the County Council has gone, the dire consequences of its axeing shout their costly message from the headlines of almost every newspaper.

Soaring rates, threats of huge cuts to key services being handed over by GMC, and the proposed loss of hundreds of council jobs, are some of the immediate and direct 'benefits' of abolition.

Of course, there are also a few disbenefits which the Government doesn't like us to talk about. So we've put them into pictures instead.

What's that? They all appear to highlight the work of a successful, caring, efficient, dynamic and enterprising county council?

Yes, that's right. But after Greater Manchester Council is buried on Monday, how long will it take before a very different picture emerges?

GMC
WE MADE GREATER MANCHESTER GREATER.

Figure 6.3 Abolition: last word from the Greater Manchester Council
Source: The Guardian, 27 March 1986.

battle over local government autonomy.

How could such a battle be pursued by the local government opposition? The Government would have the full force of the law at its disposal. Previous experience was not too encouraging. Local authority resistance to the Conservative 1972 Housing Finance Act had all but fizzled out, leaving Clay Cross as something of a sacrificial lamb and martyr. The authority might have gone into the Labour movement's annals of heroic resistance, but the reality was that councillors were disqualified and surcharged, a commissioner was sent in, and the Act was only overturned after a Labour government returned to power in Westminster in 1974. It was central power that was decisive. The real lesson of Clay Cross was more the way resistance to the 1980 Housing Act had so easily been overcome (see chapter 4). No council had wanted to be another Clay Cross. So although some, like the GLC, stated that they would refuse to implement rate-capping cuts and others predicted 'a social explosion' in the inner cities and if the cuts went through, most observers saw opposition going the same way as in the past: reluctant obedience.

With rate-capping, however, there seemed to be more hope of successful opposition. This was partly because of the experience of earlier cuts combined with the politicization of local government in general. But also, it looked as though many councils would not be left with any real choice. The 1984/5 spending targets had left 'offending' councils with three options:

1 make cuts as demanded;
2 go for partial compliance but protect services as much as possible, using rate income and hence also attracting severe penalties for overspending (and hence possible inclusion on a future rate-capping list); or
3 refuse to implement the cuts or to raise rates to cover costs and penalties, hence risking bankruptcy and illegality.

Most councils, helped by creative accounting, took the second course. There is of course a large gray area between options 1 and 2. Liverpool City Council, dominated by councillors from the 'hard-Left' Militant Tendency within the Labour Party, took the third course – refusal. And a few councils, mostly controlled by the right wing of the Labour Party, saw no option but to take the first course and to make cuts.

The rationale of this third group was clear enough. The leader of South Tyneside, for instance, said 'We would rather make the cuts ourselves and be left to govern rather than let central government do it by defying the targets' (*The Guardian*, 14 January 1984). In Cleveland, the council leader emphasized another aspect of the same argument: 'The Labour group takes no pleasure in these decisions which it believes are wrong, unnecessary and damaging to the Cleveland community. It accepts them only because the alternative imposed by the Secretary of State would be worse' (ibid., 6 January 1984).

But these councils not only found themselves implementing cuts in services they had been elected to improve, and at the expense of those they claimed to represent. They also severely strained local labour movements and local Labour Parties. At times this tension resulted in open and damaging splits. For instance, in Durham NUPE (National Union of Public Employees) campaigned against self-imposed education cuts, and in Cleveland a joint union committee saw the decision to cut spending as a betrayal and recommended industrial action to oppose the council. The Labour group split in Newcastle, when service cuts of £4m still led to 10 per cent rate increases. In Wakefield, the local Labour Party actually passed a vote of no confidence in the council's controlling Labour group, after cuts in social services were announced. Dissident councillors and protesters occupied two nurseries that were to be closed while the council replied with legal proceedings. Quite apart from councillors being elected for Labour only to carry out Conservative policies, overt compliance with the Government looked an easy way to destroy local Labour Parties and Labour groups.

The situation in Liverpool worked out rather differently (see also Parkinson, 1985). As early as the summer of 1983 the City Council's Labour group forecast open confrontation with the centre. Despite debts of £25m, they would continue a programme of job creation and house-building without making cuts or increasing rates. This, they claimed, was justified by a substantial Labour majority on the council and among the city's MPs – not to mention Liverpool's pressing social needs. Mr Jenkin replied by invoking the spectre of a commissioner (as well as publicizing government spending in the city). The crisis rumbled on for the next nine months, periodically hitting the headlines. While the Government drew back from asking for parliamentary legislation to send in commissioners (perhaps a wise decision in view of the rate-capping and abolition debate) Liverpool steadfastly refused to draw up a budget and set a rate. To everyone's surprise, it found it had no legal duty to provide a budget by a particular date. Spending was maintained by using reserves as well as by drawing on financial support from other councils (for example, the GLC and other London boroughs lent £30m with council property as security). On the other hand the national Labour Party baulked at risking illegality and recommended a compromise deal involving a 60 per cent rise in rates (similar to local Liberal/Conservative alternative budgets), although this was still less than the massive 120 per cent rise necessary both to support the council's spending plans and make up for government penalties. In contrast to those councils accepting cuts, Liverpool's stand seemed to strengthen the local Labour Party and increase its support. Most local unions took strike action to support the council, while six councillors who wished to opt out of confrontation and vote against any illegal budget with the Government became an irrelevance when the May local government elections returned Labour with a boosted 17-seat majority. The Cabinet and Patrick Jenkin in particular had apparently expected reverses for the 'militant Marxists', as they saw Liverpool's council. Flabbergasted at the actual election result, and perhaps their determination weakened by the Paving Bill, they organized a compromise. The Liverpool councillors, although publicly unyielding, had little option left but to do a deal.

The financial concessions made by the Government were, in reality, quite small. The most important concession was to continue funding urban programme projects which had been running for more than three years and no longer attracted government grants, although some extra Rate Support Grant was found under the remit of earlier 'miscalculation'. However, for every £1 the Government gave back, another £2 was saved in penalties. The council also trimmed future spending plans quite substantially and in the event got away with a 17 per cent rate rise, as well as vindication of its 'no cuts, no redundancies' stance. But however minor the financial concessions, the political impact was enormous. As an angry *Times* editorial stated the following day:

> Today in Liverpool municipal militancy is vindicated. . . . What matters is not so much the size of Mr Jenkin's concession but the example set. . . . By exempting Liverpool from the consequences of spending above its target the Government subverts its whole local government financial policy of the past four years. It issues an open invitation to councils to say the caps don't fit and they won't wear them. (11 July 1984)

As it became clear that the Government's rate-capping legislation would succeed, leading local authority opposition figures began to call for defiance. At the Labour Party local government conference in Nottingham, in February 1984, Ken Livingstone argued for non-compliance with any rate-capping law. Accepting Neil Kinnock's directive that councillors should not resign or disqualify themselves, Livingstone saw united non-compliance and refusal to cut budgets by 20 or 30 councils as a way to nullify such a law. He was strongly supported by David Blunkett, who noted the necessity for local government to act in its own defence – councillors could not 'wait crouching behind dustbins hoping that someone will bail us after a general election'. However, although the chair of the NEC Local Government Affairs Committee quoted Poplarism as an example of how breaking the law helped make better laws, the conference was not united on non-compliance. Pointedly, the stance of the parliamentary Labour Party and the NEC as a whole remained one of sympathy rather than active backing. The non-compliance strategy was, it is true, fleshed out over succeeding months. Livingstone warned against accepting the bribe of gentle cuts in the first year and showed the electoral advantages of resistance, while David Blunkett reaffirmed the need for unity and 'sophistication': 'We are not running at the first brick wall that appears in front of us and allowing the government to scoop our brains up off the floor – we don't want martyrs. We don't want another Clay Cross. We want to succeed' (*The Guardian*, 31 May 1984).

Nonetheless, these plans could now be dismissed easily, by the more cynical or realistic, as ritual intonations without long-term effects. Any unified non-compliance would break down, leaving one or two isolated councils. Indeed, Liverpool was already leading the way in the role of martyr while, as we have seen, several councils were implementing cuts even in advance of rate-capping. On the 23 May, leaders of Labour councils met in secret to thrash out a common policy – and they failed (Rentoul and Wolmar, 1984).

Three factors helped to change this scenario. First, the political climate appeared to favour opposition. Labour had done quite well in the May local government elections and the June Euro-elections. Together with the results of public opinion polls on local government issues, these suggested that public support could be gained for confrontation and that the electoral results could well be advantageous for the Labour opposition. The Government's use of rate-capping – 'constructing a hit list' as it became known – also played right into its opponents hands. Despite the official attempt to portray rate-capping as a neutral and objective procedure brought about by unfortunate circumstances, everyone concerned knew that there was a 'hit list' of Labour councils that the Government found particularly objectionable for political reasons. Rate-capping would allow the centre to cripple these councils. This identities of most of these were well known in advance of the rate-capping procedure: the GLC, ILEA, Camden, Hackney, Greenwich, Islington, Lambeth, Southwark, Basildon, Sheffield, Merseyside and South Yorkshire. Around this core hovered a group of between 10 and 15 other councils on the margins of government tolerance, with another 20 or 30 identified as 'overspending councils'. A remarkably similar list of 'primary targets' had appeared in Conservative election manifesto guide-lines (for candidates) in 1983. The question was how to make this list 'official'. A *Financial Times* article conveys this well:

> The benchmark the Government said it would use is the grant related expenditure assessment (GREA). . . . This, however, produces the wrong list politically and only negligible savings. The only way to compile a list of 12–20 Labour councils and achieve any savings is to measure the cash excess of budgets over targets. While this gives the biggest savings and lists the Government's biggest bêtes noires, it is highly contentious because targets are arbitrary figures. The Government will need to find a way to link the hit list in the table to the GREA system, at least nominally. (21 February 1984)

The Environment Minister himself confirmed in so many words that this was how rate-capping would proceed. In the committee stage of the Bill (February 1984) he was asked to give some illustration of how the selection procedure would work. He gave 11 different tests which could have been applied to 1983/4 council budgets, using a number of criteria such as spending over 20 per cent above GREA, spending 2 per cent over target, spending increases and rates increases over the past three or four years. A list of 33 councils were selected by some test, but the GLC, ILEA, Islington, Greenwich, Basildon and Merseyside appeared on all. Other 'hit lists' habituees appeared on many of the other test runs but, the Minister said, he only wanted between 10 and 20 councils on the final list for 1985/6. The validity of this exercise was further undermined when the crudity and subjectivity of the supposedly most objective part of the 'hit list' calculation, the GREA level, was again exposed. Not only were there simple errors (like underestimating the length of motorways) and technical limitations (such as using local rateable values first fixed in 1973), but just as the 'hit list' was being constructed evidence came out suggesting that GREAs had been directly manipulated to give the desired

political results. In a leaked memo, George Younger (an environment minister) described as 'political dynamite' the way in which
GREA estimates of necessary expenditure for inner-city housing
had been arbitrarily reduced (*The Guardian*, 25 September, 25
October 1984). The councils affected were predominantly Labour
councils including those on the 'hit list'. This whole flavour of
political bias and subjectivity was exacerbated by the financial
treatment meted out to probable 'hit list' authorities. It appeared
that sharply reduced spending targets for 1984/5 for the Metropolitan
County Councils, and corresponding reductions in RSG announced
in December 1983, was designed to set up these councils as easy
political targets. According to *The Guardian* the Government was
desperately worried about Tory opposition to rate-capping but:

> Mr Jenkin knows that, by setting unachievable targets and stepping
> up the penalties for failing to make the required cuts, he will raise
> the temperature of the rates debate next spring. His legislation can
> then be presented as the only measure which can cope with the
> problem. (Ibid., 19 December 1983)

So the political climate favoured opposition. But, secondly, it
appeared that a means had been found for actually carrying out
this opposition. Liverpool had shown the tactical advantages of not
setting a budget or a rate which, it had now been discovered, was
not illegal. The Government had been put on the defensive and
the debate had shifted from one of 'overspending' to local electoral
legitimacy and the social need for services. Finally, the 'hit list'
authorities had established their own organization centred on the
Local Government Campaign Unit. As well as increasingly good
reasons for non-compliance, they now had a mechanism to organize
unified non-compliance. A conference of threatened Labour councils
'Forging the Links', was organized in Sheffield for 6/7 July to try
to reach a common strategy.

In the end the conference largely went along with a three-point
plan put forward by David Blunkett. First, Labour councils – rate-
capped or not – should refuse to cut jobs or services for 1985/6.
Secondly, if rate-capped, no council should ask for 'derogation'
(revision of the budgetary ceiling). Under the Rates Act this would
give the DOE the power to set down precise guide-lines about
spending for years ahead. If there were to be any negotiations over
rate-capping, this should only be in the form of mass meetings
between the DOE and all the councils. Finally, the campaign should
be co-ordinated to achieve unified action and timing by the affected

councils, who should also make use of local union and public support. While the centre could easily pick off isolated councils, it would baulk at the prospect of taking on 20 or 30 at once.

But what form was this united action to take? It was here that Liverpool had shown the way. Councils should refuse to set a rate. This would also naturally co-ordinate action in tune with the financial year. Another advantage was that the action, although clearly disobedient, was not illegal, although in the long term councils would be bankrupt and councillors would be liable to surcharge and disqualification. But in the short term it would be the DOE that would be under most pressure. (See Fielding and Seyd, 1984; Rentoul and Wolmer 1984; *The Guardian*, 2 July 1984; *New Statesman*, 13 July 1984).

Most of the threatened authorities agreed for this plan, although some, like Birmingham with more room for financial manœuvre as well as more right-wing leadership, dissented. On the other hand Islington – where rate-capping was inevitable – went ahead and set a draft 1985/6 budget well in excess of likely DOE guide-lines. Nonetheless, although there was now a plan and some sort of pledge, the overall problem remained. How could the line be maintained and co-ordinated civil disobedience undertaken successfully when some individual councils and councillors might well be able to do better alone through 'fudging and nudging' – especially when the DOE, well used to tactics of divide and rule, would help them to do so?

Luckily, the Government came to the rescue. First it settled with Liverpool. Although the financial concessions were relatively minor, the Government had backed down and the confrontation strategy was seen to work. If just Liverpool had caused so much trouble, think what 20 councils could do. This settlement was established just after the Sheffield conference and was a major fillip to its conclusions. But even more importantly the Government enforced unity – on 26 July it announced the rate-capping 'hit list'. This seemed to leave these authorities with little choice but non-compliance. Although Patrick Jenkin had considered the obvious ploy of going very softly the first year and using the 'thin edge of the wedge' method, he found his hand was tied. Partly because of the 'Pym pledge' to shire counties (a deal ensuring that the Rates Act was passed) he needed £1bn extra from the Treasury for local government spending. The Treasury pressed for as much rate-capping as possible. This also meant that any plan to destabilize the rebels by leaving Sheffield off the list (widely seen as ringleader but not among the very hard core of 'overspenders') had to be abandoned. Even though rate-capping was still kept as low as Jenkin could manage (level cash funding for 15 authorities and a 1.5 per cent cut for the GLC, the ILEA and Greenwich) it looked as if the combined effect of inflation and past 'creative accounting' would mean much heavier real cuts. 'Fudge and nudge' did not seem to be possible, leaving (it appeared) only the options of capitulation or non-compliance.

The way the 'hit list' was constructed and announced politicized the affair even further. Fourteen councils appeared on a list constructed by combining those councils spending 4 per cent and more above targets and 25 per cent above GREA (GLC, ILEA, South Yorkshire, Leicester, Basildon, Portsmouth, Thamesdown, Islington, Southwark, Camden, Greenwich, Lambeth, Lewisham and Haringey). Even this list, however, did not catch all those councils the Government wanted, and so Hackney, Sheffield, Merseyside and Brent were added at a final ministerial meeting. The inclusion of Portsmouth (Conservative-controlled, like Brent) was part of a bizarre episode in which the list was kept under wraps until a by-election was fought there in July – but in the event leaks suggesting the city's inclusion contributed to a dramatic defeat for the Conservatives.

As soon as rate-capping was announced leaders of the 16 Labour councils involved agreed to a policy of total non-compliance. As a first step, none would apply for derogation. This action received unanimous support from Labour's NEC as well as backing from the TUC General Council, reaffirmed at both the TUC and Labour Party conferences in the Autumn. The NEC even sent a letter to all Labour council groups and local parties endorsing the Sheffield conference plan and urging them to join in a common strategy of non-compliance. The significance of all this was that both the Labour Party and the TUC had come out explicitly in support of potentially illegal action. This was quite encouraging solidarity compared with the local government campaigns against the 1972 Housing Finance Act and the 1980 Housing Act.

There were, however, several large gaps in the councils' defences. First, would Labour groups actually be able to hold out against the threat of surcharge and disqualification? Evidence from Liverpool and elsewhere suggested that not all councillors would go along with such a decision. Another problem was whether council work-forces would go along with policies that could well leave them without pay if funds finally ran out. In Liverpool both NUPE and the National Union of Teachers (NUT) had already registered opposition to going bankrupt, and had not participated in a 24-

hour strike in support of the council because of this (although other unions were more supportive). One way round this might be to default on interest payments rather than wages, as the London Labour authorities agreed at one stage to do. But this was also illegal, as councils are obliged to pay debt charges before all else. Similarly, would local communities support their councils? While local polls showed widespread opposition to rate-capping, only a minority registered support for illegal action on the part of councils. Nor were councils necessarily popular – in one London borough, councillors even admitted that 'They aren't on speaking terms with their tenants' (quoted in Fielding and Seyd, 1984). Finally, even the tactics of the Blunkett plan were not watertight. It was in fact a legal duty for *precepting* second-tier authorities to set a rate by 10 March, including rate-capped GLC, ILEA, Merseyside and South Yorkshire. This would disrupt unified action. There were also internal complaints that the whole strategy of non-compliance was still too defensive in a broader political sense. It would still be about 'overspending' rather than the links between public services with social needs and economic growth (for example, Morrell and Bundred, 1984). In the event it was a combination of these factors, plus a need for cuts substantially less than the 'end of (local socialist) civilization' scenario sometimes propounded, that led to the collapse of the campaign.

6.3 The Collapse of Resistance

The first round in the battle went to the councils. Initial unity was maintained when no council applied for derogation including, to everyone's surprise, Conservative-run Portsmouth and the hung council of Brent. It was widely thought that Portsmouth had been included just to show that the procedure would work, but apparently even here councillors could not stomach the prospect of the DoE taking detailed control of their budget. They decided to implement cuts of £1.4m (9 per cent) instead (Smith, 1984). It seemed as if a parliamentary by-election loss had been quite in vain. The Government tried to pick off what it thought were less determined councils (see Smith, 1984 for details). Even before the derogation deadline, approaches were made to the traditionally more compliant council of Thamesdown (Swindon) just before councillors voted on the issue. One of the area's Conservative MPs, who was also Parliamentry Private Secretary to the Minister for Local Government, implied that sympathetic treatment would be forthcoming if the council caved in. The attempt failed.

The story of Lewisham is even more bizarre. It would only need one council to break ranks to give the Government considerable public leverage over the rest (as events were finally to show). Lewisham believed it faced a rate-cap cut of something like 13 per cent even on a standstill budget for 1985/6, implying savage cuts with something like 3,000 job losses. But early in October, Lewisham's treasurer had been given 'signals' that the DOE would allow councils suffering from the effects of creative accounting to apply for a form of partial derogation. They might receive 'special funds' without triggering the wide powers of DOE control specified by the Rates Act. Council officials estimated that this could mean reducing the cut by £8m, leaving only a 7 per cent cut on a standstill budget.

These signals had been relayed to Lewisham through the Chartered Institute of Public Finance and Accountancy (CIPFA). But soon afterwards *The Guardian* picked up a scent of the story (3 October 1984). Next day, Thursday, the DOE reacted 'like a scalded cat' as one Lewisham councillor put it, and called the story of a generous verbal offer to relax Lewisham's spending limit 'complete rubbish' (ibid., 4 October 1984). Despite this denial, later the same day the offer was confirmed at a direct meeting between Lewisham officials and Peter Owen, Deputy Secretary at the DOE. It was only at the council's policy committee meeting on Thursday evening that the offer was finally turned down.

Clearly, the DOE and the Government were rattled about repeating the Liverpool experience, only this time on a much larger scale. It had now decided that the derogation deadline would be flexible, rather than expiring on 1 October as originally indicated. Meanwhile, the Labour rate-capped councils agreed to refuse to provide ministers with information about their financial position as required under the Rates Act. This amounted to a first act of defiance of the law. The AMA, already boycotting all talks about abolition, threatened to withdraw from all contact with the Government. At the same time, shire counties expressed dismay at the 1985/6 RSG. The 'Pym pledge' had run out, while Jenkin had been concerned with channelling extra grants to Labour inner-city authorities to smooth rate-capping. At the time of the Liverpool settlement the Government had been criticized from its own back-benches for 'suddenly forking out millions of pounds for socialist Liverpool while loyal Tory councils faced cuts' (*Financial Times*, 11 July 1984). Would rate-capping repeat the Liverpool experience, but now many times over?

It seemed that the first test of non-compliance had been passed, but the basic contradictions of the campaign remained. Publicly, and especially in the eyes of their active supporters, councils were pledged to go the whole way into illegality. But for most councils leaders and councillors, the threats of surcharge, bankruptcy, disqualification and losing control of their councils were too much to countenance. In private most council leaders probably saw the rate-capping campaign more as a means of protest by causing as much trouble and getting as much favourable publicity as possible, while in the end staying legal. This is in fact what Liverpool had done with some success. But the Government meanwhile had learnt from its propaganda defeat at the hands of Liverpool's Militant councillors. Jenkin had no desire whatsoever to repeat the experience. He also knew of the inherent splits and contradictions of the rebels' positions. Rather than let himself be drawn into endless negotiations, he could afford to let the rebels stew in their own juice. This would be all the more effective with judicious financial intervention, in order to introduce rate-capping gently and leave councils with a way out.

The first crack in the councils' facade appeared early in 1985. It had been agreed that on 7 March the rate-capped councils would declare that they would not set rates and so move into illegality. This would ensure unity between the upper-tier councils that were legally required to set a rate by 10 March, and the lower-tier councils where no time-limit was specified. But Merseyside and South Yorkshire had already signalled that they did not intend to go illegal. Moreover, at a private meeting on the 19 February, council leaders resolved only to declare that 'It will be impossible for the authority to make a rate at the present time.' Their document pushed home the implications of this decision: this wording was 'not a declaration of a fixed intention not to make a rate, which would be unlawful' (*New Statesman*, 22 March 1985).

This situation would isolate the GLC and ILEA, which were still committed to going illegal on 10 March. The Government's soft-pedalling approach made a climb-down all the easier. The rate-cap level had been revised upwards for six authorities, while a redistribution of RSG towards the cities (despite vociferous protests from Conservative shires and back-bench MPs) eased things further. Perhaps cuts need not be made after all. This would clearly take the wind out of the sails of the campaign and this is what happened with the GLC and with ILEA. The GLC rate-cap had been set quite high at 36.5 pence. By February 1985 it had become clear that this did not mean the massive £140m cuts originally feared –

these might only be as low as £30m and creative accounting might even turn this into growth. In this case, many argued, what was the point of illegality?

The Labour groups in both the GLC and ILEA split publicly over the issue. After a number of all-night meetings a coalition of Conservative and dissident Labour councillors succeeded in setting a rate even lower than the rate-cap, defeating 'ultra-left' proposals for illegality and 'centre-left' plans for the rate-cap level to be followed by a deficit budget. Despite lower rate income, and because of lower government penalties, this would mean a cut of only £11m and hence – with creative accounting – even some growth. Things went the same way for ILEA.

The GLC was widely regarded as the flagship of local socialism. Its defection from the no-rates position provided the Government with a massive propaganda coup just when other councils were deliberating whether to go into illegality. To rub it all in, the coal miners' year-long strike ended in their defeat shortly afterwards. This had sometimes been regarded as the other side of a Labour movement pincer attack on Thatcherism and it seemed that both sides had failed.

One by one other councils fell into line. But this was no easy business, for the councils had pledged precisely the opposite. As Lansley (1985) points out in a detailed commentary, the battle was no longer against the Government but within Labour Parties. This was because, as Ken Livingstone (leader of the GLC) later admitted, 'Some council leaders made the mistake of exaggerating their ability to deliver what was being agreed and this led to the unions and Constituency Labour Parties expecting more than we finally knew we could deliver'. (*New Statesman*, 22 March 1985), see also *Marxism Today*, March and May 1985, for interviews with Livingstone and David Blunkett, leader of Sheffield City Council).

By this time the Government was letting its considerable legal powers pile on the pressure. District auditors issued warnings of surcharge and disqualification, and the Audit Commission went as far as to send each councillor on the remaining rebel councils a letter warning them of imminent surcharge. In a separate action the High Court gave Hackney Borough Council until the end of May to set a rate, and this date also became a deadline beyond which the auditors threatened legal action.

Sheffield set a rate early in May, again when a coalition of Labour dissidents and opposition councillors defeated the Labour leadership. In Lewisham, the Conservatives set a rate while the Labour group was temporarily absent from the council chamber, leading to the resignation of its leader. Rates were set in Hackney and Southwark only after 'ugly scenes of abuse, recrimination and intimidation' (Lansley, 1985, p. 31). The leader of Southwark collapsed with nervous exhaustion while in a bizarrely ironic gesture, Labour councillors voting for a rate were sent white feathers. Only four councils – Camden, Lambeth, Greenwich and Liverpool – survived to flout the auditors' 31 May deadline, and of these Camden and Greenwich set rates early in June. After a particularly byzantine wrangle within the Merseyside Labour movement, including strikes, counter-strikes and deals with foreign financiers, Liverpool council set a rate in mid-June. This left only Lambeth, headed by 'Red Ted' Knight.

By this time the district auditors had taken legal action against 81 councillors in Liverpool and Lambeth who had voted against setting a rate. They were to be surcharged for the losses supposedly resulting from rate delays. Again, the Audit Commission let the political cat out of the legal bag. Cases would only be brought against Liverpool and Lambeth in the first instance because of the difficulty of proving wilful negligence elsewhere and because of the 'political situation'. The Director of the Commission was even more explicit: Liverpool and Lambeth were

> a tragedy enfolding day by day. . . . The case of Liverpool and Lambeth has nothing to do with waste and incompetence, it has to do with the law; and the commission I serve is here to see that the law of the land is obeyed and it will be obeyed and those who are willing to flout the law will have to pay the consequences. The process is 'irreversible'. (*The Guardian*, 28 June 1985)

The affected councillors appealed, but the High Court found against them early in 1986. They had been 'a pinnacle of political perversity' according to one judge. At this the auditors threatened action against other councillors in the remaining six authorities which did not set rates until May or June 1985 (Camden, Islington, Greenwich, Hackney, Islington, Southwark and Sheffield). The Liverpool councillors determined to appeal further, but the Lambeth council-lors did not and were disqualified. The three Labour councillors remaining in office were able to run the council for several weeks (at one stage only with the help of a High Court order barring a Conservative rates decision) until new elections in May 1986 resulted in a renewed Labour majority. Meanwhile, the rate-capping process continued. In the autumn of 1985 the Government announced that 32 authorities were to be rate-capped in 1986/7 – although many of these were the joint boards and quangos which were being set up to take over the functions of the soon-to-be-abolished GLC and Metropolitan County Councils. In these cases the imposition of central control over local autonomy was less direct. There were no direct elections to these bodies and the Government had already taken control of their budgets and staffing. In summing up the defeat of the 'local socialists' Lansley concluded that 'First the wrong strategy was adopted; and secondly even that strategy was badly handled' (1985, p. 29). Moreover, the Liverpool propaganda coup had been misleading.

Indeed the Liverpool–Conservative Government conflict had gone on throughout the rate-capping campaign, and as the council also refused to set a rate it became a part of it. But if this account shows the capacity for autonomous local action, (and also the way in which local social relations help produce different results in different places) it also shows up very well the weakness of the local position.

The Liverpool council was set on building good-quality council homes and renovating existing local authority stock. This provoked some local opposition from housing associations and linked community groups, and even more from the Government, which were pushing for owner-occupation. In February 1985, and smarting from his propaganda defeat, Patrick Jenkin threatened to use a forgotten clause of the 1980 Local Government Act allowing the Government to veto contracts which would take capital spending over centrally determined limits. However, the Liverpool council neatly side-stepped the Government's attack by selling its interest in municipal mortgage repayments to a consortium of foreign banks. This raised £40m and was enough to keep central spending on council house-building going. Rather late in the day, the Government began to look at ways of making this dodge illegal in the future.

This was by no means the end of the story. The council was not prepared to raise rates, in order to pay for its programmes, beyond 9 per cent and in June 1985 set a deficit budget on this basis. As the council and many commentators had pointed out, council spending had been run down during previous Liberal–Conservative coalition administrations and as the city had a very low base from which to calculate spending targets like GREA. These could not, therefore, reflect the city's real needs (see Parkinson, 1985). This argument did not, of course, impress the Government or the auditors, who noted that, while there was no such thing as an illegal budget, legal action could still be taken on the grounds that losses would result. Learning from his past experiences, Jenkin refused to negotiate and let the council stew. By the end of July the auditor was warning that the money would soon run out and most of the council's 30,000 staff would face dismissal.

This effectively turned the issue – as in the rate-capping campaign – from a battle against the government to a battle within the Labour movement. This was intensified by the conflicts within the Labour Party over the influence of the Trotskyte Militant Tendency, and what should be done about it. The council's manual work-force was the major power base of Liverpool's Militant-dominated Labour group, but the threat of dismissal ruptured this accord. Instead of strikes in support of the council, strike action was threatened against it and at one stage councillors had to force their way past angry pickets from their own work-force to enter the council chamber. The Government turned the screw further by blocking loans from the Public Loans Works Board. A £30m loan from a firm of London stockbrokers delayed the crisis slightly, but by the end of September the council issued 90-day redundancy notices to 31,000 employees. NALGO members refused to process the notices whereas other employees refused to accept them. In a bizarre twist, council officers hired a fleet of taxis from which they threw the offending notices into school playgrounds.

The whole issue of Labour Party–Militant relations threatened to sour Labour's annual conference, just when it was beginning to recover in the opinion polls. David Blunkett, leader of Sheffield City Council, set up a deal with the Liverpool Labour group backed by trade union leaders, the NEC and Labour front-bench MPs. Liverpool would open its books to this group, look to accept their recommendations and in return other councils could find some extra financial help. The redundancy notices were withdrawn, although replaced by plans for a one-month lay-off avoiding redundancy payments, although this perhaps had more to do with a High Court decision declaring them illegal than with the revised plan. Meanwhile, further public conflicts between Liverpool Militants and Neil Kinnock, the Labour Party leader, almost broke up the rescue attempt.

The rescue plan, engineered by the Director General of the GLC who was in fact gaining a reputation as the local government financial wizard, went like this. Rates would increase by 15 per cent to produce £19m extra income, various creative accounting dodges would raise £25m (for example by capitalizing housing repairs and leasing central-heating plant). Loans from other councils increased charges for services and increased council rents would bridge the remainder of the £15m budget deficit and provide £19m surplus. Blunkett, the NEC, Kinnock, national unions and local unions supported the plan.

Liverpool City Council did not, sticking to its original 9 per cent rate rise and asking for bigger loans from other councils. Liverpool was now living from day to day, with British Telecom beginning to take action over unpaid bills and bailiffs arriving to impound council-owned cars. By mid-November only seven days money was left – only voluntary emergency services would be left running. Another improved rescue plan, needing only a 10 per cent rate rise and higher loans from other councils, was proposed by Blunkett. But it was the threat of the final withdrawal of its own local support, in the council manual unions, that changed the council's mood. Again cocking a snoop at all and sundry the council fixed a £30m deal from Swiss banks allowing it to avoid rate increases (later increased to £60m over two years) and accepted the rest of the Blunkett plan. A balanced budget was now possible – but only on a 'live now, pay later' basis. Early in 1986 a new crisis was developing with another emerging deficit unless rates were increased dramatically. But yet again, the Militant-dominated council side-stepped the problem by doing a deal with international capital. This time the Japanese Yasuodo Bank lent a further £30m which, in addition to creative accounting, would allow Liverpool to balance its 1986/7 budget without rate increases or any significant service cuts. But huge municipal debts were building up in Liverpool as elsewhere and Labour leaders were beginning to wonder if this would prejudice their reflation plans – to be led by council spending on infrastructure – if they won the next election.

The local government rebels and the Thatcher Government had by now reached a stand-off. Abolition and rate-capping had clearly succeeded in a technical sense: offending councils were abolished and rates were capped. It remained doubtful, however, if these measures contributed very much to the Government's macroeconomic aims and in pushing through the legislation the Cabinet had scored something of a political own-goal. The Government's actions were widely seen as undemocratic and unnecessary, and had even alienated many of its own supporters. On the other hand, the opposition had overreached itself with the rate-capping campaign. The might of legislative power remained with central government and against this the rebel councils were left in disarray.

The first response of the Government to its political defects was to try to extend its powers even further, into those areas like political campaigning where the opposition had come off best. But soon it also became obvious that the rate-capping legislation had

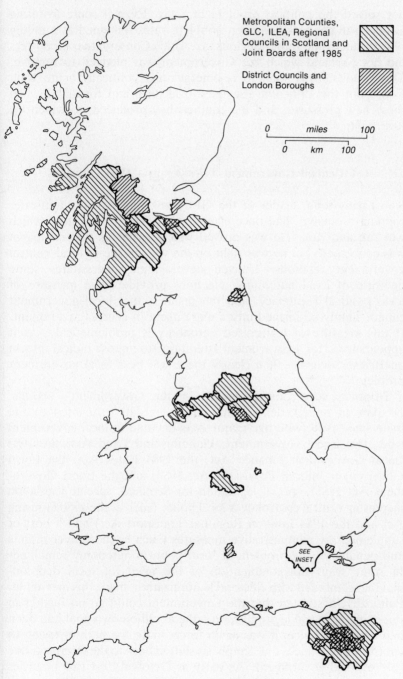

Metropolitan Counties,
GLC, ILEA, Regional
Councils in Scotland and
Joint Boards after 1985

District Councils and
London Boroughs

0   miles   100

0   km   100

SEE
INSET

Figure 6.4 Councils hit by rate-capping up to 1986

not solved the political problem of rates. Even if some irritating Labour-run councils had been nobbled, rates remained as a mildly redistributive and rather obvious tax, which Conservative supporters did not like and which the Government was pledged to remove. This problem was soon to re-emerge in a politically acute way. Could not this difficulty also be solved once and for all? It is to these new pressures, and the conflict they produced, to which we turn next.

6.4 Central Government Tries Again – 1985 Onwards

Ken Livingstone, leader of the GLC, talking about the anti-rate-capping campaign, had once claimed that 'This is one story which will run and run.' He was proved wrong as far as that campaign was concerned, but he was right on the wider issue of local–central government relations. Uneven development necessitates some measure of local autonomy, elections provide some measure of local political legitimacy, and the result is that local government cannot simply be formed into a mere agent of central government. If this measure of legitimized autonomy is problematical – as it appears to be for a government attempting to impose radical reform on British society – then clearly there will be a local government problem.

This was very soon confirmed by the Government's actions. Despite an unprecedented amount of legislation devoted to the issue since 1979, with five major Acts devoted to local government (the 1980 Local Government, Planning and Land Act; the 1982 Local Government Finance Act; the 1984 Rates Act; the Local Government Interim Provisions Act 1984; and the Local Government Act 1985), special legislation for Scotland, specific legislation increasing central control over local policy (such as the 1980 Housing Act and the 1984 London Regional Transport Act) and a host of supplementary administrative measures (such as those over targets and penalties), the problem of local political autonomy remained. In some ways the combination of the need for local decision-making, combined with electoral legitimization, made this inevitable. Politically, it seemed that the Government could go no further in removing electoral legitimization – the abolition own-goal had been bad enough. Hence, it was again forced onto the path of trying to control what councils did. Emphasis shifted back to the interpretative role of local government. As early as October 1984 two inquiries were set up to try to deal with these problems. One was concerned more with guarding the Government's flank against the successful publicity campaigns like that mounted against abolition, and at the same time restricting the scope that local governments had for making political points. According to Mr Jenkin, these features were 'a cancer' which threatened local democracy. The second inquiry was even more wideranging, covering the whole question of local government finance and functions – although its central concern soon became the problem of rates. We will look at each in turn.

THE LOCAL GOVERNMENT PROBLEM WON'T GO AWAY: POLITICS

The first inquiry was set up in February 1985, with the distinguished Labour Queen's Counsel David Widdicombe as chair. But this was always something of a façade. Before the inquiry was even set up a government committee – chaired by William Waldegrave, Junior Environment Minister – was already planning legislation of the sort required to curb counter-attacks from local government. Apparently, it was well on the way to draft legislation before the Widdicombe committee made its interim report in August 1985 (Campbell and Forbes, 1986).

The interim report was probably rather disappointing for the Government. The need for legislation had always been presented as a matter of stopping 'party political propaganda on the rates'. The trouble was, party political propaganda had always been illegal. The report in essence recommended little more than a clarification of the situation (and noted in passing that most public complaints had been generated by the government's own campaign to sell British Telecom shares). It proposed a statutory ban on council publicity of a party political nature (which was already illegal), monies from sector 137 of the Local Government Act – used widely by opposition councils for a variety of purposes – should not be used for publicity, and councils should keep a separate publicity account. Even this was challenged by a minority report stressing the need for local advocacy, while Widdicombe himself had concluded that:

It is important that at all times, particularly in times of wide political differences, our political system should accommodate the free expression of opposing views... it is right for local authorities to be able to explain their views on controversial matters affecting them. (Quoted in Campbell and Forbes, 1980, p. 113).

This did not go far enough for the Government, which nevertheless tried to make the best of it in public announcements. Its concerns were demonstrated much more by the submissions made by the DOE to the committee, objecting to council support for such things as nuclear-free zones, police-monitoring units, enterprise boards and benefit-uptake campaigns. Using Widdicombe as much as possible, new legislation – the Local Government Bill 1985 – was introduced in November. This would introduce a detailed code of conduct specifying the style, content, distribution and cost of publicity material and require separate publicity amounts. Such measures would prevent campaigns like that against abolition being repeated. The Bill would also require rates to be set by 1 April each year – preventing another rate-capping campaign – and also require councils to receive written assent from each borrower before selling their mortgages. This would stop councils emulating Liverpool and side-stepping government financial controls.

From then on the Government ran into a number of difficulties. First, single-issue campaigns were to be exempted, although it is not clear if this was because of pressure from bodies like the National Council for Voluntary Organizations or because William Waldegrave's wife worked for the Coronary Prevention Group. Even more telling was opposition to the code of practice, which again united Conservatives in local government with their formal Labour opponents. As one objector put it, the Bill was short, hastily drafted, exceptionally wide-ranging, unnecessary to the purpose for which it was said to be required – and in many places so badly set out as to be virtually meaningless. Its provisions really could ban local authorities from telling you the time. Or they could ban almost nothing (Campbell and Forbes, 1986, p. 11). The House of Lords apparently agreed, stipulating that only material which appeared to be designed to increase public support for a political party should come under the proposed legislation, and that it should be up to complainants to prove this. Waldegrave stopped the code of conduct, proposing a new version which the House of Lords decided should only be advisory. Finally, the Bill was dropped in March 1986 until after the next election. Perhaps, by then, better ammunition could be found.

Something of this nature finally appeared in June 1986 with Widdicombe's final report (Widdicombe, 1986). Claiming that 'At its worst, politics can be a malign influence', Widdicombe recommended that local ombudsmen could consider complaints about council publicity, that any electors or ratepayers could seek a judicial review of publicity with power for courts to disqualify or surcharge councillors, and that a ban should be imposed on public-sector employees receiving more than 28 days paid leave a year for council duties. This would effectively remove 'twin tracking' where it was estimated that about 10 per cent of paid local government officials were also councillors elsewhere. The proposals would directly threaten many Labour councillors who also had local government jobs, while as many as 70,000 local government workers would become ineligible to stand as councillors. But these proposals were still hedged around with qualifications, which implicitly recognized a right to local government autonomy. The new Environment Secretary, Nicholas Ridley, postponed any legislative control until after the next election. He preferred the more concrete course of forcing councils to privatize their service delivery still further.

THE LOCAL GOVERNMENT PROBLEM WON'T GO AWAY: FINANCE

If one dimension of local government is the political autonomy granted by the electoral system, the other is the financial autonomy necessary for adequate local management. By 1986, the Thatcher Government had spent seven years searching for a way out of both these problems and, despite increasingly severe controls over local governments, seemed in the end to be banging against a brick wall. The Widdicombe inquiry and the failed Local Government Bill 1985 represented the latest attempt to deal with political autonomy in the local state. Similarly the same old problem remained of controlling local taxation and local spending.

The 'Scottish solution' of rate-capping had provided the model for the most far-reaching attempt to deal with these problems – but it was the 'Scottish problem' over rate taxation that forcefully pointed out that this was no real solution. For in early 1985 rates in Scotland were revalued – that is, increased to reflect current property values – again as a test of what might happen in England and Wales. At the same time cuts in RSG meant that higher rate income would be necessary in any case. The result was politically frightening for the Conservatives. Large and heavily increased rate bills dropping through people's front doors led to an uproar among Party activists and alienation among key supporters like small shopkeepers and richer owner-occupiers. The problem was brought forcefully to ministers' attention at a Conservative Party conference in Newcastle-upon-Tyne in March 1985. Scottish councillors saw their own political demise, 'If we are not protected we will soon be extinct' according to one representative, while others feared that when the problem reached England and Wales it would lose the next general election for the Conservatives. Something had to be done, quickly.

An immediate response was to spend a way out of trouble. Much against the opposition of the Treasury, a relief package was put together of £40m for commercial ratepayers and £10m for domestic (the Treasury later managed to have this reduced to a total of £30m). But this was too little too late. Grass-roots Conservative dissatisfaction was unabated, even leading to resignations of important local activists. Not only did this seem like electoral suicide if exported south of the Border, but any relief package would have to be far larger. A more radical response was clearly necessary. The old Conservative rallying cry – abolish the rates – a particular favourite with Mrs Thatcher – was adopted again.

Thatcher called a Cabinet meeting at the end of March and charged environment ministers and officials with producing proposals for reforming the rating system. These ministers and officials had already concluded that a local income tax was both the fairest and most rational system, but of course that would only reintroduce the very problem that two Conservative Governments had spent five years fighting – so they had to go away and think of something else.

The Cabinet–level committee on local government finance now constituted (the 'ELF' committee), chaired by the Prime Minister, disinterred the notion of a poll tax previously rejected in the aftermath of the 1981 Green Paper *Alternatives to Domestic Rates* (DOE, 1981). This would be combined with a nationalization of business rates. Immediately, all the old technical and political problems spotted in 1983 re-emerged. How could a poll tax be collected without appearing to be taxing the right to vote by using electoral registers? What about problems of equity between rich and poor, and what to do about those too poor to pay? Should a new register be set up, should social security be extended to pay for the charge, or mortgage tax relief cut to make up for gains at the other end of the spectrum? (See Midwinter and Mair, 1987). That the committee continued to work through this minefield is a measure of the political fright taken from Scotland, especially when the Treasury remained adamantly opposed to any change threatening the control over local government finance it had built up so assiduously over the previous six years. These technical and political problems did not go away, however, and by the summer of 1985 ministers were reduced to admitting that the rates reform was a long-term hope which would not be realized before the next general election. This, of course, might well mean never, and indeed Kenneth Baker, the Minister for the Environment, admitted as much. The Conservative Party, he said, would lack credibility if it had not at least published a Reform Bill before the next election, but legislation could not possibly take effect before 1990 (*The Guardian*, 10 October 1985).

The ELF committee and DOE officials continued to play around with various combinations of poll tax (now hopefully desensitized to 'community charge'), reformed property taxes and nationalized business rates, and this mixture was reflected in the Green Paper published in January 1986 (see *Local Government Chronicle*, 31 January 1986, for details). Non-domestic rates would be set by central government and redistributed to local authorities on a simple population basis, all adults would pay a flat-rate 'community charge' (with government power to 'community charge-cap'). This would mean new 'householder' registers, with a new criminal offence for withholding information, as well as the end of the redistributive element of rates. Finally, RSG would be replaced by a standard grant based on population, backed up by a needs grant to meet the extra costs of providing services in authorities of greater need. Capital expenditure would need central permission while safety nets and transitional arrangements would shield councils from over-abrupt charges. As usual, the reforms would go through first in Scotland.

This immediately attracted condemnation from politicians, professionals and political commentators alike. Perhaps the most damning reaction came from the Association of District Councils, which embodied the sort of grass-roots local Conservative whom the reform was supposed to placate. The reform would be 'an utter nonsense' which would only allow 'further steps to central control' (*Local Government Chronicle*, 7 February 1986). Most people were liable to end up paying more local taxes and this would include large increases in traditional Tory areas.

But despite all this, it was obvious that if the Government was to retain any credibility at all in the area of local government it would have to do something about rates. The issue could not be fudged for a third election. At the same time it was essential for the Conservatives to regain the initiative after the abolition fiasco. Legislation for Scotland – where the community charge would come into effect during 1988–9 – was put in place before the 1987 general election and legislation for England and Wales was promised for after the election. Having won the 1987 election, the Conservatives became embroiled in the messy practicalities of trying to make a community charge work. The implications were all the more worrying to Party managers as the Conservatives had polled disastrously in Scotland – winning a mere 11 of 72 Scottish Parliamentary seats – and the suspicion was that the 'poll tax', as it was now universally known, had made a major contribution to this defeat.

6.5 Conclusion: Towards the Regional State

Our discussion of uneven development and state forms in chapter 2 ended with the conclusion that local states are necessary for the adequate management of societies. In franchise democracies like Britain this means two things: first, local states are subject to the encroachments of electoral accountability and hence gain an autonomous political legitimacy. Secondly, local states need financing and this gives their political autonomy some measure of material backing. These two dimensions of local government underlie the whole history of local–central conflict throughout the period of the Thatcher Governments. Even after various solutions of increasing severity, the same old problems remained. The Widdicombe inquiry and the failed Local Government Bill 1985 were just the latest attempts to confront the problem of local political autonomy, while the poll tax is the latest attempt to curb local financial autonomy.

As long as the system of government remains one of franchise democracy these problems will almost certainly also remain in some form or other. So in the aftermath of the 1987 Conservative election victory, the new Environment Minister for the inner cities, David Trippier, promised that 'incompetent or downright loony' councils who stood in the way of the Government's plans would be 'swept away' (*The Guardian*, 1 July 1987). Another round of abolition, perhaps? But in acting against the problem of local government in this way the Thatcher regimes have come close to destroying elements of this democracy. This has ricocheted against the Conservative Government, which in effect threatens its own political legitimacy through such actions – a point not lost on the Party's political managers. On the other hand central administrations require sub-national state institutions if they are to govern and administer effectively.

The way out of this – in the search for the best of both worlds – is perhaps the 'regional state solution'. That is, the removal of subnational state functions to non-electoral local states, while electoral local governments are left formally in position but with much reduced powers. Because, in Britain, there is no tradition of electoral accountability at the regional level, it is here that subnational powers have been extended most. We turn to this regional state solution in the next chapter.

7

The Regional State

7.1 Introduction: Regional State Institutions and Removing Electoral Influence

In some policy areas the local government problem has been solved essentially in favour of the centre. Sometimes this has proceeded by what we might call 'nationalization'; policy is decided at the centre and regional and local offices exist only as administrative units. The social security system run by the Department of Health and Social Security (DHSS) is the major example. When near-universal male suffrage was established in the 1880s, poor-relief and Poor Law administration became open to significant local electoral influence. This was at least an irritant to central government but at worst, as with Poplarism (see preface and chapter 1), created a direct political threat. From the 1920s onward, this local influence was whittled away until by 1948 the expanded social security services were run by a central department of state using a vast network of secretive regional and local offices. Local representation in social service administration today is confined almost entirely to local committees, which merely have some appellate jurisdiction over certain discretionary parts of the system. Even in this case, committee members are nominated by local civil servants. This centralized structure has been crucial to the success of the Thatcher Government's policy in this area; it is difficult to see how the substantial cuts and policy changes since 1979 (see Alcock, 1983) could have been achieved if local government or local electorates had retained significant influence over policy.

'Regionalization' is a variant on the 'nationalization' of local autonomy. Local electoral influence and accountability is reduced or removed by creating regional-scale corporatist bodies of appointees and nominees, heavily subject to central direction. Councils may have some nomination rights, but government-favoured interest groups would normally dominate and in any case councillor nomination is quite different from direct electoral accountability. Similarly, the local government legislation on publication of minutes and public access to meetings will not usually apply to these bodies. As Saunders (1985b) has pointed out, even if this reduction and removal is not the conscious aim of regionalization it has certainly been the consequence.

But why create public bodies at all; if removing policy from elected local government is all that is required why not stay with nationalization? The problems of uneven development create a need for policy formulation that can remain sensitive to local variations (a good example is water-supply, given the quite different geological conditions that exist in different parts of the country). This local sensitivity is not so dangerous politically when there is no tradition of electoral accountability at the regional level in Britain, hence the 'technical' reasons for regional policy formulation (concerning, for example, the size of drainage areas or client catchment areas) fit in nicely with the social reasons for narrowing electoral influence. These regional bodies are accountable to the centre and their autonomy is often strictly defined by legislation.

In addition to blocking popular political aspirations, Saunders (1985b, 1985d, on which we draw heavily) lists a number of other explanations for the piecemeal development of the regional tier of the state. These include a pragmatic response to economic recession; and concerns with internal and external security; with developing a coherent planning machinery; with devolving detailed administration; and with dealing with the problems and requirements of specific areas. The first and last explanations have an explicit spatial determinant. In the rest the influence of uneven development is more implicit, but we can still see its importance.

The development of the regional state began in earnest during the 1930s, although the establishment of 10 regional offices under Civil Commissioners had taken place in 1925 as part of the preparations for the General Strike. As Dearlove and Saunders note, 'It is no coincidence that regional agencies should have begun to grow at the same time as local councils began to lose their powers, for many of the responsibilities which were taken out of local hands were passed over to newly-created regional offices' (1984, p. 393). Powers transferred from local government over the next 50 years were to include trunk roads, hospitals, gas, electricity, water, police and local health-care. The major periods of regionalization, however, have been the immediate post-war period, which has seen the national organization of a welfare state, the 1974

The Regional State

reorganization of local government (which was in practice as much 'removal' as 'reorganization'), and the centralizations conducted by the two Thatcher Governments.

Between 1979 and 1985, legislative changes in the three key policy areas of health, water and transport have been concerned with consolidating and tidying up this regionalization, and further weakening or even removing the elements of local accountability (for example, council nominees, public meetings) that still existed in 1979. For instance, the 1982 health legislation reduced local government nomination to one-fifth of the members of the District Health Authorities (compared with one-third on the abolished Area Health Authorities), ruled out elections for any District Health Authority (DHA) members, took away common boundaries with local councils and severely weakened the access, status and financing of the already weak consumer 'watch-dog', the Community Health Councils. Similarly, the 1983 Water Act abolished council member-ship entirely on Regional Water Authorities (RWAs) and removed the need to allow public audience at their formal meetings. With just one exception (the Welsh Water Authority) all the RWAs immediately went secret.

If these regional authorities are closed off from local electoral pressure, and similarly consumers seem to have little influence, then who does make the decisions? This was the principal question posed by Saunders' research, which was carried out in conjunction with our own work on the local state (see Saunders, 1984b, 1985c, 1985d). He studied health and water provision in South-east England, interviewing key individuals within the Regional Health and Water Authorities as well as representatives of various interests and organizations outside them. His conclusion was basically that decision-making in the region's health authority was dominated by professional and bureaucratic interests (i.e., consultants and administrators), while that in the water authority reflected the close relationship between office-holders and business interests, represented through organizations like the regional Confederation of British Industry (CBI), the National Farmers' Union and the House Builders' Federation. In the case of water authorities, large producer interests are enormously influential. The regional scale of these institutions means that regional offices of the CBI can be involved directly in decision-making over issues such as pricing and pollution. Such arrangements are mutually convenient, as the following quotes indicate:

> 1974 backwards, we had trouble dealing with a whole lot of authorities and all the rest of it. Collect them all together and at least you have one point to go in at the top. (Regional CBI)

You see, the CBI is a nice convenient bunch of people to interact with. (Southern Water Authority; quoted in Saunders, 1984b, p. 22)

This interaction takes place through formal liaison meetings and less formal personal contacts. The CBI informant was obviously pleased with the results:

Public bodies do not have rapport. They are made up of individuals. Rapport has to be created between individuals, and that's what we do. We influence their ideas and they influence ours – in the nicest possible way. there's nothing underhand about it. . . . It's not a token involvement. Take charges . . . we have made an impression to the benefit of our members in terms of charges. And there are a lot of areas too where, from the point of view of chemicals and the type of chemical in effluent and so on, where agreement has been reached that possible, er, certain, erm, requirements were too stringent. (Ibid., pp. 20–1).

Similarly, developers (whether individually or through groups such as the House Builders' Federation) are able to negotiate policy in areas such as site water-charges and new infrastructural developments. Again liaison takes place through both official forums and through more personal means:

If we've got a problem, we just phone up. It's as simple as that. Fix a meeting. I think we can probably come to a solution of the problem much more quickly than actually going through some sort of formal consultation machinery. . . . We do have a formal meeting about once a year . . . and if we have a special problem which crops up halfway through the year, then we'll phone them up and say we want a meeting now. (House Builders' Federation regional officer; quoted in ibid., p. 23)

On a smaller scale, the apogee of the democratic vacuum is perhaps reached with the 273 Internal Drainage Boards. Members are elected on a restricted constituency of landowners and farmers but then have the power to levy rates on their members. These rates are matched pound-for-pound from the public purse via the Ministry of Agriculture. Together with the Land Drainage Committees (dominated by agricultural interests organized through the National Farmers' Union and the Country Landowners' Association), these bodies have considerable power to order drainage schemes (often with considerable environmental impact), drawing heavily on public funds with little or no outside intervention. Not surprisingly, the

National Farmers' Union (NFU) and the Country Landowners' Association (CLA) see nothing wrong in these arrangements:

> I think generally speaking the land drainage committees of the Southern Water Authority, because they have remained fairly local, still work pretty well . . . if you mean that they're dominated by farmers and growers, absolutely right! Yes. On the other hand, the implications of land drainage primarily fall upon farmers and growers. . . . So I think, who the hell has a better right to be involved? (NFU regional officer; quoted in ibid., p. 17).

One might venture that the implications of reductions in hospital funding, or increases in water charges fall mainly on the consumers, yet they are denied any meaningful involvement whatsoever in policy-making. Even the water authorities are somewhat unhappy about these arrangements. As a senior officer of the Southern Water Authority put it:

> It is the most indefensible thing that I have ever met in my public life! We are spending millions of pounds subsidising people who are very wealthy in their own bloody right. . . . The system is quite, quite indefensible and I will not defend it. And, of course, it's run by bloody farmers! It's quite extraordinary (Ibid., pp. 17–18).

Extraordinary it may well be, but the system continues, along with the one that gives the NFU and CLA regular access to administrators and officials at the regional level itself, especially with regard to pricing policy.

Health authorities by comparison have very little big-business involvement. Quite simply the private sector (with the exception of the drug industry) has little interest in influencing health policy below the national level. Instead the 'democratic vacuum' is filled by those who do have a direct interest – health service managers and professionals. (Consumers are as usual excluded from all but the most token forms of representation.) In his research, Saunders found that the main policy battles were internal, especially those between managers and hospital consultants over funding priorities. Thus 'Where the managers of the water authorities are obliged to share their power with key producer–sector interests, those in the health authorities share their power with no one' (1985b, p. 10). This situation has increasingly become the norm as doctors themselves have become involved with administration. A regional officer of the British Medical Association (BMA) rationalized this move in the following terms:

The district general manager is in the position to take decisions. The unit general manager is accountable to him or her. This is the place where the doctors see their chance. Consultants will probably agree to spend two or three days a week as unit general managers. If consultants don't do it, then administrative or nursing officers will. Some consultants are now say 'OK, let's do these jobs, then we can stop anything we don't like'. (Saunders, 1984b, p. 33)

Thus, between them administrators and consultants are increasing the strength of their own positions at the expense of other employees and consumers alike.

In this way the interests of vested groups, rather than of the electorate as a whole, are built into the everyday practice and the accepted role of regional state institutions. It is hardly surprising then, that regionalization of this sort is intimately linked to a new definition of policy-making. These regional bodies are less able, and less willing, to resist central demands that provision should be seen in terms of a commodity rather than a service. For instance, since 1974, water services have been expected to be self-financing through charges to consumers. The principal monitor of organizational success has increasingly been the balance sheet, especially as parts of the water system are beginning to be prepared for privatization. As one water authority officer put it, 'The government come and talk to us about our performance aims, return on capital and so on....We have to have a target that's set by government' (ibid., p. 8).

Similarly, the 1980 Health Services Act required health authorities to remain within centrally determined cash limits, although it took legal action and central government commissioners to force some recalcitrant area authorities into line. The 1982 reorganization extended financial controls over the new structure, through the appointment of the Rayner Committee to increase health service efficiency according to commercial criteria. According to the chair of a District Health Authority, 'I think what we miss enormously is an independent source of finance. . . . I've found the funding of the NHS extremely constraining. You've just got this statutory amount of money that's given to you to spend' (ibid., p. 36). In order to oversee this extension the Thatcher Governments have taken an increasingly interventionist line in appointing health authority chairs. Indeed it has recently been alleged by one appointee that Conservative Central Office is vetting the new appointments of all 191 District Health Authority chairs. (*The*

Guardian, 13 March 1986). A BMA officer referred to the increasing importance of these 'political' appointments:

> They are a new breed of people – no longer retired colonels but business people with all their marbles. . . . They have had a significant effect on our members. Our members are treated with less deference. . . . They are political appointments to a man and a woman. . . . Being called to account is the theme tune for the future. (Saunders, 1984b, p. 33)

In practice as well as in theory then, appointed regional-level institutions are less likely than elected local authorities to oppose central demands for expenditure reductions – hence their attractiveness to the present Conservative regime, and their extension at a time of economic recession and contentious public expenditure cuts. The situation was put succinctly by a senior local government officer, when he contrasted the National Health Service (NHS) with the organization of local authority social services:

> The people who run our committee know perfectly well that they've got to go back to local electors. . . . The question arises as to how are local people to make their wishes felt if their DHA refuse to hear – what sanctions have you really got? What can local residents do? I'm not sure what the answer to that is. (Ibid., p. 44)

The Government seems to know the answer, which in practical terms amounts to very little. After all, as we shall see, it makes sense for the centre to keep policy-making away from the hands of potentially troublesome opponents in the local authorities. This is what has happened in the case of passenger transport services.

7.2 Transfer to the Regional State: the Case of Public Transport

Public transport is a particularly interesting but in some respects anomalous case. Local government and electoral influence has been substantially diluted from the 1930s onwards, but was much restored in the metropolitan counties following the 1974 local government reorganization. It seemed for a while as if regionalization would be hoist with the petard of its own technical justification – for now regional-scale elected authorities had come into existence, and substantial conflict resulted between the new authorities and the centre over transport, especially after 1979. But the solution to the conflict proceeded along similar lines to those described in chapter 5. The solution to the problem was largely one of abolition, and local authority influence was removed once again in favour of appointed regional bodies.

THE ISSUES: COMMERCIAL OR SOCIAL LOGIC AND UNEVEN DEVELOPMENT

The history of policy control in passenger transport since the 1930s provides a case-study typical of local–central relations in Britain. Emerging from a situation of commercial provision by private firms interspersed with 'municipal socialist' services, it has never been clear whether passenger transport remains a commercial or a social/ environmental service. The problem has been particularly acute when wider commercial criteria (for example, getting workers to workplaces) conflicts with narrower operating ones (for example, making a profit from a bus service). This is exacerbated by the difficulties of uneven development. Local areas quite clearly differ in their transport needs, suggesting that local policy formulation is essential (indeed the Greater London Area is apparently so different as to require separate legislation). But at the same time, local political relations also vary significantly and councils have reflected this by holding quite different views from each other, and from the centre, on the social service/commercial service divide. Central nationaliziation has been one solution – as with British rail, and at times parts of road haulage and air transport – with local government influence limited to a consultative role strengthened by a subsidy role especially over commuter and 'social' railway services. But with passenger transport by bus and underground, probably because of its more local orientation compounded by a long history of municipal service, the result has been a confusing variation, over both time and space, of national, regional corporatist and local government policy competence.

We can distinguish three broad periods, however. First, one of nationalization and regionalization of previously independent commercial and council services, from the 1930s to about 1968. This is followed by a short period when council influence was reintroduced, from 1968–74. Finally, the pendulum has swung back to increased centralization, reaching a peak during the Thatcher Governments. We will deal with these periods in turn, concentrating on the last. But first we will deal with a crucial element of passenger transport policy-making that remained corporatist throughout the entire period: the licensing system (drawing extensively on Evans,

1983). This system represented an attempt to rationalize, control and regulate passenger transport 'in the public interest' without replacing the commrcial form of provision by private and municipal companies and, as far as possible, without involving subsidies to these companies.

CORPORATIST CONTROL WITHOUT PUBLIC SUBSIDY:
THE LICENSING SYSTEM, 1930–84

The licensing system for public transport was introduced by the 1930 Road Traffic Act (which has set guide-lines up to 1984) in order to rationalize a clearly inefficient plethora of competing services. The definitions of efficiency and hence of rationality are not neutral, however, and are open to challenge. The solution was to set up regional corporatist licensing bodies directly answerable to the centre – which although insulated from local political pressures, could deal with local policy problems. Nevertheless, as part of the process of creating such a structure, the existing large operators were able to gain protected status.

The 1930 Act set up 13 Traffic Areas, each with a Traffic Commission using an elaborate system of licenses for both services and vehicles. Each Commission was answerable directly to the Secretary of State for Transport (later the Secretary of State for the Environment) and those outside London were run by a centrally appointed chair assisted by two council nominees. The London Traffic Commission, which extended for 1,800 square miles far into South-east England (compare the London County Council of 117 square miles), consisted of the centrally appointed chair alone. As we shall see, this special arrangement for London echoes a continuing fear of the capital's combination of regional scale, unique transport problems and political coherence in the LCC and later in the GLC. Finally, the 1930 Act protected the interests of existing large operators through the licensing criteria and also the criteria for making public objection to proposed new routes. Both allowed existing commercial interests considerable significance. Entry to the industry was made extremely difficult and small firms were effectively left unable to expand and so ready to be taken over by larger competitors.

The first substantial revision of the 1930 guide-lines was the 1980 Transport Act with the supplementary 1981 Passenger Vehicles Act. These simplified and weakened the licensing system, and greatly reduced the commercial protection available to existing operators. The 1980 Act also allowed 'trial areas' to be set up on a county basis as a guide to further legislation. In these areas the 1930 framework would be relaxed substantially. In Devon and Norfolk this took the form of allowing new minibus services to operate in rural areas deserted by bus companies, although in the old county of Hereford the experiment took the wider form of removing the statutory duty for operators to co-operate (rather than compete) and the relaxation of safety requirements, etc. The result was a greater number of cheaper services in some built-up areas. The other side of the coin was fare rises or a withdrawal of services in rural areas and, on the most profitable routes, a return to the inefficiencies of buses racing for passengers followed by delays and some disturbing cases of unsafe vehicles.

Despite such evidence, and objection from the Conservative-controlled Association of District Councils and the County Council Association of County Councils, as well as from the Labour-controlled Association of Metropolitan Authorities and their transport organizations, these experiments were used to justify further legislation later in 1986 which removed most elements of licensing except for safety regulations. But as with Enterprise Zones, the political aims of this legislation are at least as important as the technical ones – the demonstration that a new commercialization does work.

Regional Corporatism and Nationalization, 1930–68

We will only summarize this period, noting some of the political issues behind its formal arrangements. Looking first at London, over the period 1933–69 non-railway public transport (buses and underground) was run by the Ministry of Transport through various corporatist bodies (The London Passenger Transport Board 1933–48, the London Transport Executive 1948–63 and the London Transport Board 1963–9). The members of all these bodies were appointed by the Ministry of Transport (and later the DOE), although sometimes in consultation with the national quangos to which they were formally subordinate. (The British Transport Commission, representing the nationalized railway interests which included substantial bus services especially in London, and its successor for road and water interests, the Transport Holding Company). The London boroughs and the LLC had no statutory representation, while the various transport bodies were composed overwhelmingly of transport professionals and representatives of the transport industry. Although the policy problems of London Transport changed considerably over this period (especially with the nationaliz-ation of the railways in 1947 and declining custom by the 1960s), the framework of who should make policy was essentially laid down in the 1933 London Passenger Transport Act. Like the 1930 Road Traffic Act introducing licensing, this was introduced to rationalize the inefficient results of private competition complemented by municipal hole-plugging – but without replacing the existing commercial logic. The fear was that local politics would be allowed into transport. Herbert Morrison expressed this very well in the parliamentary run-up to the 1933 Act: 'We ask ourselves whether or not this vast business is necessarily appropriate for politicians with electoral minds at all, for politicians trying to win elections with concessions to electors on questions of fares, wages, and salaries' (1931; quoted in Evans, 1983). Morrison both echoes worries about the municipal socialism of Poplarism and anticipates the recent conflicts over the 'municipal Marxism' charge levelled against the GLC's cheap fares policy. Both, somewhat illogically, were sometimes seen as revolutionary movements in the making and were feared as much for that as for the challenge they presented to narrow commercial logic.

In the rest of Britain (Scotland had slightly different arrangements from England and Wales) responsibility for passenger transport policy-making remained in limbo up to 1968–72. This was partly because the centrally accountable licensing system and central legislation provided overall constraints; similarly, as passenger transport was split between municipal, commercial and (after 1947) nationalized services it seldom became identified with coherent and oppositional political units. (Although some towns had gained local municipal monopolies, other quite large towns, such as Bristol, had no municipal services at all.) Many bus services were in fact run by the British Transport Commission/Transport Holding Companies through the Passenger Transport Executive, accountable to the central ministry responsible. These bodies controlled the bus interests of the nationalized railway companies, which were soon considerably enlarged through take-overs of independent operators. Nonetheless, conflicts broke out between the centre and councils in a few cases where local policies went too far in disturbing commercial logic and also had the transport influence to put this into practice. Birmingham Corporation, for instance, was successfully taken to court in 1953 for introducing subsidized fares for pensioners.

Reinforcing Local Government Influence 1968–74

Local electoral influence on passenger transport was reinforced substantially following the 1968 Transport Act, the 1969 Transport

(London) Act and the local government reorganization of 1972–4 (1963–5 in London). The technical justification for corporatist regionalization – the regional scale of transport problems, etc. – were hoist by their own petard. For now, regional-scale but elected councils were created in the GLC, the Metropolitan County Councils, the County Councils and Scottish Regional Councils. We should be clear, however, that this reintroduction was never more than partial even in the GLC and Metropolitan County Councils, where it was most effective. Substantial elements of bus transport were still run by national quangos (as, of course, was British Rail), while the overall constraints of the licensing system and central legislation remained. Nevertheless, this experience was apparently so disturbing to government that corrective centralization measures were taken from the mid-1970s culminating in centralization by abolition in 1984.

The rot started in London with the creation of the GLC in 1965. The GLC was given wider powers than its predecessor, the LCC, including powers over 'transportation'. The GLC was created partly in response to technical arguments for metropolis-wide local administration (where the LCC had covered inner London only) but it was also seen as a way of dispensing with the Labour-controlled LCC which sometimes reached the status of a Labour 'government in exile'. The GLC with increased suburban representation was confidently expected to be run permanently by the Conservative Party, just as the LCC had been by Labour. This expectation was, however, quite wrong and power has alternated between the two parties.

The Transport (London) Act 1969 transferred London Transport responsibility to the GLC from 1 January (it was to be removed once again on 29 June 1984). Although the GLC was the policy-making body, day-to-day management and operation was to be undertaken by the London Transport Executive (LTE). The latter was composed of transport professionals who were to respond to the statutory directions of the GLC, and this distinction was to be a source of conflict. One result was GLC nomination of its own supporters to the LTE. There was also a Users Body which could consider complaints – unless these concerned fares! Further confusion was to be added by the remit of the 1969 Act. According to section 1 it would be the GLC's duty 'to develop policies and to encourage, organise and where appropriate, carry out measures, which will promote the provision of integrated, efficient and economic transport facilities and services for Greater London'. What 'efficient and economic' actually means is of course open to question. The courts were later to pronounce that this meant making a profit.

The situation remained more complicated outside London. The 1968 Transport Act created four Passenger Transport Authorities (PTAs) in Greater Manchester, Tyne and Wear, West Midlands and Merseyside. These were the policy-making bodies for passenger transport in their areas, with subordinate 'Executives' (PTEs) carrying out operational management. They were vested with existing municipal services, bought out some independent operators and established agreements with the remainder, including British Rail (BR) and the National Bus Company (NBC).

At first PTAs were composed of part-time nominees from the constituent councils; they therefore lacked political cohesion and left considerable autonomy with PTEs. The 1972 Local Government Act changed all this by creating unified, regional-scale Metropolitan County Councils all of which (including also South Yorkshire and West Yorkshire) became PTEs. All were dominated by the Labour Party, which in some cases had ruled Metropolitan County Councils continuously from their inception in 1976. This reintroduced the problem of local political autonomy buttressed by electoral legitimization.

Outside the GLC and the Metropolitan County Councils, policy-making for bus transport remained split between councils, commercial companies and nationalized undertakings, all operating under the licensing system. The 1968 Transport Act set up the NBC which took over the assets of 64 bus companies. Responsible to the central ministry, the Secretary of State appointed both the full-time chief executive and the part-time members of the NBC board. Again, the operational instrument was separated and staffed by professionals. The national network was broken into four regional divisions and a long-distance group. These are responsible to the centre and have no council representation. Nevertheless, 49 District Councils continued to run their own services as local authority departments. Although these were unable to budget for deficits, they could, as in the past, use support from local rates. Finally, the 'shire' County Councils were also designated PTAs in the 1972 Local Government Act, although with less powers than their metropolitan counterparts. Municipal services were not vested in the PTAs, nor were the remaining commercial operators bought out. Rather, the County Councils had a controlling and co-ordinating role where District Councils and commercial companies were to respond to County Council policy in return for revenue support.

Curbing Local Government Influence, 1974–84

The only subsidy finance available to PTAs was their own rate revenue supplemented by RSG. There was no specific subsidy support until the 1974 Local Government Act introduced what became the Transport Supplementary Grant (TSG). This was composed of both revenue and capital subsidies and was administered under criteria recognizing the social and environmental importance of public transport. It seems, then, as if the 1974 Act reflected the anti-capitalist (or at least anti-narrow commercialism) and environmentally conscious aspects of the victorious Labour Party's manifesto of that year. This breakthrough did not last long, however. By 1977/8 the Labour Minister of Transport had already withdrawn TSG from Sheffield in punishment for the latter's cheap fare policies, and the whole system was considerably tightened up by the 1978 Transport Act. (This paralleled the Housing Investment Programme System introduced in 1977.) TSG would be allocated in response to detailed PTA plans concerning their transport problems, policy responses and expenditure estimates – but local freedom to plan became in fact central ability to cut and TSG allocations inevitably became lower than requested (for South Yorkshire no grant was made at all!). In 1980 TSG was partly replaced by the transport element of the Block Grant.

It was in London and the metropolitan counties that the major battles were to be fought out – precisely because it was there that local government influence was greatest. By 1979, with central government attempting to reinforce narrow monetarist and commercial logic, while the Metropolitan County Councils resisted and some attempted to work according to a wider social(ist) logic, the mixture became explosive. After Labour gains in the 1981 local government elections, many Metropolitan County Councils carried out manifesto promises for cheap fares, funded from supplementary rates. The issue was brought to a head later in 1981 when the GLC initiated its 'Fares Fair' policy. This saw London's public transport as a service, and among other things meant an average fare cut of 32 per cent (the first ever in London). Before this, 57 per cent of London Transport revenue was from passenger receipts, with a 33 per cent GLC rate subsidy, but under Fares Fair (October 1981–March 1982) subsidies rose to 50 per cent of total expenditure. Although this subsidy was still lower than in other cities in Europe and North America, the new policy breached the predominantly narrow commercial logic on which London Transport's operations had rested until then. Eventually the GLC was taken to court by the right-wing Conservative Bromley Council (clearly with government support) who argued that the GLC had ignored their ratepayers who would have to contribute to this bill, pointing out that 'If Parliament had intended the transport system to be run on social welfare principles they (*sic*) would have said so' (*The Guardian*, 29 October 1981).

Basing its judgement partly on the 1969 Transport (London) Act, the London Divisional Court found in the GLC's favour, but noted that the GLC's actions might be on the margin of what was permissible. The Appeal Court reversed this decision, portraying Fares Fair as 'a crude abuse of power' (*The Guardian*, 11 November 1981). According to the three judges, the GLC had failed to balance properly its two conflicting duties to the ratepayers and the travelling public: 'fiduciary duty' was paramount in any case, and (in their interpretation of the 1969 Act), London Transport's duty to promote 'integrated, efficient and economic transport facilities' meant making a profit. Wider economic and social criteria, such as the significant reductions in road congestion, traffic accidents, pollution and overall travel times (see ibid., 27 April 1983; *New Statesman*, 21 October 1983) were ignored or dismissed as 'political'. *The Guardian* leader article commented that the judges had 'grossly overstepped the mark' since

> the judgement that the ratepayer has had a rotten deal to the benefit of the farepayer is not one which should be made in the courts. It ought to be made at the ballot box, as it always has been in the history of democratic elections. (27 April 1983)

Although this sentiment was shared widely, the five Law Lords nevertheless upheld the appeal decision unanimously. The immediate result was a 100 per cent fare increase in the attempt to get nearer the break-even point. Commuting by car to central London increased to 14 per cent and traffic accidents rose sharply (ibid.).

The GLC counter-attacked using the ambiguity of the 1969 Act, which apparently empowered it to promote public policies 'to the benefit of Londoners as a whole'. This was supported by the provisions of the Greater London Development Plan, drawn up in the early 1970s but still binding on both the GLC and central ministries. In May 1982, the 'Just the Ticket' policy was implemented, again reducing fares (by 25 per cent on average, to the level before Fares Fair in October 1981) and planning transport provision on the basis of social as well as more strictly commercial criteria.

Again, the law was party to local government policy formulation. The London Transport Executive (LTE) approached the High Court for a legal ruling on 'Just the Ticket' (formulated by the GLC in December 1981). This approach was presented purely as a means of clearing the legal air, although it has since emerged that key LTE members were always opposed to the GLC's wider social (or 'political') policy formulation. Despite the fact that the GLC's revenue subsidy would clearly be in excess of the £125m the Minister of Transport had declared as the absolute maximum under the statutory provision of the 1983 Transport Act (passed 28 March 1983), the High Court upheld the GLC's directive. (In fact the 1983/4 revenue subsidy was to reach £182m, although London Transport travel was to rise by 16 per cent and a loss was turned into a profit of £36m.)

This legal decision was reached partly on the technical grounds that the GLC had sought proper legal advice before taking policy decisions, and that this advice had not ruled out such policy (although of course this meant the GLC using lawyers favourable to their overall aims). We also suspect that the considerable opprobrium over the legal suppression of Fares Fair also encouraged the court to be a little more cautious this time. The pendulum was also pushed further over to the GLC's side by events in the metropolitan counties. A High Court case brought by a large retail firm against Merseyside County Council, opposing its supplementary rate to finance a cheap fare policy, failed. The judgement appealed to the wording of the 1968 Transport Act (for PTAs outside London) which – unlike the 1969 Transport (London) Act – could not be so easily interpreted to mean breaking even in strict commercial terms. Again, the council was judged to have taken proper legal advice (an eventual fares cut of 22 per cent over two years was to increase passenger miles by 15 per cent and so increase revenue).

Nevertheless, in the period of confusion after the GLC Fares Fair case West Midlands County Council had withdrawn its cheap fares scheme before a similar case (initiated by the Conservative-run Solihull District Council) came to court. At the same time, many other councils modified or retreated from more radical policy decisions for fear of legal intervention. This fear was all the more potent because it seemed that a new legal restriction on local government action – 'ficuciary duty' to ratepayers – had been created by the Fares Fair case. Certainly the Government played on these fears. According to the Minister of Transport, for instance, the final Fares Fair court decision meant that 'All local authorities will now need to take careful note of the block grant consequences in framing their budgets....Everything that this Government has been saying about the need for all local authorities to achieve expenditure reductions has been vindicated' (*The Guardian*, 18 December 1982).

One reason for the partial success of the local government fight-back was that both judiciary and central government were widely seen to have overreached themselves. Not only this, but the decision had pushed the whole issue of local–central relations and local democracy firmly into the limelight. We can illustrate the tone and direction of this debate by quoting the words of a leading academic commentator on legal affairs: 'The moral seems to be that the great wave of judicial intervention . . . is still rolling forward. Who knows what it might not seek to submerge if some future left-wing government applies more generally even the moderate measure of Ken Livingstone's socialism' (Griffith, 1982, p. 31).

The Fares Fair decision had elevated both the GLC and its leader – and hence by implication local government autonomy – to public popularity. In one opinion survey Ken Livingstone was the second most respected 'man of the year' in Britain (after the Pope, who was visiting at the time, see Carvel, 1983). This is all the more remarkable when we remember that most of the national press, as well as London's local press, had consistently vilified 'Red Ken' ever since he had become GLC leader. Similar political reactions occurred elsewhere. In Sheffield, for instance, support for cheap fares brought strikes in engineering and steel, as well as in public transport, and the collection of 100,000 supporting signatures in just over a week (the number was soon to reach 250,000). South Yorkshire's cheap fares policy was propelled firmly into the local public mind and added substantially to the council's popularity. The Government drew back from scoring another political own-goal and this is probably why the provisions of the 1983 Transport Act – which apparently made the GLC's 'Just the Ticket' of dubious legality – were not enforced. Central weakness in this respect is highlighted by the 1982 Transport Act, which was passed specifically to *reinstate* concessionary fares to pensioners in London, where the Fares Fair decision apparently made them illegal.

Rather than risk repeating the self-inflicted damage of stamping directly on a democratically elected body following a broadly popular policy, the Government took the well-worn path of restructuring local–central relations. The problem could then be removed at source. The Government began its attack with counter-propaganda on the subject of local democracy. For South Yorkshire to have pursued cheap fare policies since 1975 in accordance with overwhelming electoral mandates was, according to the Minister of Transport 'a distorted view of how our system of democracy should work' (*The Guardian*, 21 February 1983, in a speech to the Conservative local government conference). The GLC had already been warned that the Government might 'have to consider whether the arrangements that allow them to preside over the destruction of the city's transport undertaking can continue in their present form' (ibid., 15 January 1982). Sir Peter Mansfield, Chair of London Transport, giving evidence to the House of Commons Transport Committee, stated that control of London's transport should, in the interests of professional neutrality, be taken from the GLC and given to the Government. The Conservative-controlled Committee endorsed his view and its report (July 1982) and asked for a Metropolitan Transport Authority which, although able to precept rates from London boroughs, would be directly under the control of the Minister of Transport.

The 1983 Transport Act followed this lead and began the restructuring of local–central relations in public transport, or, as the Minister of Transport put it in Parliament: 'to discourage city authorities from the reckless course on which some of them have been set, with their excessive commitment to high rates, which destroy jobs with deadly efficiency, and the ultra-low fares which destabilise our transport system' (15 November 1982; quoted in Evans, 1983).

The Government would set 'guide-lines' for the maximum subsidy levels that the GLC and Metropolitan County Councils could pay to their Local Transport Executives. Subsidies within these limits were likely to be quite legal, but while payments in excess were not necessarily illegal, councils would be wide open to challenge in the courts and councillors could easily be surcharged. At the same time, a section of the Act withdrew the need of London Transport to submit proposals for fare alterations to the GLC in response to the latter's policy directives.

As we have seen, however, the 1983 Act did not give the Government the immediate level of control it desired and might be counter-productive. Cheap fare policies could struggle on in the short term, and the presence of opposing elected bodies was always dangerous. The GLC, for instance, nominated five (later seven) additional members of the London Transport Executive, giving the council a majority position where the professional members and chair had already signalled their opposition to the GLC policies. As all the nominees were Labour supporters or activists based in

London, including traffic campaigners and trade union representatives, these appointments infuriated both the Government and the professional members of London Transport Executive (for some reason they were especially incensed by the appointment of a Black woman office-worker from Brent in October 1983). It was these GLC members who were later to carry the day for the GLC's three-year plan (submitted under the provisions of the 1983 Act) for a fares freeze, increased service provision and lower staff reductions. The plan implied about twice as much subsidy as the Government guide-lines and the London Transport Executive chairman and three professional members insisted on attaching a dissenting letter to it.

Despite the 1983 Act, it seemed that challenges to central policy could still be mounted and the Government might lose the political battle that followed even if it won in technical terms. The transport unions, for instance, were beginning to organize in support of GLC and Metropolitan County Council policy while public opinion polls showed increasing support for the GLC and its transport policies. The Government decided that the Fares Fair fiasco should not be repeated. Effective abolition of local government influence seemed to be the best solution. The planned abolition of the GLC and Metropolitan County Concils would solve this problem like so many others. In their regions public transport would be run by regional quangos drawing on District Council nominees and budgets and rate precepts would be controlled from the centre. Many other metropolitan transport functions would devolve to District Councils, despite probably expensive losses of scale and linkage economies. The 'distortion of democracy' led by South Yorkshire could be removed. But in the case of the GLC, waiting for abolition in 1986 was, apparently, far too dangerous. Special legislation was brought forward to strip the GLC of all control over London Transport, creating a new quango – London Regional Transport (LRT) which would be accountable directly to the Minister of Transport. This transfer of power took place on 29 June 1984 under the London Regional Transport Act. Local government autonomy had lasted just $13\frac{1}{2}$ years.

The next day the Minister of Transport dismissed the GLC representatives and announced his new LRT board. The existing chair of London Transport and the three professional members heading buses, underground and finance (who had shown themselves opposed to GLC policy) moved over to equivalent posts on LRT. A consultative body, the London Regional Passengers' Committee was set up – but members would be appointed by the Trade

Secretary! The Minister of Transport called this 'a day of liberation for management from political interference' (*The Guardian*, 30 June 1984). Further provisions required London Transport to cope with a reduction of central subsidy from £190m to only £95m in three years, while precepted rate subsidies from 33 boroughs should not exceed 66 per cent of total aid. (This had been 50 per cent on the first draft but was changed to 66 per cent, in handwriting, four hours later!). London Transport assets could now be sold to the private sector and the operating guide-lines were changed from 'to meet the needs of Londoners' (as in the 1969 Act) to 'with due regard to passenger needs'.

The way would now be clear to implement government-preferred policy without local interference. This includes higher fares, lower subsidy, service cuts, large-scale redundancies and privatization. 'Free market' competition could be introduced on the more profitable bus routes (despite the judgement on an earlier minibus scheme, dismissed by an independent inspector as 'folly'). Nevertheless, fare increases and service cuts were to be introduced slowly at first. The *Evening Standard* leader comment points out why:

> Bus and tube fares will be seen by Londoners as the litmus test of what Margaret Thatcher has in store for their city after the abolition of the GLC. To promise a better run London and begin with high fare increases would be disastrous. (24 July 1984)

In like manner, the Government took care to see that pensioners' concessionary fares were not left to the boroughs to support. Already under Block Grant pressure, many Tory authorities would probably abolish them. LRT was given rights to rate precepts to avoid this vote-losing situation.

The 1986 Transport Act and abolition of the Metropolitan County Councils in the same year effectively brought local–central conflict to a close. With abolition, PTEs in the metropolitan counties were reduced to the role of administrative co-ordinators, under joint boards (composed of council nominees) no longer directly accountable to the public – and hence without either electoral legitimization or political cohesion. Their operational functions will disappear with the intended break-up of both the NBC and the regional bus operators into smaller competitive groups. Privatization will be encouraged as far as possible, although in many urban areas only municipal operators seem interested in taking over. At the same time TSG was reorientated towards new roads (the 1985/6 grant was to be spent entirely on roads, although in 1984/5 25 Labour authorities spent all their TSG on public transport) and with reductions in RSG combined with rate-capping, council subsidies will be far less possible. In any case, the Act allows subsidies only to particular routes, hence cutting out cross-subsidization between profitable and unprofitable routes. At the same time deregulation from the licensing system will allow 'free market' competition, allowing private operators to concentrate on the profitable routes which will further undercut cross-subsidy.

The implications of this for public transport as a social service are of course severe, if not fatal. The jewel in the crown of attempts to show that there is an alternative to private car-ownership – South Yorkshire's cheap fares policy (see Hill, 1986) – has now effectively ceased. Fares went up about 200 per cent in 1986, with service cuts and 1,600 job losses. In other abolished metropolitan counties integrated transport systems – for instance Tyne and Wear's metro and bus system – have been dismantled with components forced to compete against one another. Finally, local government influence over local transport policy has been reduced to a minimum once more. Public transport will be run by a combination of central ministry, regional quangos and private companies. Removing what powers local government had to the regional level has allowed a further shift from state subsidy to market provision. Local operational autonomy has been separated successfully from local political autonomy. As we noted at the beginning of this chapter, these regional bodies, isolated from local political influence, are an attractive way for the centre to neutralize popular opposition. If the way the local state manages and interprets capitalist society is not the centre's liking, service provisions can always be shifted to other more amenable local state institutions.

8

Concluding Comments

In the previous five chapters we have described some of the major changes that have taken place in local–central relations since 1979. As well as the more general legislation, we also looked at central attempts to control specific policy areas and through this combination we hope to have provided a fairly comprehensive picture of legislative, administrative, financial and political change. Throughout, we have tried not only to summarize these particular changes in a descriptive manner, but also to relate one to another within an overall concept of local–central relations. Accordingly, the early chapters of the book raised several issues concerning the use of concepts such as the local state and uneven development. Returning to these issues, we can now examine them in the light of the descriptive material detailing local–central changes.

The story detailed in this material has generally been one of increasing central control over local state institutions – whether elected or appointed, whether regional or local. This has not, however, been a passive or a one-way process, far from it. For the central state has been responding to the problems and actions of local state bodies, particularly local government. It is here that the political and financial autonomy of local states, although always only partial, was best developed and expressed following the emergence of mass representative democracy in Britain. Nor, as we have seen, has central government had matters entirely its own way, and its 'success' remains to be proven. Centralization is by no means some smooth and inevitable process which is necessarily functional to British capitalism. If anything, the opposite seems nearer the mark. Indeed, in political terms, local government has probably caused the Conservatives more problems than any other issue between 1979 and 1987.

If a final evaluation of these measures cannot yet be undertaken, a clear picture has emerged that the overall progress of centralization jars with the rhetoric that surrounds it. The official story from the centre has been one of rolling back the state and freedom from bureaucratic control. For instance, the 1980 Local Government, Planning and Land (No. 2) Bill announced itself as 'a Bill to relax controls over local government'. In fact, as we have seen, it laid the basis for probably the biggest attack seen on local government up to that time. Similarly, the 'market freedom' supposedly represented by Free Enterprise Zones and Urban Development Corporations is supported by an almost unprecedented level of state subsidy and support. It would be nearer the mark to say that the events that we have detailed show a dramatic restructuring, rather than a rolling back, of the state.

Nevertheless the rhetoric continues – rate-capping and abolition supposedly 'free' the local ratepayer from town hall interference – and is important in pointing to the conections between restructuring local government on the one hand and restructuring social institutions and social relations elsewhere in society. Homilies about 'freedom', 'thrift', 'good housekeeping', 'realism' and other 'Victorian values' have become commonplace, as the Conservatives have sought to impose their version of a new Britain on the country (see Hall and Jacques, 1983). In her opening speech in the 1983 general election campaign, in which local government was to occupy a larger role than ever before, Margaret Thatcher announced:

> The choice facing the nation is between two totally different ways of life. And what a prize we have to fight for. No less than the choice to banish from our land the dark divisive clouds of Marxist Socialism and bring together men and women from all walks of life who share a belief in freedom. (*The Guardian*, 14 May 1983, p. 1)

This statement, like so much else in the rhetoric of the Thatcher Governments, leaves a large gap between presentation and the real world. But it is against this background that the restructuring of local–central relations should be viewed – especially as 'Red Ken' and the Greater London Council represented the British version of the dark divisive clouds of Marxist Socialism. It is crucial to realize that local state institutions, as we stressed in chapter 2, are themselves both a major element and a major arena in the struggle to decide what replaces Britain's collapsing post-war consensus.

As a major element in this struggle local state institutions undertake a significant share of public spending and public borrowing. But as we have seen, this is not enough to explain the degree and type of control desired by the centre – very often the

Conservative Cabinet has been concerned with curtailing particular authorities or specific policies, which have only an infinitesimal direct significance in relation to the national economy. This is partly because local state institutions are a major site of collective service provision – acting not just as something which spends public money but also as the site of an attitude and an ideology. To put it simply, for the centre the money is being spent on the wrong people in the wrong way. And this can quite easily result in undesired effects on how people expect society to operate. David Blunkett (leader of Sheffield City Council) expresses this well:

> Mrs Thatcher is intent on changing the economic, social and political life of the country in a way that, to quote her own words, 'sweeps socialism from this land'. By that she does not simply mean the proposals of the Labour Party but collectivist and community socialisation in all its forms. Hence the obsession with destroying local government. (Ibid., 17 June 1983).

That it is a local council leader who says this hints at why local state institutions are a major arena for this conflict. For local government in particular is not just an object in the struggle, it is also a participant. Both Left and Right may use this opportunity to participate. The privatization plans of the Government, for instance, have been tried out at the local level in a few Tory authorities, and the lessons learnt there are being incorporated in future general legislation. More usually though, local governments, by their very nature as providers of collective services, preserve 'collectivist and community socialization'. But more than this, they may try to present practical alternatives of what British society should, and could, be like. This possibility is heightened when, as at present, opposition parties control most of local government – at the time of writing the Conservatives control only 2 out of 12 inner-London boroughs, 7 out of 20 outer-London boroughs, 1 out of 36 metropolitan authorities and 11 out of 39 shire counties (*New Statesman*, 17 October 1986). Restructuring local economies for labour, providing cheap public transport and building houses for rent, not sale, are just three examples of local government alternatives to central policy. To quote David Blunkett again:

> Local government is threatened so severely by Thatcher not because it challenges macro-economic policies but because it offers a genuine and legitimate defence against the encroachment of the new order. It is a living example of community as opposed to private endeavour.

In key areas it offers a coherent socialist alternative which genuinely
wins popular support. (Ibid.).

Although we would accept the major thrust of Blunkett's argument
concerning the importance of local government as both an element
in, and an arena for, the restructuring of British society, it must
be said that we find it difficult to view local government as 'a
coherent socialist alternative'. Indeed, the moribund bureaucracy
of many Labour-led local authorities over the post-war period has
done much to lend credence to Conservative attacks on 'welfare-
statism', and the appalling record of many councils has contributed
to the ease with which local welfare provision has been eroded.
Moreover, the power of local government officials, together with
the continued restrictive application of centrally imposed limits,
severely curtail the likelihood of local government at present
offering a socialist alternative. The point is, however, that local
government does offer a key site (perhaps the key site outside
Parliament) where such potential can be developed. It was the
awakening of this potential which contributed substantially to the
tightening of these centrally imposed limits through the legislation
we detailed above, and hence to the forming of the current local
government crisis.

To understand why this is the case we need to go back to two
crucial conceptual dichotomies identified in chapter 1. First, the
local state is both an agent of, and an obstacle to, central control,
and secondly, it performs both an interpretive and a representational
role. The latter dichotomy underpins the former, in that the local
state is both a key site for interpreting and managing capitalist
social relations, and also an institution that can represent local
interests. These two processes allow it to be at once agent and
obstacle. In order to see how these dichotomies have been felt
recently it is interesting to look at the experience of the GLC,
where perhaps the first stirrings of this awakening were felt. A left-
leaning Labour administration was elected in London on a fairly
radical manifesto in May 1981. In discussing the lessons to be learnt
from the GLC story, Stuart Hall (a leading political commentator
of the Left) claims that 'The question of the GLC and local
authorities...has become the most important front in the struggle
against Thatcherism.' He points out that along this front

we have the two essential conflicting principles of English political
life in direct confrontation...the camp of the profit motive and
possessive liberalism which Thatcherism represents; and the camp of
collective social need and the public interest, which the labour

movement, even in its most degenerated form, has always represented. Thatcherism put that fundamental divide squarely on the political agenda. The local authorities are contesting it on that very ground. (*New Socialist*, September 1984, p. 37)

Hall has clearly highlighted the interpretative role played by the local state, and the consequent confrontation with the centre that can result. He then moves on to discuss the representational aspect of the GLC (although he does not conceptualize events in these terms) by noting the way in which the authority has united and built on the diverse political and cultural movements operating in the capital. He concludes by noting the potential for social change that can appear when these two roles coalesce:

> It is one of the aspects of GLC politics – rooting itself in the everyday experience of popular urban life and culture, and becoming the leading force in moral and cultural life – which most holds out the promise (not everywhere much in evidence) that socialism could become the politics and culture of the future, and has something to say to life and living in the twenty-first century. (Ibid).

Drawing on this we can perhaps postulate that at those occasional times when a truly oppositional interpretative role joins with a significantly widespread representational role, the resulting potential is something that the centre is quick to neutralize – as in the case of the GLC, and as in the case of Oldham, Poplar and Clay Cross in the past. The centre quickly decides that both roles must be curtailed, so that alternative interpretation and effective representation of oppositional voices is stilled. When this happens the resultant changes in local–central relations will not just be felt in the authority concerned, but will instead affect the social relations of the state on a much more general level.

It is our contention that this is what happened over the past few years, and that this is why the current 'crisis' has developed. But of course the crisis of local government is much deeper and wider than just the GLC and its metropolitan counterparts. 'Red Ken' and abolition are only the highly visible tip of a whole iceberg of central–local change. To understand its extent we need to appreciate how uneven development has activated and sustained the contradictions inherent in the representational and interpretive roles of the local state.

As we stated earlier, the most recent round of this uneven development has resulted in wholesale changes to British economy and society. Post-war consensus, constructed around a fairly uniform geography as well as a uniform society, has given way to diversity and disjuncture. Places, as well as people and social groups, have become less alike and there is a greater disparity between various parts of the country. (And note that, in the passage by Hall on Thatcherism quoted above, he was commenting on '*English* political life' – presumably recognizing that political life in Wales, Scotland and not least Northern Ireland was different.) The run-down and poverty-stricken inner cities and other older industrial areas, afford an increasing contrast with suburban and 'green-field' developments. It is ironic that the former, with an ever-growing percentage of population dependent upon welfare provision, are almost entirely controlled by the Labour Party. This gives the Government an opportunity to attack its political opponents at the same time as it cuts public expenditure. As Michael Heseltine put it succinctly, when Secretary for the Environment: 'The city that is all subsidy is the city that is all Labour, because those who might choose, those who might resist, they go and in going the problems are compounded and the hold of the (professional) left is compounded' (*The Guardian*, 8 October 1982).

It is an opportunity that has not been wasted. As we have shown in some detail, central control has been used increasingly to restrict the activities of a small number of mainly urban Labour-controlled authorities. What began as a general attack has turned into a specific vendetta. Both fronts have produced positive results for the Government. In some cases local authorities have been prevented from operating the policies that they wished to – such as subsidized public transport systems – and in others they have been forced to operate those that they did not wish to – such as selling council houses. A general reduction in central grants has obviously limited the scope of local councils to extend and diversify services, especially once they have streamlined their management practices and service delivery structures. Rate-capping has tightened this limitation in certain authorities, and abolition has made sure that the Labour-controlled Metropolitan County Councils have no policies at all to implement.

It is difficult at this stage to draw a detailed conclusion as to the effects of central legislation, mainly because so many authorities have indulged in what has become known as 'creative accounting'. Services in general have been maintained through such means as rescheduling existing loans, mortgaging council buildings, borrowing money from overseas institutions and switching finance from revenue to current accounts. These methods will eventually produce an even greater financial shortage in the future, but for the present they have staved off immediate reductions in council services. Currently the effects of centralization are being more clearly felt in individual policy areas than they are in general financial terms.

Nevertheless it is clear that local autonomy has been seriously eroded by the wealth of central legislation that has been passed. Again it remains to be seen exactly what the impact of this will be. This is partly because the changes have not had time to make their full impact. But it is also because the largest curbs have been placed on the *potential* of local authorities to initiate and demonstrate change. In other words, future activities have been restricted as much as present ones – and we will never know if they would have been put into operation in any case, for it remains true that a few highly visible, large, Labour-controlled urban authorities were at the forefront of exploring the interpretive potential of local government. The vast number of local authorities have operated largely bipartisan policies which the centre has no real wish, or need, to restrict. But it also remains true that the reaction that these few councils provoked from the centre indicates how seriously their threat was taken. Moreover, the contents of counter-legislation, for example, to make councils put contracts for service provision out to private competition, shows that the Conservatives themselves see local authorities as important elements and arenas of social change.

This means that those processes operating locally in and around the institutions of the local state will remain important politically, as the local state continues its contradictory relationship as agent and obstacle to the centre. Moreover, the processes of uneven development are also likely to continue as the effects of the recession bite deeper. These in turn will promote more responses from local coalitions determined to alleviate decline in their particular area, and as in the past the local authorities will play a key role in promoting and sustaining these coalitions. Of course, their make-up and demands will differ from place to place – but this will only serve to highlight the effects of uneven development. The current crisis of local government that we have described will thus continue as long as the larger social and economic crisis of which it is a part remains unresolved. The social relations of the local state ensure that this will be the case, and we need to appreciate them and the contradictory processes they generate before we can understand the contemporary crisis of local government.

References

Alcock, P. (1983) 'Social security', in 'Banishing Dark Divisive Clouds: Welfare and the Conservative Government 1979–1983', *Critical Social Policy*, 8.

Alcock, P. and Lee, P. (1981) 'The Socialist Republic of South Yorkshire?', *Critical Social Policy*, 1, 2.

Alcock, P., Bennington, J., Cochrane, A. and Lee, P. (1984) 'A Parable of How Things Might be Done Differently', *Critical Social Policy*, 9.

Ali, T. (1984) *Who's Afraid of Margaret Thatcher?* (Verso, London).

Alt, J. (1971) 'Some Social and Political Correlates of County Borough Expenditure', *British Journal of Political Science*, 1, pp. 49–62.

Alt, J. (1977) 'Politics and Expenditure Models', *Policy and Politics*, 5, 3, pp. 83–92.

Anderson, B. (1983) *Imagined Communities: Reflections on the Origin and Spread of Nationalism* (Verso, London).

Anderson, J. (1983) 'Geography as Ideology and the Politics of Crisis: The Enterprise Zones Experiment', in Anderson, J., Duncan, S. and Hudson, R. eds *Redundant Spaces in Cities and Regions?* (Academic Press, London).

Ashford, D. (1974) 'The Effects of Central Finance on the British Local Government System', *British Journal of Political Science*, 4, pp. 305–22.

Ashford, D. (1975) 'Resources, Spending and Party Politics in British Local Government', *Administration and Society*, 7.

Ashford, D., Berne, R. and Schramm, R. (1976) 'The Expenditure Financing Decision in British Local Government', *Policy and Politics*, 5, pp. 5–24.

Audit Commission (1984) *The Impact on Local Authorities' Economy, Efficiency and Effectiveness of the Block Grant Distribution System* (HMSO, London).

Audit Commission (1985) *Capital Expenditure Controls in Local Government in England and Wales: A Report by the Audit Commission* (HMSO, London).

Bacon, R. and Eltis, W. A. (1978) *Britain's Economic Problems: Too Few Producers* (Macmillan, London).

Ball, M. (1978) 'British Housing Policy and the Housebuilding Industry', *Capital and Class*, 4, pp. 78–99.

Ball, M. (1982) 'Housing Provision and the Economic Crisis', *Capital and Class*, 17, pp. 60–77.

Ball, M. (1983) *Housing Policy and Economic Power* (Methuen, London).

Banham, R., Barker, P., Hall, P. and Povie, C. (1969) 'Non-Plan: An Experiment in Freedom', *New Society*, (20 March).

Barnett, R. and Topham, N. (1977) 'Evaluating the Distribution of Local Outputs in a Decentralised Structure of Government', *Policy and Politics*, 6.

Bassett, K. and Short, J. (1980) *Housing and Residential Structure* (Routledge and Kegan Paul, London).

Bevan, P. (1980) *Social Reproduction and the Reproduction of Labour Power: Beyond Urban Sociology* (University of Sussex, Falmer, Brighton), Urban and Regional Studies Working Paper, 22.

Blondel, J. and Hall, R. (1967) 'Conflict, Decision-Making and the Perceptions of Local Councillors', *Political Studies*, 15, pp. 322–50.

Blunkett, D. and Green, G. (1983) 'Building from the Bottom: The Sheffield Experience', *Fabian Tract*, p. 491.

Boaden, N. (1971) *Urban Policy-Making* (Cambridge University Press, Cambridge).

Boaden, N. and Alford, R. (1969) 'Sources of Diversity in English Local Government Decisions', *Public Administration*, 47, pp. 203–23.

Boddy, M. (1984) 'Local Councils and the Financial Squeeze', in Boddy, C. and Fudge, M. eds *Local Socialism?* (Macmillan, London), ch. 9.

Bonjean, C., Clark, T. and Lineberry, R. eds (1971) *Community Politics* (Free Press, New York).

Boyle, R. (1983) 'Privatising Urban Problems: A Commentary on Recent Anglo–American Urban Policy'. Unpublished paper presented to Political Science Association Working Group on UK Politics, Oxford (August).

Bramley, G. (1984) 'Mr Jenkin's Cudgel' *Roof*, July/August.

Branson, N. (1979) *Poplarism 1919–26: George Lansbury and the Councillors' Revolt* (Lawrence and Wishart, London).

Budge, I., Brand, J., Margolis, M. and Smith, A. (1972) *Political Stratification and Democracy* (Macmillan, London).

Bulpitt, J. (1984) 'Thatcherism and Monetarism: The Development of Territorial Management', in McAllister, I. and Rose, R. eds *The Nationwide Competition for Votes: the 1983 British Election* (Francis Pinter, London).

Burgess, T. and Travers, T. (1980) *Ten Billion Pounds: Whitehall's Takeover of the Town Halls* (Grant McIntyre, London).

Byrne, D. (1980a) 'The Standard of Council Housing in Inter-War North Shields – A Case Study in the Politics of Reproduction', in Melling, J. ed. *Housing, Social Policy and the State* (Croom Helm, London), pp. 168–93.

Byrne, D. (1980b) 'Reproductive Politics and Class Politics in a Different Place'. Unpublished paper given at Institute of British Geographers Annual Conference, Manchester, January.

Byrne, D. (1982) 'Class and the Local State', *International Journal of Urban and Regional Research*, 6, 1, pp. 61–82.

Cabinet Office (1985) 'Lifting the burden' (HMSO, London) Cmnd 9571.

Campbell, D. and Forbes, P. (1986) 'Gags for Local Authorities', *New Statesman* (21 February).

Carr, M. and Weir, S. (1986) 'Sunrise City', *New Socialist*, 41, pp. 7–10.

Carvel, J. (1983) *Citizen Ken* (Chatto and Windus, London).

Castells, M. (1977) *The Urban Question* (Edward Arnold, London).

Castells, M. (1978) *City, Class and Power* (Macmillan, London).

Castells, M. and Goddard, F. (1974) *Monopolville* (Mouton, Paris).

Cawson, A. (1985) 'Corporatism and Local Politics', in Grant, W. ed. *The Political Economy of Corporatism* (Macmillan, London), ch. 5.

Cawson, A. and Saunders, P. (1983) 'Corporatism, Competitive Politics and Class Struggle', in King, R. ed. *Capital and Politics* (Routledge and Kegan Paul, London).

Cheetham, T. (1980) 'Forlorn Hopes of Improvement to the Bill', *Local Government Chronicle* (25 July).

Clavel, P. (1986) *The Progressive City: Planning and Participation 1969–1984* (Rutgers University Press, New Jersey).

Cochrane, A. (1983) 'Local Economic Policies: Trying to Drain the Ocean with a Teaspoon', in Anderson, J., Duncan, S. S. and Hudson, R. *Redundant Spaces In Cities and Regions?* (Academic Press, London).

Cockburn, C. (1977) *The Local State* (Pluto, London).

Cohen, A. ed. (1982) *Belonging. Identity and Social Organisation in British Rural Cultures* (Manchester University Press, Manchester).

Cole, T. (1983) 'Life and Labour in the Isle of Dogs'. Unpublished Ph.D. thesis (University of Oklahoma, Norman, Oklahoma).

Community Development Project (1976) *Whatever Happened to Council Housing?* (Home Office, London).

Community Development Project (1977) *The Costs of Industrial Change* (Home Office, London).

Cooke, P. (1983) 'Regional Restructuring: Class Politics and Popular Protest in South Wales', *Society and Space*, 1, 3.

Cooke, P. (1985a) 'Radical Regions: A Comparison of South Wales, Emilia and Provence', in Rees, G. ed. *Political Action and Social Identity: Class, Locality and Culture* (Macmillan, London).

Cooke, P. (1985b) 'Class Practices as Regional Markers: A Contribution to Labour Geography', in Gregory, D. and Urry, J. eds *Social Relations and Spatial Structures* (Macmillan, London), ch. 10.

Coopers and Lybrand Associates (1983) *'Streamlining the Cities': an Analysis of the Government's Case for Reorganising Local Government in the Six Metropolitan Counties* (London).

Coopers and Lybrand Associates (1984) *'Streamlining the Cities': an*

Analysis of the Costs Involved in the Government's Proposals (London).

Cowell, D., Jones, T. and Young, J. (1982) *Policing the Riots* (Junction Books, London).

Crompton, P. (1982) 'The Lothian Affair: A Battle of Principles, in McCrone, D. ed. *The Scottish Government Yearbook 1983*. (Research Centre for Social Sciences, University of Edinburgh, Edinburgh).

CSE State Group (1979) *Struggle over the State: Cuts and Restructuring in Contemporary Britain* (CSE Books, London).

Dahl, R. (1961) *Who Governs?* (Yale University Press, New Haven).

Damer, S. (1980) 'State, class and housing; Glasgow 1885–1919' in Melling, J. ed. *Housing, Social Policy and the State* (Croom Helm, London) pp. 73–112.

Danemark, B., Elander, I., Strömberg, T., Söderfeldt, B. (1985) *A Success Story? Housing Policy in Three Swedish Communes* (University of Örebro, Örebro, Sweden), Research Report, 85–4.

Danziger, J. (1976) 'Twenty-Six Outputs in Search of a Taxonomy', *Policy and Politics*, 5.

Danziger, J. (1978) *Making Budgets* (Sage, Beverley Hills).

Darke, R. and Walker, R. eds (1977) *Local Government and the Public* (Leonard Hill, London).

Davies, B. (1968) *Social Needs and Resources in Local Services* (Michael Joseph, London).

Davies, B., Barton, A., McMillan, I. and Williamson, V. (1971) *Variations in Services for the Aged: A Causal Analysis* (Bell and Sons, London).

Davies, B., Barton, A. and McMillan, I. (1972) *Variations in Children's Services Among British Urban Authorities* (Bell and Sons, London).

Davies, J. (1972) *The Evangelistic Bureaucrat* (Tavistock, London).

Dawson, D. (1976) 'Determinants of Local Authority Expenditure', *Report of the Committee of Enquiry into Local Government Finance*, (HMSO, London), appendix 7.

Deacon, A. and Briggs, J. (1974) 'Local democracy and central policy. The issue of paper votes in the 1920s', *Policy and Politics*, 2, 347–64.

Dearlove, J. (1973) *The Politics of Policy in Local Government* (Cambridge University Press, Cambridge).

Dearlove, J. (1979) *The Reorganisation of British Local Government* (Cambridge University Press, Cambridge).

Dearlove, J. and Saunders, P. (1984) *Introduction to British Politics* (Polity Press, Cambridge).

Dennis, W. (1972) *Public Participation and Planners' Blight* (Faber and Faber, London).

Department of the Environment (1977a) *Policy for the Inner Cities* (HMSO London) Cmnd 6845.

Department of the Environment (1977b) *Housing Policy* (HMSO, London) Cmnd 6851.

Department of the Environment (1981) *Alternatives to Domestic Rates* (HMSO London) Cmnd 8449.

Department of the Environment (1983a) *Rates* (HMSO, London) Cmnd 9008.

Department of the Environment (1983b) *Streamlining the cities* (HMSO, London) Cmnd 9063.

Department of the Environment (1986) *Paying for Local Government* (HMSO, London) Cmnd 9714.

Dickens, P., Duncan, S. S., Goodwin, M. and Gray, F. (1985) *Housing, States and Localities* (Methuen, London).

Direct Labour Collective (1978) *Building with Direct Labour: Local Authority Building and the Crisis in the Construction Industry.* (Housing Workshop of the Conference of Socialist Economists, London).

Direct Labour Collective (1980) *Direct Labour under Attack* (Housing Workshop of the Conference of Socialist Economists, London).

Duncan, S. S. (1981) 'Urban Research and the Methodology of Levels: The Case of Castells', *International Journal of Urban and Regional Research*, 5, 3, pp. 231–54.

Duncan, S. S. (1986) *What is Locality?* (University of Sussex, Falmer, Brighton), Working Paper in Urban and Regional Studies, 51.

Duncan, S. S. (1988) 'What is a Locality?', in Peet, R. and Thrift, N. *New Models in Geography* (George Allen and Unwin, London), ch. 19.

Duncan, S. S. and Goodwin, M. (1980) *The Local State and Restructuring Social Relations: Theory and Practice',* (University of Sussex, Falmer, Brighton), Working Paper in Urban and Regional Studies, 24.

Duncan, S. S. and Goodwin, M. (1982a) 'The Local State: Functionalism, Autonomy and Class Relations in Cockburn and Saunders' *Political Geography Quarterly* 1, 1, pp. 77–96.

Duncan, S. S. and Goodwin, M. (1982b) 'The Local State and Restructuring Social Relations', *International Journal Urban and Regional Research*, 6, 2, pp. 157–85.

Duncan, S. S. and Goodwin, M. (1985a) 'The Local State and Local Economic Policy: Why the Fuss?', *Policy and Politics*, 13, 3, pp. 227–53.

Duncan, S. S. and Goodwin, M. (1985b) 'Local Economic Policies: Local Regeneration or Political Mobilisation', *Local Government Studies*, 11, 6, pp. 75–96.

Duncan, S. S. and Goodwin, M. (1985c) *Central Control versus Local Autonomy: The Local Government Crisis in Britain 1979–84,* (London School of Economics, London), Discussion Paper in Geography, 13–15.

Dunleavy, P. (1980) *Urban Political Analysis* (Macmillan, London).

Dunleavy, P. (1981) *The Politics of Mass Housing in Britain 1945–75* (Clarenden Press, Oxford).

Dunleavy, P. (1984) 'The Limits to Local Government', in Boddy and Fudge, eds *Local Socialism* (Macmillan, London).

Dye, T. (1966) *Politics, Economics and the Public* (Rand McNally, Chicago).

Elliott, B. and McCrone, D. (1982) 'Austerity, Autonomy and the Politics of Resistance', in McCrone, ed. *The Scottish Government Yearbook 1983*, (Research Centre for Social Sciences, University of Edinburgh, Edinburgh) ch. 5.

Erikson, R. A. and Syms, P. M. (1986) 'The Effects of Enterprise Zones on Property Prices', *Regional Studies*, 20, 1, pp. 1–14.

ESRC (1985a) *Research Initiative on Social Change and Economic Life* (Social Affairs Committee, ESRC, London).

ESRC (1985b) *The Changing Urban and Regional Systems in the UK* (Environment and Planning Committee, ESRC, London).

ESRC (1986) *'Changing Urban and Regional Systems in the UK'*, Research Programme Bulletin, 2 (ESRC, London).

Evans, C. (1983) 'The Administrative Structure of Public Transport in England and Wales, 1930–1983'. Unpublished paper, Urban Policy and Local–Central Relations Project, (Urban and Regional Studies, University of Sussex, Falmer, Brighton).

Fielding, N. (1984) 'Who is Subsidising Whom', *Roof*, 9, 2, pp. 11–14.

Fielding, N. and Seyd, P. (1984) 'Cities in Revolt', *New Socialist*, (September).

Fine, B. and Harris, L. (1985) *Peculiarities of the British Economy* (Lawrence and Wishart, London).

Flynn, N. (1985) 'Direct Labour Organisation', in Jones, S. and Jones, G. *Between Centre and Locality* (George Allen and Unwin, London), ch. 7.

Flynn, N., Leach, S. and Vielba, C. (1985) *Abolition or Reform?* (George Allen and Unwin, London).

Forest, R. and Murie, A. (1984) *Monitoring the Right to Buy* (University of Bristol, School for Advanced Urban Studies, Bristol), Working Paper 4.

Forest, R. and Murie, A. (1985a) *An Unreasonable Act? Central-Local Government Conflict and the Housing Act 1980* (University of Bristol, School for Advanced Urban Studies, Bristol), Occasional Paper 1.

Forest, R. and Murie, A. (1985b) 'Marginalisation and Subsidised Individualism: The Sale of Council Homes in the Restructuring of the British Welfare State', *International Journal of Urban and Regional Research*, 10, 1.

Foster, J. (1974) *Class Struggle and the Industrial Revolution* (Methuen, London).

Foster, J. (1979) 'How Imperial London Preserved its Slums', *International Journal of Urban and Regional Research*, 3, 1, pp. 93–114.

Foster, J. (1980) 'Scottish nationality and the origins of capitalism', ch. 1. in Dickson, T. (ed.), *Scottish Capitalism* (Lawrence and Wishart, London).

Foster, C., Jackman, R. and Perlman, M. (1980) *Local Government in a Unitary state* (George Allen and Unwin, London).

Fothergill, S. and Gudgin, G. (1982) *Unequal Growth* (Heinemann, London).

Francis, H. and Smith, D. (1980) *The Fed: A History of South Wales Miners in the Twentieth Century* (Lawrence and Wishart, London).

Fried, R. (1975) 'Comparative Urban Policy and Performance', in Greenstein and Polsby (eds), *Policies and Policy Making: Handbook of Political Science*, vol. 6 (Addison-Wesley, Reading, Mass.).

GLC (Greater London Council) (1984) *The Future of the GLC* (Greater London Council, London).

Gamble, A. (1981) *Britain in Decline* (Macmillan, London).

Giddens, A. (1981) *A Contemporary Critique of Historical Materialism* (Macmillan, London).

Giddens, A. (1984) *The Constitution of Society* (Polity Press, Cambridge).

Ginsberg, N. (1981) 'Housing Policy under the Tories', *Critical Social Policy*, 1, 1.

Glyn, A. and Harrison, J. (1980) *The British Economic Disaster*, (Pluto, London).

Goldsmith, M. (1981) *Politics, Planning and the City* (Hutchinson, London).

Goodwin, M. (1984) 'Council Housing, the Social Democratic State and the Locality'. Unpublished Ph.D. thesis (University of London).

Goodwin, M. (1986a) *Locality and Local State: Sheffield's Economic Policy* (University of Sussex, Falmer, Brighton), Urban and Regional Studies, Working Paper, 52.

Goodwin, M. (1986b) *Locality and Local State: Economic Policy for London's Docklands* (University of Sussex, Falmer, Brighton), Urban and Regional Studies Working Paper, 53.

Goodwin, M. (1988) 'Replacing a surplus population: the housing and employment policies of the London Docklands Development Corporation' in Hamnet, C. and Allen, J. (eds) *Housing and Labour Markets* (Hutchinson, London).

Goodwin, M. and Duncan, S. S. (1986) 'The Local State and Local Economic Policy: Political Mobilisation or Economic Regeneration', *Capital and Class*, 27.

Goss, S. (1983) 'Restructuring London Government – A Southwark Case Study'. Unpublished MA thesis (University of Sussex, Falmer, Brighton).

Gough, J. (1985) 'Class Relations and Local Economic Planning', in Hoggart, K. and Kofman, E. eds *Politics, Geography and Social Stratification* (Croom Helm, London), ch. 7.

Gray, F. (1976) 'The Management of Local Authority Housing' in *Housing and Class in Britain* (Housing Workshop of the Conference of Socialist Economists, London).

Griffith, J. (1982) 'The Law Lords and the GLC', *Marxism Today*, (February).

Gyford, J. (1976) *Local Politics in Britain* (Croom Helm, London).

Gyford, J. (1985) *The Politics of Local Socialism* (George Allen and Unwin, London).

Halford, S. (1987) 'Women's initiatives in local government: tokenism or power?' (University of Sussex, Falmer, Brighton) Urban and Regional Studies Working Paper, 58.

Hall, P. (1977) 'Green Fields – Grey Areas', (Royal Town Planning Institute Annual conference 15 June).

Hall, S. and Jacques, M. (1983) *The Politics of Thatcherism* (Lawrence and Wishart, London).

Hampton, W. (1970) *Democracy and Community* (Oxford University Press, Oxford).

Harloe, M. (1978) 'The Housing Policy Review', in Baldwin, S. and Brown, M. eds *Year Book of Social Policy in Britain 1978* (Routledge and Kegan Paul, London).

Harloe, M. (1979) 'Marxism, the State and the Urban Question', in Crouch, C. ed. *State and Economy in Contemporary Capitalism* (Croom Helm, London).

Harloe, M. (1980) 'Housing and the State. Recent British Developments', in Ungerson, C. and Karn, V. eds *The Consumer Experience of Housing* (Gower, Farnborough).

Harvey, D. (1982) *The Limits to Capital* (Basil Blackwell, Oxford).

Harvey, D. (1985a) 'The Geopolitics of Capitalism', in Gregory, D. and Urry, J. eds *Social Relations and Spatial Structures*, (Macmillan, London) ch. 7.

Harvey, D. (1985b) *The Urbanisation of Capital* (Basil Blackwell, Oxford).

Hill, R. (1986) 'Urban Transport: From Technical Process to Social Policy', in Lawless, C. and Pabon, C. eds *The Contemporary British City* (Harper and Row, London), ch. 5.

Hipkin, B. (1984) 'Writing on the Wall for the GLC' *Marxism Today*, August.

Hoggart, K. (1986) 'Geography, Political Control and Local Government Policy Outputs', *Progress on Human Geography*, 1.

Hooper, A. (1985) 'Estimating Land Availability for Private Home-Building: Some Methodological Issues', in Barrett, S. and Healey, P. eds *Land Policy: Problems and Alternatives* (Gower, London).

House of Lords Select Committee on the London Docklands Development Corporation (1981) (a) Transcript of sittings, (b) Final Report (HMSO, London).

Howe, G. (1978) 'Liberating Free Enterprise: A New Experiment'. Speech given to Bow Group, Isle of Dogs, 26 June 1978. Reprinted in Sternlieb, G. and Listat, D. eds (1981) *New Tools for Economic Development* (Rutgers University, Centre for Urban Policy Research, New Jersey).

Hunter, F. (1983) *Community Power Structure*. (University of North Carolina Press, Chapel Hill).

Jaggi, M., Muller, R. and Schmid, S. (1977) *Red Bologna* (Writers and Readers Publishing Co-operative, London).

Jessop, B. (1980) 'The Transformation of the State in Post-War Britain', in Scase, R. ed. *The State in Western Europe* (Croom Helm, London).

Johnston, R. J. (1983) 'The Neighbourhood Effect Won't Go Away', *Geoforum*, 14, pp. 161–8.

Johnston, R. J. (1985) *The Geography of English Politics: The 1983 General Election* (Croom Helm, London).

Jones, G. (1969) *Borough Politics* (Macmillan, London).

Jones, G. (1975) 'Varieties of Local Politics' *Local Government Studies*, 1, 2, pp. 1–16.

Jones, G. ed. (1980) *New Approaches to the Study of Central–Local Government Relationships* (Gower/SSRC, London).

Jones, G. and Stewart, J. (1983) *The Case for Local Government* (George Allen and Unwin, London).

Jordan, G. and Reilly, G. (1981) 'Enterprise Zones: Non-Intervention as a Form of Intervention. The Clydebank Enterprise Zone and Policy Substitution', in Drucker, A. and Drucker, N. eds *The Scottish Government Yearbook 1982* (Research Centre for Social Sciences, University of Edinburgh, Edinburgh), ch. 7.

Karn, V. (1985) 'Housing', in Ranson, S. and Jones, G. eds *Between Centre and Locality* (George Allen and Unwin, London), ch. 10.

King, A. (1987) *New Directions in Urban Policy: The Merseyside Development Corporation and Task Force* (University of Sussex, Falmer, Brighton), Urban and Regional Studies Working Paper, 57.

King, P. (1973) 'Why Do Local Authority Rate Poundages Differ?', *Public Administration*, 51, pp. 165–73.

King, R. (1985) 'Corporatism and the Local Economy', in Grant, ed. *The Political Economy of Corporatism*, ch. 8.

Klausner, D. (1985) *Behind the Dock Walls: Popular Planning in Newham*, (London School of Economics, London), Geography Discussion Paper, 17.

Korpi, W. (1978) *The Working Class in Welfare Capitalism* (Routledge and Kegan Paul, London).

Lansley, S. (1985) 'The Phony War', *New Socialist*, (July).

Layfield, F. (Chair) (1976) *Report of the Committee of Enquiry into Local Government Finance* (HMSO, London) Cmnd 6453.

Leys, C. (1983) *Politics in Britain: An Introduction* (Heinemann, London).

Lojkine, J. (1985) 'The Working Class and the State: The French Experience in Socialist and Communist Municipalities', in Szelenyi, I. ed. *Cities in Recession: Critical Responses to the Urban Politics of the New Right* (Sage, Beverley Hills), pp. 217–27.

Loughlin, M. (1981) 'Local Government, Planning and Land Act: Local Government in the Welfare Corporate State', *Modern Law Review*, 44.

Loughlin, M. (1982) 'Developments in Central–Local Fiscal Relations', *Journal of Law and Society*, 9, 2.

Loughlin, M. (1986) 'Municipal Socialism in a Unitary State', in McAuslan, P. and McEldonney, J. *Law, Legitimacy and the State* (Sweet and Maxwell, London).

Mackenzie, R. and Rose, D. (1983) 'Industrial change, the domestic economy and home life', in Anderson, J., Duncan, S. S. and Hudson, R. eds *Redundant Spaces in Cities and Regions* (Academic Press, London).

MacIntyre, S. (1980) *Little Moscows: Communism and Working Class*

Militancy in Inter-War Britain (Croom Helm, London).

McCulloch, D. (1982) 'The New Housing Finance System', *Local Government Studies*, 8, 3.

Mark-Lawson, J., Savage, M. and Warde, A. (1985) 'Gender and Local Politics: Struggles over Welfare 1918–1934', in Murgatroyd, D. et al. eds *Localities, Class and Gender* (Pion, London).

Marx, K. (1975) *Early Writings* (Penguin, London).

Massey, D. (1977) 'Industrial Location Theory Reconsidered' (Open University, Milton Keynes), D204, Unit 25.

Massey, D. (1979) 'In What Sense a Regional Problem?', *Regional Studies*, 13.

Massey, D. (1984) *Spatial Divisions of Labour* (Macmillan, London).

Massey, D. and Catelano, A. (1978) *Capital and Land: Landownership by Capital in Great Britain* (Edward Arnold, London).

Melling, J. ed. (1980) *Housing, Social Policy and the State* (Croom Helm, London).

Mellor, R. (1977) *Urban Sociology in an Urbanised Society* (Routledge and Kegan Paul, London).

Middlemas, K. (1979) *Politics in Industrial Society* (André Deutsch, London).

Merrett, S. (1979) *State Housing in Britain* (Routledge and Kegan Paul, London).

Midwinter, A., Keating, M. and Taylor, P. (1982) *Excessive and Unreasonable: The Politics of the Hit List* (University of Strathclyde, Glasgow), Working Paper Department of Administration; and *Political Studies*, 21, 3.

Midwinter, A. and Mair, C. (1987) *Rates Reform: Issues, Arguments and Evidence* (University of Strathclyde, Glasgow).

Miliband, R. (1969) *The State in Capitalist Society* (Weidenfeld and Nicholson, London).

Miller, W. L. (1977) *Electoral Dynamics in Britain Since 1918* (Macmillan, London).

Miller, W. L. (1978) 'Social Class and Party Choice in England: A New Analysis', *British Journal of Political Science*, 8, pp. 257–84.

Minns, R. (1974) 'Who Builds More?', *New Society*, 603, pp. 184–6.

Morrell, F. and Bundred, S. (1984) 'No Short Cut', *New Socialist*, September.

Murgatroyd, L., Savage, M., Shapiro, D., Urry, J., Walby, S. and Warde, A. (1985) *Localities, Class and Gender* (Pion, London).

Murray, R. (1977) 'Value and Theory of Rent: Part I', *Capital and Class*, 3.

Murray, R. (1978) 'Value and Theory of Rent: Part II', *Capital and Class*, 4.

Neale, R. S. (1981) *Bath, 1680–1850. A Social History* (Routledge and Kegan Paul, London).

Newton, K. (1976) *Second City Politics* (Oxford University Press, Oxford).

Newton, K. and Karran, T. (1985) *The Politics of Local Expenditure* (Macmillan, London).

Nicholson, R. and Topham, N. (1971) 'The Determinants of Investment in Housing by Local Authorities: An Econometric Approach', *Journal of the Royal Statistical Society*, series A, 134, pp. 273–320.

Nicholson, R. and Topham, N. (1972) 'Investment Decision and the Size of Local Authorities', *Policy and Politics*, 1, pp. 23–44.

Nicholson, R. and Topham, N. (1975) 'Urban Road Provision in England and Wales, 1962–68, *Policy and Politics*, 5, pp. 3–29.

North Southwark Community Development Group (1983) *Annual Report* (NSCDG, London).

NUPE/Titterton (1983) *Excessive and Unreasonable: The Case Against George Younger* (NUPE Scotland, Edinburgh).

Oliver, F. and Stanyer, J. (1969) 'Some Aspects of the Financial Behaviour of County Boroughs', *Public Administration*, 47, pp. 169–84.

Open Group (1969) 'Social Reform in the Centrifugal Society', *New Society*, (11 September).

Page, E. (1982) 'Why Should Central–Local Relations in Scotland be Different to those in England?', in Jones, ed. *New Approaches to the Study of Central–Local Relationships* (Gower/SSRC, London).

Pahl, R. (1975) *Whose City?* 2nd edn (Penguin, London).

Parkinson, M. (1985) *Liverpool on the Brink* (Hermitage, Berks.).

Parkinson, M. and Duffy, J. (1984) 'Government's Response to Inner-City Riots: The Minister for Merseyside and the Task Force', *Parliamentary Affaris*, 37, pp. 76–96.

Pickvance, C. ed. (1976) *Urban Sociology: Critical Essays* (Tavistock, London).

Pinch, S. (1978) 'Patterns of Local Authority Housing Allocation in Greater London between 1966–73: As Inter-Borough Analysis', *Transactions of IBG*, new series 3, pp. 35–54.

Pinch, S. (1985) *Cities and Services* (Routledge and Kegan Paul, London).

Rees, G. (1986) '"Coalfield Culture" and the 1984–85 Miners' Strike: A Reply to Sunley', *Society and Space*, 4, 4, pp. 469–76.

Rentoul, S. and Wolmar, C. (1984) 'Fitting the Cap', *New Statesman*, (24 June 1984).

Rhodes, R. (1975) 'The Lost World of British Local Politics?', *Local Government Studies*, 1, 3, pp. 39–60.

Rhodes, R. (1980a) 'Some Myths in Central–Local Relations', *Town Planning Review*, 51, pp. 270–85.

Rhodes, R. (1980b) 'Analysing Inter-Governmental Relations', *European Journal of Political Research*, 8, pp. 289–322.

Rhodes, R. (1983) '"Power-Dependence" Theories of Central–Local Relations: A Critical Assessment'. Paper for the SSRC Conference on Political Theory and Central–Local Government Relations, Oxford (September).

Robson, W. (1966) *Local Government in Crisis* (George Allen and Unwin, London).

Roger Tym and Partners (1981) *Monitoring the Enterprise Zones. Year 1 Report* (London).

Roger Tym and Partners (1982) *Monitoring the Enterprise Zones. Year 2 Report* (London).

Ruggie, M. (1984) *The State and Working Women* (Princeton University Press, Princeton).

SAUS (School for Advanced Urban Studies) (1983) *Statement in Response to the Rates White Paper* (University of Bristol, Bristol).

Sack, R. D. (1980) *Conceptions of Space in Social Thought* (Macmillan, London).

Saunders, P. (1979) *Urban Politics: A Sociological Interpretation* (Hutchinson, London).

Saunders, P. (1980) *Towards a Non-Spatial Urban Sociology*, (University of Sussex, Falmer, Brighton), Urban and Regional Studies Working Paper, 21.

Saunders, P. (1981) *Social Theory and the Urban Question* (Hutchinson, London).

Saunders, P. (1982) 'Why Study Central–Local Relations?', *Local Government Studies*, (March/April), pp. 55–66.

Saunders, P. (1984a) 'Rethinking Local Politics', in Boddy, M. and Fudge, C. eds *Local Socialism*, (Macmillan, London) ch. 2.

Saunders, P. (1984b) *We Can't Afford Democracy too Much: Findings from a Study of Regional State Institutions in South-East England* (University of Sussex, Falmer, Brighton), Urban and Regional Studies Working Paper, 43.

Saunders, P. (1985a) *Social Theory and the Urban Question* 2nd edn (Hutchinson, London).

Saunders, P. (1985b) 'Urban Service Provision and the Regional State in England'. Paper prepared for 'Spatial Structures and Social Process' conference, Greece, (September).

Saunders, P. (1985c) 'The Forgotten Dimension of Central–Local Relations: Theorising the "Regional State"', *Environment and Planning C: Government and Policy*, 3, pp. 149–62.

Saunders, P. (1985d) 'Corporatism and Urban Service Provision', in Grant, ed. *The Political Economy of Corporatism*, ch. 6.

Saunders, P. (1985e) 'Space, the city, and urban sociology' in Gregory, D. and Urry, J. eds *Social Relations and Spatial Structures* (Macmillan, London), ch. 5.

Saunders, P. (1986) 'Reflections on the Dual Politics Thesis: the Argument, its Origins and its Critics', in Goldsmith, M. ed. *Urban Political Theory and the Management of Fiscal Stress* (Gower, London).

Saunders, P. (1987) 'The City, Space and the Created Environment in the Social Theory of Anthony Giddens', in Held, D. and Thompson, J. eds *Critical Theory of the Industrial Societies* (Cambridge University Press, Cambridge).

Saunders, P. and Williams, P. (1984) 'Clarity Begins at Home: some

Thoughts on Recent and Future Developments in Urban Studies'. Unpublished discussion paper, BSA Sociology and Environment Studies Group Seminar, LSE, (November).

Savage, M. (1987) *What Happened to Red Clydeside? Political Parties in the Local Social Structure* (University of Sussex, Falmer, Brighton), Urban and Regional Studies, unpublished paper.

Sayer, A. (1979) *Theory and Empirical Research in Urban and Regional Political Economy: A Sympathetic Critique* (University of Sussex, Falmer, Brighton), Urban and Regional Studies Working Paper, 14.

Sayer, A. (1982) 'Misconceptions of Space in Social Thought', *Transactions of the Institute of British Geographers*, New Series 7.

Sayer, A. (1984) *Explanation in Social Science: A Realist Approach* (Hutchinson, London).

Sayer, A. (1985a) 'The Difference that Space Makes', in Gregory, D. and Urry, J. eds *Social Relations and Spatial Structures* (Macmillan, London), ch. 4.

Sayer, A. (1985b) 'Locales, Localities and Why we Want to Study them'. Unpublished working note, (University of Sussex, Falmer, Brighton).

Schifferes, S. (1980) 'The Housing Bill 1980: The Beginning of the End for Council Housing', *Roof*, (January).

Sharp, E. (1969) The Ministry of Housing and Local Government (George Allen and Unwin, London).

Sharp, L. and Newton, K. (1984) *Does Politics Matter* (Clarendon Press, Oxford).

Sheffield City Council (1981) *Alternative Economic Policies – a Local Government Response* (Sheffield CC, Sheffield).

Short, J. (1982) *An Introduction to Political Geography* (Routledge and Kegan Paul, London).

Shutt, J. (1984) 'Tory Enterprise Zones and the Labour Movement', *Capital and Class*, 23.

Simmie, J. (1981) *Power, Property and Corporatism* (Macmillan, London).

Simmie, J. (1985) 'Corporatism and Planning', Grant, W., ed. *The Political Economy of Corporatism* (Macmillan, London), ch. 7.

Skinner, D. and Langdon, J. (1974) *The Story of Clay Cross* (Spokesman Books, Nottingham).

Smith, D. (1982) *Conflict and Compromise. Class Formation in English Society 1814–1914* (Routledge and Kegan Paul, London).

Smith, N. (1984) *Uneven Development: Nature, Capital and the Production of Space* (Basil Blackwell, Oxford).

Smith, P. and Brown, P. (1983) 'Industrial change and Scottish nationalism since 1945', in Anderson, J., Duncan, S. S. and Hudson, R. *Redundant Spaces in Cities and Regions?* (Academic Press, London).

Stacey, M., Batstone, E., Bell, C. and Murcott, A. (1975) *Power, Persistence and Change* (Routledge and Kegan Paul, London).

Stedman-Jones, G. (1971) *Outcast London: A Study in the Relationship between Classes in Victorian London* (Oxford University Press, Oxford).

Stewart, J. (1980) 'The New Government's Policies for Local Government' *Local Government Studies*, (March/April).

Stewart, J. (1983) *Local Government: The Conditions of Local Choice* (George Allen and Unwin, London).

Stewart, J. (1984) 'Storming the Town-Halls: A Rate-Cap Revolution', *Marxism Today*, (April).

Stewart, J. and Underwood, J. (1983) 'New Relations in the Inner-City' in Young, K. and Mason, C. (eds) *Urban Economic Development* (Macmillan, London).

Strathern, M. (1984) 'The Social Meaning of Localism', in Bradley, T. and Lowe, P., eds *Locality and Rurality* (Geo Books, Norwich).

Townsend, A. (1983) *The Impact of Recession on Industry, Employment and the Regions 1978–81* (Croom Helm, Beckenham).

Travers, T. (1986) 'Two Views of the Government's Rates Intention', *Local Government Chronicle* (7 July).

Urry, J. (1981a) 'Localities, Regions and Social Class', *International Journal of Urban and Regional Research*, 5, 4.

Urry, J. (1981b) *The Anatomy of Capitalist Societies: The Economy, Civil Society and the State* (Macmillan, London).

Urry, J. (1983) 'De-industrialization, Classes and Politics' in King, R. ed. *Capital and Politics* (Routledge and Kegan Paul, London).

Urry, J. (1985) 'Social relations, space and time', Gregory, D. and Urry, J. eds *Social Relations and Spatial Structures* (Macmillan, London), ch. 3.

Ward, M. (1981) *Job Creation by the Council, Local Government and the Struggle for Full Employment* (Institute for Workers' Control, Nottingham), pamphlet 78.

Warde, A. (1985) 'Space, Class and Voting in Britain', in Hoggart, K. and Kofman, E., eds *Politics, Geography and Social Stratification*. (Croom Helm, London).

Widdicombe, D. (1986) *Report of the Committee of Inquiry into the Conduct of Local Authority Business* (HMSO, London) Cmnd 9797.

Wilson, J. ed. (1968) *City Politics and Public Policy* (Wiley, New York).

Young, K. (1984a) 'The Background to the GLC Abolition and Alternative Approach' *The London Journal*, 10, 1.

Young, K. (1984b) 'Governing Greater London: The Political Aspects', *Policy and Politics*, 12, 3.

Young, K. and Kramer, J. (1978) *Strategy and Conflict in Metropolitan Housing* (Heinemann, London).

Index of Works Cited

Index of Subjects

local government
  autonomy, 97–8, 188–94, 216
  expenditure, 96–105, 108–10,
    112–25, 168–9, 171–2, 181,
    243, 246
  interpretive role, 169
  reorganization, 91, 98, 99–100,
    172–3, 256
  representational role, 169, 173
  in Scotland, 171–6
Local Government Act (1972),
    91, 97, 214
Local Government Finance Act
    (1982), 91, 115–25, 153,
    157, 168, 217
Local Government (Miscellaneous
    Provisions) (Scotland) Act
    (1981), 173–4
Local Government, Planning and
    Land Act (1980), 91,
    106–15, 124, 128, 130, 132,
    157, 168, 217, 272
Local Government and Planning
    (Scotland) Act (1982),
    175–6
local policy
  formulation, 81–8
  and local social relations, 76–89
  studies of, 17–22, 28–9
  variation in, 5–10, 48–9, 59–60
local social process, 57–61
  variation in, 58–61
local state, 1, 30–43, 69, 82, 94,
    130, 271
  as agent and obstacle, 46, 73,
    127, 274
  interpretive role, 41–2, 274–5
  representational role, 41–2,
    274–5
  social relations of, 37–43, 277
  theory of, 38–43
  see also local government; local
    policy
London Docklands Development
    Corporation, 92, 136–7,
    138–9, 205
Lothian Regional Council, 119,
    170, 174, 175, 176

Merseyside, 144–7
Metropolitan County Councils,
    46, 114, 119, 187, 261, 276
  transport policy, 262–3, 265–70
  see also abolition
monetarism, 100–1, 104, 121,
    125, 176
municipal socialism, 90, 95, 128,
    144, 176, 188–90, 236, 260,
    274

nature, 68–9
  uneven development of, 70, 72
'new right' ideology, 92–4, 95,
    104
'new urban left', 79–80, 104
Norwich City Council, 158–9

Oldham, 1–3, 275
organizational theory, 31–2
output studies, 10–16

political advertising, 104, 206,
    219–20
political consciousness, 79
political culture, 70–1, 78, 82–3
Poplarism, 2–3, 4, 189–90, 260,
    275
positivist methodology, 43
production, 62–6, 67
  social relations of, 24–5
  see also spatial division, of
    labour
public housing
  finance, 149–54
  Housing Act (1980), 152–4,
    156–61, 166
  Housing Benefit, 161–2
  Housing Corporation, 155–6
  local policy, 26–7
  sales, 115, 156–61
public sector borrowing, 94, 180
Public Sector Borrowing
    Requirement, 109, 121,
    124, 152

Rates Act (1984), 153, 176–88,
    230, 234